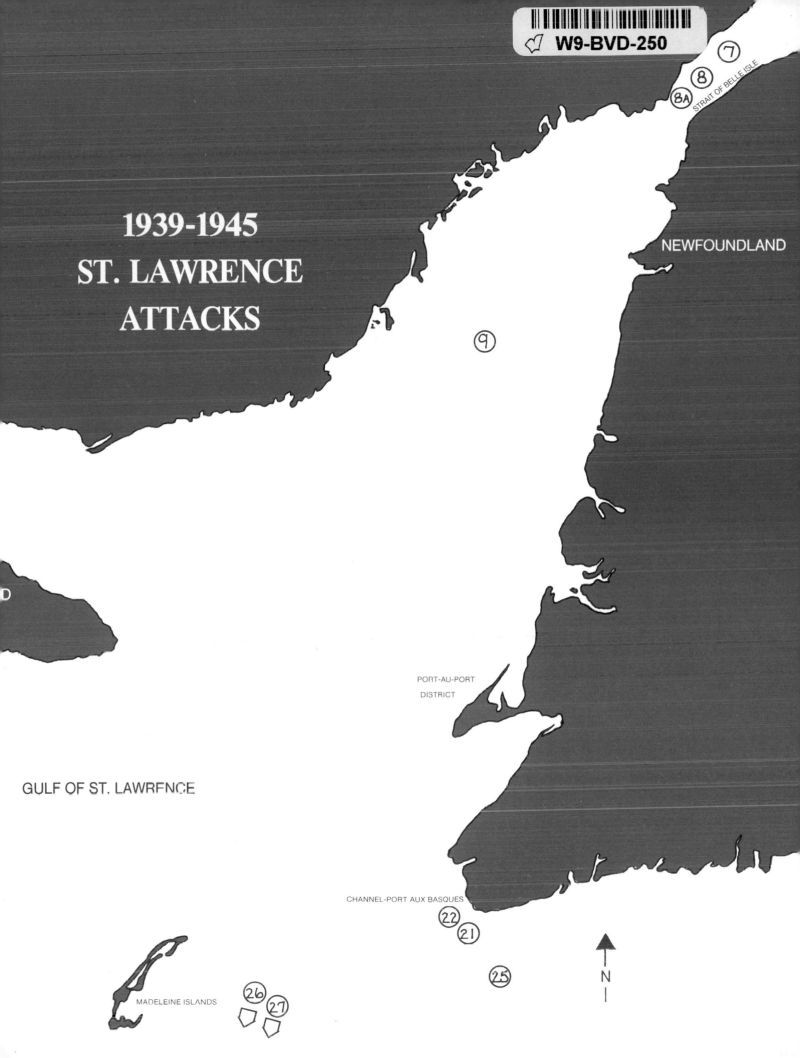

1939-1945 ST. LAWRENCE ATTACKS

NEWFOUNDLAND

STRAIT OF BELLE ISLE

PORT-AU-PORT DISTRICT

GULF OF ST. LAWRENCE

CHANNEL-PORT AUX BASQUES

MADELEINE ISLANDS

N

VICTORY
IN THE
ST. LAWRENCE
✦ JAMES W. ESSEX ✦

VICTORY
IN THE
ST. LAWRENCE

❧ JAMES W. ESSEX ❧

CANADA'S
UNKNOWN WAR

Canadian Cataloguing in Publication Data

Essex, James W. (James William), 1921-
    Victory in the St. Lawrence: Canada's unknown war

ISBN 0-919822-56-8

1. World War, 1939-1945—Naval operations,
Canadian.   2. World War, 1939-1945—Campaigns—
Saint Lawrence, Gulf of.   I. Title.

D779.C2E8 1984   940.54'5971   C84-098871-0

Published by:
THE BOSTON MILLS PRESS
98 Main Street
Erin, Ontario N0B 1T0
(519) 833-2407

Winners of the
Heritage Canada
Communications Award

American Association
for State and Local History
Award Winner

Design by John Denison
Cover design by Dave Hooton

Typeset by Linotext, Toronto
Printed by Ampersand, Guelph

We wish to acknowledge the financial assistance of The Canada
Council, the Ontario Arts Council and the Office of the Secretary
of State.

Dedicated to:

*"They that go down to the sea in ships,
that do business in great waters."*

—Psalms, CVII, 23.

table of contents

Poignant ceremony at Gaspé Reunion: Widows of naval officers who served on the ill-fated Canadian ships HMCS "Raccoon" and HMCS "Charlottetown" throw wreaths on the sea to remember their men and all who had served and been killed in action. Above, Dorothy Davidson, (left) whose first husband Lt Commander J.N. Smith went down with HMCS "Raccoon," joins Mary Bonner, wife of the late J.W. Bonner of HMCS "Charlottetown" and Mr. Vautour, Guelph Naval Vet, (left) and Chairman of the reunion committee, James Essex.

—Daniel J. Vautour

preface

This is a story which should have been told 40 years ago but, being a busy man pursuing a radio career following extensive war-service, raising a family and gardening (which I especially like to do), I've been just too busy.

However, a lengthy illness stopped all this in recent years, and I've had time to reflect. It has not been about radio—exciting as that's been—but about the Navy, my first love.

When I suggested to my wife that we take up a latent desire to re-visit some of the postings that we shared together, Gaspé was our first choice. It was while stationed there in 1942 at the height of Canada's struggle in the Battle of the St. Lawrence that my wife, then my fiancée, came to visit me. Our subsequent visit in 1977 triggered a train of memories, shared by veterans with whom we later came in contact and who fought in that war, of which most Canadians know little, even today.

Events moved swiftly: a committee was formed of Ontario navy veterans for which I was pleased to act as chairman. In Gaspé itself, Georges Allard volunteered help assisted by the enthusiastic Veterans of Branch #59, Royal Canadian Legion, "Jubilee Branch", Gaspé.

In 1979, we succeeded in bringing sailors, airmen and soldiers back to Gaspé from all across Canada and the U.S. while the Canadian Broadcasting Corporation came with a camera crew from the "Fifth Estate" Program to record the gathering.

When we placed wreaths upon the waters of the Gulf of St. Lawrence that weekend at Gaspé remembering those "who went down to the sea in ships", I unashamedly wept. The quiet widow standing next to me, was the wife of Capt. J.N. Bonner of HMCS "Charlottetown", torpedoed off Gaspé on September 11, 1942. He never returned. Her quiet tears expressed as no words could do how we all felt.

For myself, the poignancy of it all had a double meaning: Here was I, a victim of Cancer, having fought for my own life and won against an insidious personal enemy, while the men we honoured today hadn't been allowed to live out theirs because of a different kind of war. At least I'd had the subsequent 40 years and knew the joy of family and friends. All they had was a watery grave, cut off from loved-ones by an equally insidious enemy *right here in Canada*. It wasn't until the next day while standing downtown admiring the new and unique R.C. Cathedral in Gaspé, built entirely of native Canadian wood, that a sailor standing next to me brought the whole thing into perspective.

The sailor reached into his topcoat pocket and hurriedly proffered a crumpled photograph. I recognized it as a picture of the military funeral, in long-ago 1942, at the tiny Anglican Church I'd nearly forgotten about just down the road. The photo pictured the burial of one of the seamen of "Charlottetown", one of several who'd been lucky enough to be rescued, only to die later of wounds received from the hands of the enemy. He was killed *in Canada* by the Nazis; by their submarines which had invaded our waters in 1942.

This book in a real sense then is his story, and the hundreds of others who perished because of the Nazi submarines in the St. Lawrence. As Cmdr. George Bernard, Naval Officer In Command (NOIC) Gaspé from 1943 to war's end, said in later years: "In 1942, marauding U-Boats entered the Gulf of St. Lawrence and did a great deal of damage. They roamed the Gulf and River St. Lawrence at will and were seldom opposed. They sank Canadian warships and valuable merchant vessels almost with impunity."

This was Victory in the St. Lawrence.

This was Canada's Unknown War.

A narrow gravelled road swings through Gaspé's isolated hills. On north shore Anse Au Valleau, Gaspé.

—Ian Tate

introduction

Setting up the defence of a country as unique as Canada sometimes proves to be a greater problem than inspiring a "will to win" to support that defence. True, the difficulties of leadership so necessary to winning any war are often overlooked, but the problem of defending over one thousand miles of coastline is often minimized to such a degree that lack of adequate preparation courts disaster.

Examine Canada's eastern defence posture, for example. I first saw Gaspé in the early summer of 1942, at the height of Canada's greatest trial. I can still see those fog-shrouded yet beautiful rolling hills, soon to burst forth in autumn's yellows and golds. The day that I arrived on the 'Bullet', the antiquated steam train which miraculously managed to stay on long neglected tracks, found the coast of the Gulf of St. Lawrence swathed in a gentle mist, peculiarly beautiful, as the still, cool water of the Gulf reflected the gold of the setting sun. The train took the last full sweep of this beautiful vista before heading inland to Gaspé town. Historic Percé rock lay just at the water's edge outlined in shimmering yellow—a background to a coastline much as it'd been since Cartier's time. But what a change from the once peaceful, virgin waters of 1534.

Four centuries later, these very waters erupted in hatred as the Nazi incursions increased and men cried out as today's modern ships, though bereft of the encumbrances of the wooden ships of the sailor from St. Malo, found, that despite the superior steel ship of today, they were more vulnerable than even the most decrepit vessels in the era of "Wooden ships and iron men". While today's ships were steel, they were nevertheless being ripped open, not by the hazards of the sea, but by giant, hideous torpedoes, whose can opener like thrust let in the sea while a thousand tortures were inflicted on the men who manned the ships.

Neither Cartier nor Nelson—the latter who sailed this same shore in the Albermarle in 1783—ever envisaged, in their wildest dreams, anything like this. Dogged Cartier and Brave Nelson; how they would have revolted at the carnage as brave men were killed by deception and not by the sea; killed by an invisible foe. Nelson's cry, "England expects every man to do his duty" would not avail here. This enemy could not even be seen let alone be joined. While Canada mistakenly sent its sons overseas, thinking it was the place to fight the vitals of an enemy whose evil had now shocked the sensibilities of good men everywhere, we left our own shores naked. Worse, the shores of our friendly neighbour to the south also bore the brunt of the Nazi's initial attacks, after itself suffering a "day of infamy" only six months earlier at Pearl Harbour. Like us, they too were to find the extreme weapon of subterfuge, the submarine, even more menacing than that black Sunday in 1941. The ensuing slaughter caught both countries by surprise, but especially Canada.

Canada also had another problem when National Selective Service became the butt of controversy. When war hit the United States, "the Draft" was taken as a matter of course; in Canada, it got bogged down in the semantics of a dilettante Prime Minister who never really had a feel for a free people's will to fight. This lack of confidence later exploded overseas in Aldershot in 1941 when Prime Minister King, reviewing Canadian troops anxious to fight, was roundly "booed". It was no secret that servicemen listened more to Churchill and Roosevelt for direction rather than the top man in Canada.

Ignoring a signal call to battle, he uttered his now famous phrase…"Conscription if necessary but not necessarily Conscription". This dilemma reached up into the highest station of municipal government when the Mayor of Montreal, Camillien Houde, elected to go to jail rather than serve his country. Unfortunately, by this incident the rest of the country branded the Quebecers as pacifists and surprising to some, only the Church offered a call to service which was peculiarly lacking from Quebec secular authorities. Students of Quebec history knew Cardinal Villeneuve, the head of Quebec's Roman Catholics, was an irrepressible person, unflinchingly endorsing a war policy at serious variance with the apparent preferences of the majority of his provincial flock.

As a result of the Conscription dilemma the role of the men in the Army, Navy and Air Force became much more difficult; they not only had to fight the enemy in every corner of the world, but did so without the support of *all* of the "people back home". In some instances, their patriotism was compromised by jingoists who felt Canada's call "to stand" was solely their idea.

Monsignor Charbonneau, a Franco-Ontarian serving in Quebec, chose to fly the Union jack atop his Archiepiscopal Palace in Montreal as a badge of appreciation for England's brave stand against the forces of evil. Actually, all of Canada had its share of pacifists. Ontario, for example had large blocks of the population against the war. The Mennonites, a large farm group in Ontario noticeably dedicated to the soil if not the country, refused military service. Under the National Registration Act, they opted for conscientious objector status and accordingly, men of military age were shipped to British Columbia. Perhaps they unwittingly aided Canada's war effort more than if they'd gone overseas because, occupying the forests of the interior, they cut down huge Douglas Fir trees urgently needed to build our Fairmile sub-chasers and, later, Mosquito Bombers, without which victory might not have been ours.

The classic case of the Canadian-Japanese internment comes to mind when a whole populace was taken from a sensitive coastal area, after Japan entered the conflict against us, serving the rest of the war inland. In central South-Western Ontario, a large German presence in Kitchener (formerly Berlin) posed a "threat" not unlike the Japanese. However, they astounded skeptics by volunteering for overseas service, as they had in World War One, even if doing so meant they'd end up in France shooting their own uncles, cousins, and in some cases, their own fathers whom they had left behind when they emigrated to Canada.

The logistics of defence were even more difficult. Most of the ships, corvettes, minesweepers, and even the lowly Fairmile, an all-wood boat literally carved out of the forests of Canada, presented a different problem as they were largely built in Ontario over a thousand miles from the sea.

The advent, by Germany, of the submarine as a weapon of war in WW 1 was considered by the Royal Navy to be "unfair", because the submarine couldn't be seen. It was therefore considered a weapon "unchallengeable" and the Royal Navy considered it "not cricket".

By 1939, Britain and Germany each entered the war with identical numbers of submarines (57) but the Germans were already building at the rate of two boats per month.

Eventually they would outstrip "the Allies" in number of submarines, number of submariners and especially in design of specific equipment for undersea warfare. Their knowledge of underwater performance of sound waves, for example, made their submarines almost undetectable. They learned that the meeting of freshwater and saltwater caused sound waves to bend and the use of Asdic by the British, Americans and Canadians in the shoals off the Eastern U.S. and Canada's St. Lawrence River became almost useless. Asdic was the Anti-submarine detection device which originated a sound wave that bounced back off an underwater object and when measured, gave a direction and distance to that object.

The German "Schnorkel" breathing apparatus when introduced in 1944 reversed the tide of battle in favour of the Germans at a moment when victory was almost within grasp of the "Allies". The war became a "battle of wits"; our Radio Direction Finders (RADAR), their Schnorkel; our Asdic; their sound wave bending.

There were some in Canada who believed that the Germans artfully charted the waters of the St. Lawrence in peacetime, about the time that Hitler attempted to buy Anticosti Island from a wealthy chocolate bar manufacturer in France named Menier. This purchase, had it been made, would have given the Germans an unbelievable advantage and could have changed the outcome of the war.

The dilemma in Canada was further complicated by the fact that we entered the war with only six warships, and a Navy which existed only on the drawing board. Only days after Britain declared war, Canada was handed plans for a novel sub-hunter, the Corvette. Most of them would be built in Ontario.

Our Merchant fleet was practically non-existent, necessitating that Canada draw on vessels under different flags, Norwegian, Dutch, Greek, British, in order to ship the necessities of war to feed a starving and war-wracked Britain. We even had to put our "Lakers" into the breech; lake freighters designed for the smooth inland waters of the Great Lakes, not the turbulent waters of the North Atlantic. A classic example was Convoy SC-7 which brought together several of these "Lakers" from Lake Ontario loading en route at Montreal, Quebec City and Gaspé. The convoy was decimated by Nazi Wolf Packs who found the slow, lumbering, shallow draft ships easy prey. It was only a matter of time before the German Submarines using new long-distance subs supported by "Milch Cows" (tanker refueling submarines), realized that they could better attack us in the sanctuary of our own waters. This they were able to do together with the luxury of "sunning themselves" off our shores by day and holing up in the many Canadian secluded coves at night, serenaded by our own radio stations wafting music across the night air.

Canada mistakenly paid more attention to uniting our Country with powerful civilian radio transmitters like CBA Maritimes, installed at a cost of millions of dollars, instead of a concerted Science Council developing R.D.F. (Radar) and Asdic. So it was that local people on the Gaspé and New Brunswick shores, where the "subs" became most pressing, listened to

Don Messer over CFCY or CKNB Campbellton, supported by the French language station CHNC New Carlisle. Money thus spent should have gone into support for our factories now trying to develop an efficient "Radar". In haphazard fashion, Research Enterprises Limited of Leaside farmed out their components (some say to preserve secrecy) to develop model-SW1C & 2C sets. These were superseded by the British-built Micro-wave Radar utilizing the Magnetron which they developed even while bombs were falling on Britain, but which we didn't use until the press of events forced us to.

It was inescapable that the Germans would know our inland route, the St. Lawrence, was being used, to sail our hastily built corvettes, minesweepers, and fairmiles to war, and that it was an indispensable artery of support for war-besieged Britain. This artery had to be closed and in 1942 they set out to do just this, in earnest.

Our sailors most of them novices had to not only traverse the circumspect navigation of at least three canal systems just to reach the St. Lawrence, but also the gauntlet had to be run with ships not yet fully "worked up", compromising our defence. At least two of the first 14 corvettes sailed the St. Lawrence with wooden posts sticking from their gun turrets, later to be outfitted in England. Our merchant ships had little more than "Bren guns" for defence. Many were torpedoed in transit, even before they reached the "theatre of war" in the Atlantic.

This is *Canada's Unknown War*: a war Canadians, through the heavy hand of the Censor, knew nothing about. A recalcitrant Government, fearful their own fellow-Canadians lacked a will to fight, surreptitiously kept it from us under the mistaken idea we might panic and submit, rather than fight.

That we did fight should be credited solely to our men who went down to the sea in ships, not to forget the soldiers who manned our shore fortifications, much of it in deadly silence not knowing fully why they were there. Later the airmen would venture forth each day seeking the elusive submarine. As Rev. Burton, at the time a leading seaman on HMCS Arrowhead, put it; "We thought we were doing our duty". How well they did and how eventual Victory was won is the message of our story.

Percé Rock, Canada's southern defence anchor for "the Defended Port of Gaspé" during the Second World War.
— *Peter Donald*

The "Narrows", a strip of water separating Gaspé's inner and outer harbours. "Sandy Beach" may be seen opposite. A submarine net between that point of land and Peninsula in the foreground was installed to prevent enemy subs from entering the inner harbour. — David Essex

preparation for war

In 1812, invasion of Upper and Lower Canada by the United States tested the "Nationhood" of Canada like no other war, with one exception. Unfortunately, the structures of this exception left no room for heroics to be catalogued. The commitment of the Government to secrecy has left this segment of our "National Dream" untold. However, the imposition of silence, lest it give aid and comfort to the enemy has remained generally in place, and Canadians today still know little about the enemy which challenged our shores and spilled Canadian blood on our doorstep. Men are dead and can't tell the tale, but to those of us who took part in the battle, it was no less a struggle compared to the War of 1812; just 130 years later.

If the test of Nationhood is the stopping of a real or potential incursion into the Nation's sovereignty, then the long, hot summer of 1942 contains all the ingredients necessary for that test, even if the heavy hand of Government Censorship must carry the blame for Canadians not knowing. Military censorship imposed in the early years of WW 2 it would seem has really not been lifted yet.

Perhaps a nation of 12 million can be forgiven for omitting its own defence, when it is better recognized for its peaceful pursuits than its military prowess. Historians generally concede Canada found its soul on Vimy Ridge in 1917, and became a Nation fifty years after Confederation. How then did we find ourselves prostrate in 1942 before the greatest scourge that Hitler unleashed against the Allies—the submarine? This was the weapon that Churchill himself despaired might cause us to lose the fight for Freedom.

While Dieppe is remembered, and rightly so, those who fought and died in Canada's inland waters are unknown.

Early in the war, Churchill, fearing the imminent fall of France and with it, the capitulation of the French Navy, conferred with Roosevelt on the possible use of Gaspé Harbour in case Britain should also fall. Accordingly, Canada agreed to the use of Gaspé for safe anchorage for the British Fleet and as a base for Quebec-Sydney Convoys; tacit recognition of the importance of this area of the St. Lawrence Seaway. A direct result of these earlier plans, laid first in 1940, was the St. Lawrence Conference in which Canada offered, not only financial help, but an avuncular care as well.

It wasn't easy. Canada cajoled the almost morbidly modest young men to take to the colours, providing thereby Canada's best picture of a Nation uniting for a common cause. While Prime Minister Mackenzie King, perhaps, didn't epitomize war as did Churchill, he somehow managed to get the message across. Roosevelt rushed north to sign a mutual defence pact, and even American citizens flocked north across the border and enlisted.

In industrial Ontario, only recently inhabited by mere wrecks of men as a result of the hungry Thirties; real men emerged overnight. These were the same men who epitomized the poverty of our times when Denton Massey put the poverty picture so eloquently into words in his famous Massey Hall lectures. Even the most critical said that his talks "kept them off the streets". The lectures were broadcast every Sunday afternoon and received national prominence across Canada. There were few exceptions to this scene, and most people agreed, that Canada did the right thing in declaring war on Germany on September 10th, 1939.

Canada was merely an observer in the war, in every sense of the word, not a participant. For Captain Colin D. Donald of the Navy, appointed to head up Canada's Naval defence at Gaspé in early 1940, it was a "brooding Canada". An aide succinctly put it into words, describing exactly how he and Donald felt when they got their first glimpse of historic Percé Rock, "No more would this Rock, readily seen in posters in most railway stations across Canada, inspire tourists. This would now be our southern defence anchor; Canada's undefended 'Rock of Gibraltar'".

For Canada, the task was a formidable one. Canada's scant forces which remained after the Allied victory in WW 1, were now really only a microcosm of what the whole Allied effort against the overwhelming forces of the Kaiser had been. Now, it was the Axis Power who had us undermanned and ill-prepared. Canada, in 1940 for example, had a naval force of some 20 men of all ranks at Gaspé to help prepare a Naval Base big enough to support the British Fleet.

Canada at this point chose not to say too much about our lack of preparedness. This, unfortunately, left an uninformed public forced to follow rumour rather than fact.

In contrast, in Britain, each enemy plane downed in 1940 was catalogued and people watched the events with the same gusto as a soccer match, instilling pride in their forces as well as galvanizing the country's will to win. In Canada, only the military actually on the job at Gaspé enjoyed such pride. Only they were aware of the progress that was being made toward defence, even if the defence was epitomized by the recent arrival of a civilian engineer, Mr. Goldie.

For Goldie, the logistics on the job were simple enough. He had already moved into a site just 1.5 miles from the edge of town. There he utilized a jetty built over two decades earlier, in 1914, to handle the First World War's needs. A meagre start for a naval base.

The trickle of men that now began to arrive found adequate billets in Gaspé homes, a hopeful sign for Canada as barriers of language and custom evaporated in the face of a desire to put country first. The ubiquitous barracks, so familiar in this area since the earliest times, would come next, accompanied by all the paraphenalia of workshops and supplies necessary to service a fleet. Next would come the submarine gate at the narrows at Sandy Beach.

Actually, arming this Peninsula was nothing new. When Robert Flowers of the 29th Regiment was forced to travel the long sea route with his family to their new home in the Gaspé after 1759, he echoed the desire of many for a more direct and safer link with Quebec City. He was the only married man of the five soldiers discharged the day before Christmas in 1783 at St. John, Quebec. The Crown offered free land to those remaining loyal during the War of Independence and the five soldiers were only a few of the many who accepted the offer of free land in the Gaspé. It was inevitable that in time the enthusiasm which followed the mosaic of people tumbling into this new "Commonwealth"—Loyalists, Acadians, immigrants from the Jersey Isles and the United Kingdom and those from Denmark—would demand better passage that the St. Lawrence could provide.

By the middle eighteen hundreds, with the coming of the railway, the pioneers were less dependent on and vulnerable to the elements and to the mighty St. Lawrence. For the military now arriving in 1940 at Gaspé, the railway would once again provide a vital link with the rest of Canada and the vulnerability of travel on the St. Lawrence would not be confined to the elements. The new enemy, however, would approach not from the South as in the war of 1812 but from the East....and under the water.

Canada is a benevolent country known to not act with alacrity. For the incoming Military, care had to be exercised, not so much with the actual construction, but the choice of defence positions. The military walked the tightrope of local sensitivities, careful not to upset the townspeople nor the Church, while at the same time satisfying Ottawa which recognized Quebec's unique relationship within Confederation.

Ferguson, a lighthouse keeper, one of many on the north shore, maintained his light at Cape des Rosiers just opposite the headland at Fort Prevel. He provided a good example of local co-operation with Scottish and Irish regiments were now coming into Fort Prevel. The Military, accustomed as they are to labelling everything superficially, concluded that with a name like Joseph Ferguson, this lightkeeper just had to be a Scot, perhaps even one of their own.

"Ferguson?" queried an Aide, "I'm told most lightkeepers here actually came from a long line of lightkeepers, originally from the Cornish Coast".

Mr. Goldie, Supervisor of Construction for the "Defended Port of Gaspé"— Fort Ramsay's Base Engineer in 1940.
— Peter Donald.

Cape des Rosiers Lighthouse.

"Oh?" returned the inquisitor, his interest now piqued; "Yes," he returned, suggesting in a veiled reply, "not all was complimentary"." How's that?" the officer mumbled ,to himself thinking it was because they'd learned Ferguson was French-Canadian and that he couldn't speak a word of English. (another of the many contradictions already noted here in Quebec) "No, it's what happened on the Cornish Coast, in the old days, when they'd pass the word around whenever rich cargoes came their way". "So?" "Well", they'd simply move their light; that way they fattened their lot in life off the wrecks of others". While the officer smiled in mute assent, as if acknowledging the joke for what it was, he couldn't help but notice the parallel with his own men. Here they were on a mere $1.30 per diem, while manufacturers now making munitions would reap huge monetary rewards back home in industrial Montreal and Toronto.

Ferguson's allegiance to Canada—nor for that matter any of the hundreds of lighthouse keepers stretched along a thousand miles of Canada's coast-line, was never in question. His unique position atop the 120 foot light maintained safe passage for the hundreds of cargo ships, soon to pass the broad

Joseph Ferguson, keeper of the lighthouse at Cape des Rosiers, proudly holds his "glass" in this photo taken in 1942 by his daughter, Yvonne. Ferguson is credited with sighting the first German submarine to invade Canadian waters.

—Georges Allard/Cassidy's Photos, Gaspé

wastes of the Gulf of St. Lawrence, allowing them safe passage this side of Anticosti Island some 30 miles distant. Canada was fortunate this key position was maintained by Ferguson who would one day prove to be Canada's best watchman and win, not one, but two coveted awards for devotion to duty in the face of the enemy. How the circle had shrunk. Here Canadians were now arming themselves to the teeth to fight an enemy we'd once had on the run in Europe in 1918; Now, our own lightkeepers and even our fishermen would be asked to help intercept the Boche.

We hadn't learned the lesson the League of Nations valiantly held out in the postwar years after 1918: The "War to End Wars" had cost the lives of 1.8 million Germans, 1.4 million French and nearly a million British. If you added the Russians, Austrians, Hungarians, Italians, Turks and Americans to Canada's, the conflagration was unimaginable. Samson, Donald and Goldie felt the irony of their particular situation: Gaspé was to mount an unparalleled Naval Defence in 1942. Not two decades earlier, 10,000 Canadians embarked from these shores, sailing from Gaspé Oct. 3rd and 4th 1914, arriving unscathed in England October 14th and 15th, safely shepherded by the Royal Navy. This time, however, Canada would have to do it alone, and defend our own shores with our own Navy, which we didn't yet have.

At first, it looked easy. The "Phoney War" overseas in France remained a stalemate with opposing forces serenading each other over loudspeakers. One song, "We're Going To Hang Out The Washing On The Siegfried Line", perhaps best illustrated our confidence. Our troops only stopped singing when the Germans swept through the low countries of Belgium and Holland by-passing the Maginot Line in that horrible May of 1940 when France fell. Dunkerque followed and the interlude of false hopes evaporated.

In late 1940, two Corvettes, the vanguard of 14 Corvettes to come in early 1941, moved silently down the St. Lawrence. They were the first of over 70 destined for Canada's main armament, now shaping up in the Battle of the Atlantic. However, there were none for Gaspé. Incoming personnel to Gaspé had more immediate worries in 1940. For example, how would we be received in a Province cradled mainly in the history of Europe? For it was matter of fact, and readily accepted that Canada really was the handmaiden of the French and English where attitudes were therefore fashioned on two founding races—not the mores of the common weal. This attitude was older than even the country itself and while obvious pride in our service was plain by the fact that we had all volunteered to serve our country for $1.30 a day, it didn't go unnoticed that we might have stayed home and bettered our lot earning top dollar in local industry, making the stuff we'd soon be called upon to throw at the enemy.

The Commanding Officer of the Army, Col.

Samson, saw it a different way. He had to reconcile the fact that volunteers from across Canada were expected to defend a largely French Province in a Quebec already known to list 25,000 deserters. One soldier jokingly remarked that this was not counting "those who'd already taken to the woods". Early enlistees felt, perhaps with some justification, that they had worked as hard to get into the service as those in Quebec had worked to keep out. The RCMP, responsible for arresting delinquents from the National Registration Act, already had a lengthy list in Quebec and it was still growing. Small wonder then that Donald of the Navy, Samson of the Army and Mr. Goldie, the civilian engineer felt undue concern, while a dilettante Prime Minister beat every effort to ameliorate Quebec's growing fears of Conscription by promising none, in order to retain office. No parallel existed before in Canada. When Mackenzie King visited Aldershot, England the next year, he'd be booed by his own soldiers.

It was perhaps paradoxical that men like Samson, Donald and Goldie found themselves in Gaspé at this point in history, when to a man they felt their services could better be employed elsewhere. A seasoned soldier, Samson really saw his role better served in Europe; Donald, who joined the Navy, like all sailors, to see the world, wondered at his shore-based appointment; and Goldie, the engineer, wondered when he found his initial task appeared mainly to be to clear woods rather than build a naval base. It was, indeed, a very strange way to wage war.

Col. Samson is shown seated on motorcycle as Army units assemble at the "Defended Port of Gaspé".

—Peter Donald

the eve of battle

Gaspé is a huge complex of tree-covered hills, with three rivers cutting swaths through the solid slopes which ramble haphazardly down to the water's edge. The Dartmouth and York Rivers form an estuary upon which the town itself has been carved on the southern slope; while the St. John River, down harbour, takes up its mile-wide course to lead the five mile gut out to the open sea. For defence, the setting is ideal and the Military hadn't failed to see the potential

Nor did the guns, placed in solid concrete bunkers along the harbour's perimeter,fail to bring a sense of security to the townspeople, even though the guns had lain idle in storage since the First World War. The largest, a 10 inch mammoth, brought up from Panama (some said it was the largest on the continent), really proved to be a big problem. Due to the terrific explosion when test fired, it caused the CO of the gun crew, Major White, to topple from the parapet to the concrete floor below. He sustained a concussion and all of the barracks windows were shattered.

Guns for our corvettes would present a different sort of headache. Canada's lack of a concerted Naval program left no guns for our ships. Our two corvettes, the first to go to England, would sail with wooden guns. With fence posts sticking out of their gun mounts, it was the closest Canada could come to the real thing, and we only hoped the silhouette would be enough to fool lurking German subs now in the Atlantic. The corvettes would be fitted with real guns when they arrived in Britain.

For Captain Donald, this was all too typical of Canada's ersatz preparation. Even the choice of the Robin's Warehouse as a temporary Naval Base in Gaspé until HMCS "Fort Ramsay" could be completed was typical. Especially humiliating was Canada's choice of an escort vessel for Gaspé. Named "Oracle", it was really only a motor boat donated by a sympathetic Montreal businessman who loved Canada and wanted to help. Our next "donation" wouldn't be much better, coming as it would from the rum-running days of Prohibition. However, it would have twin engines and an enviable record as a

customs boat off Cape Breton. Neither would have any type of gun, but for now, Donald would take satisfaction in running "Oracle" into the Harbour to challenge any and all ships which entered. He would also take pride in circling anchorages ear-marked for leviathins of the Royal Navy like HMS "Prince of Wales", HMS "Renown" and HMS "King George V" that he was sure would soon come.

Robin's Warehouse was the real annoyance. Being no more than a stone's throw from downtown Gaspé, the obvious military preparations just might alarm the local people who suddenly would find the war right on their doorstep! He consoled himself with the fact that the Cenotaph, located on a hill just off Main Street, bore the names of local men who had died for King and Country two decades earlier, even if they were mostly Irish, Scottish and English names —with few French-Canadians. He hoped, for the cause of unity, that he might have more French-Canadian personnel this time.

So far, he could count on Captain Paul Belanger and Skipper Lieutenant George Allard. When Britain declared War on September 3, 1939 George Allard spent his last 65¢ and telephoned Ottawa, volunteering his services. He waited, while Canada vacillated; and although Canada finally declared War on Germany a week later on September 10th, Allard never received an acknowledgement from Ottawa until the following January 7th, 1940. He immediately signed on and received his rank of Skipper Lieutenant RCN (R). He was sent to Halifax for basic training and next was assigned to Gaspé.

People like bilingual Reg. DeGruchy, originally from the Jersey Isles, were already there. After the British conquest of "New France", Jerseymen with French names and English tongues came to struggle for control of the Gaspé fish trade. Charles Robin was one of them and the little jetty and warehouse was named after him. Also, DeGruchy was a descendant of one of the fishermen from Jersey. Today, however, the struggle for the fish trade had been forgotten and national origin had faded. All were Canadian with one common cause.

One of the several concrete bunkers installed at Fort Peninsula opposite Gaspé in 1940, a 4.7 inch converted Naval gun peers out upon the neighbouring water of the Harbour. —*David Essex*

The outer harbour beyond Fort Peninsula. Fort Prevel on headland at right. —*David Essex*

"Oracle", a former pleasure launch, pictured at the jetty below Robin's Warehouse, Canada's first Naval Base at Gaspé.
                                                                    —*PAC 105434*

"Donald's Bridge" named after Captain Colin Donald RCN, the first Naval C.O. Gaspé Harbour is seen in left foreground and Gaspé Town at opposite end of the bridge. The York River which divides the two centres is at the middle of the photograph with the lift span connecting the two truss sections.
                                                                    —*Peter Donald*

The real concern at Gaspé was the electric generator: the sole supplier of electricity for the whole town and environs. While it was fascinating to observe the simple gasoline motor rotate the aging alternator, wheezing and grunting as the load increased and the town lights came on each night, it was too visible and too vulnerable. That it worked at all, continually amazed everyone. It also supplied the electricity needed to operate the bridge linking Gaspé with Gaspé Harbour opposite. The generator was the sole means of opening the lift section at the bridge's centre whenever ships wanted in or out of the inner harbour. This was an extra burden on Naval authorities, and appropriately, the Navy posted a guard on the generator until more permanent quarters for it would be available down-harbour at the new "Fort Ramsay". Donald knew should the enemy ever succeed in getting men ashore in a rubber dinghy (something they would actually succeed in doing at New Carlisle later), Gaspé would be done. Enemy agents could effectively isolate Gaspé Harbour—on the opposite shore of the York River by merely blowing up the generator, thus disabling the bridge's centre span.

Gaspé Harbour contained two essential services for Canada's war effort: a terminal for the CNR trains from Matapedia and Montreal; and a Hospital, where the Roman Catholic Sisters would receive our dead and dying in the months ahead.

Near this bridge ran the slender wires carrying the electricity from the generator on the Gaspé side, reaching along the gravelled main street on hydro poles to the opposite shore, and Donald equated these with the slender thread now strung in a hundred Convoys linking Canada's war effort to Britain's. Should that be severed—(and Churchill already had expressed fears that our salvation depended on the Battle of the Atlantic victory)—all was lost.

The proposal by Imperial Oil to look after oiling our ships, under the expert care of Mr. Reg De-Gruchy, was seen as a sign by local people of our common cause. The fact Imperial Oil was an American company (parent company was Exxon, a U.S. firm) didn't seem to strain relations with our neighbour to the South who, so far, had managed to remain neutral in this war. Reg DeGruchy proved he wasn't neutral, however; nor did he disguise his hatred for an enemy threatening Canada's shores. Good Anglican that he was…he shared the sentiment of all the sailors soon to arrive best expressed by a Truro youth Rod Van Buskirk from Nova Scotia; "Love your enemy…etc.…might be o.k. but we can't beat 'em that way: Seek and destroy should become our motto."

This mood extended right through the town, and included Mr. Annett, the local bank manager, who felt Canada had been asleep too long and he said so. He even remembered when German agents—posing as real estate salesmen, walked these streets seeking land purchases of seashore properties. It was well-known by now that Hitler wanted to purchase

Anticosti Island in the late 30's! A faded copy of the Montreal Gazette dated December 1937 proved this. "To get a foothold on the North American Continent, that's what", Annett readily pointed out. It became a cause célèbre at the time, but in typical Canadian indifference, it soon died down. Annett's service to the community was only outdone by his pleasant wife and the ladies of the community—among them Jean DeGruchy, Hazel Clark, Gladys Kruse, and all who attended local clubs and generally reflected the determination of the community to win.

It was perhaps appropriate that they were the first ones to voice concern over the fact that the local military had not seen fit to pay their respects to the Roman Catholic Bishop. After all, this was a Catholic Province. Both the Anglicans and United Church enjoyed a minority presence here, and taken together they were not as big in total as the Catholics. All denominations shared the attitude that not enough of the military attended church. So far as the troops were concerned, largely Protestant, the conglomerate of Convents and Seminaries which dotted the Gaspé hillside offered a somewhat stoic presence, perhaps better ignored. The Seminary situated as it was on the hillside offered stark contrast to the worldliness posed by Patterson's Cafe. There, on the main town thoroughfare, the fun-loving matelot congregated regularly in off-duty hours, especially when the street lights, now coming on earlier with approaching winter, illuminated the boardwalk-lined gravelled street as if it were home. This illusion would persist through winter until ice breakup in spring. Then with the coming of summer, the Seminary would shed its silent, yet visible, reminder of the Church and burst forth with Bach and Beethoven from open windows causing a cacaphony of sound to clash with Patterson's ubiquitous jukebox, playing the latest Jazz hits.

For the military, especially Captain Colin Donald ensconced in the lower town at Robin's Warehouse, the Seminary and the cafe delineated, perhaps too well, the separation of the Church and the variance of war. For the men, anxiously awaiting the first enemy onslaught, the discipline of war was perhaps sufficient, never mind the discipline of the Church. Both Capt. Donald and Bishop Ross, in his hilltop retreat, were now engaged in parallel fights.

The Seminary had turned out priests to war on sin in faroff outposts, in deepest Africa while the military had produced servicemen from Ontario and the West now serving in faroff Gaspé: both men, equally isolated, felt a peculiar malaise not solely the military's but common with men too far from home. Such was the plight of the homesick servicemen even here in Gaspé.

Mrs. Hazel Clark felt the isolation also, not without some trepidation, when every civilian was given a phone number they could call, "to help feel secure". Residents were instructed to call a particular number "should they notice anything amiss", and report it to

"Sandy Beach" where a temporary Rifle Range was installed: Note "spotters" at extreme right of picture and men firing from the prone position in centre-foreground. —Peter Donald

"Johnny-on-the-spot" reporter photographs embarrassing moment when the Naval Van tipped over rounding a curve. It was a victim of loose gravel, typical of Gaspé roads of that day. —Peter Donald

the authorities. It was one such phone call the Robin's (Navy) Warehouse received now!

"The transport, Sir", the voice at the other end hollered, "It's flipped over". Donald recognized the voice to be one of his seamen. Incredibly he listened as the voice described what happened.

They were returning from Sandy Point following rifle practice when the van skidded off the edge of the road and turned on its side. The accident scene was very close to the temporary rifle range located at the spot where the Submarine Net would eventually be installed. "Likely the men were getting a little edgy", he reasoned, "but this was no time to get careless." For Donald, the incident was a subtle sign that they were perhaps all becoming a little hyper, and he didn't like it. "Was it the truck?" He hoped it wasn't his prize Van. The Van was something the Military used regularly to "show the flag" and instill a sense of confidence in the townspeople, tantamount to saying they knew what they were doing. So far as the Navy was concerned the "Van" was the one indispensable compensation for the ships they did not have in Gaspé.

"No sir," the seaman replied, as if reluctantly anticipating what he knew would be a blast. Then, he blurted out—"it was the Van". For a man normally even-tempered, Donald exploded. He saw it as a sad day for Canada, especially when a news photographer appeared "Johnny-on-the-spot" to take pictures of the Van—ingloriously upended at the roadside. The treacherous gravel roads became another of the many incongruities facing the Military and served, however, as a suitable excuse for the accident. Donald's wife and son, Peter, recently arrived from the West Coast to spend the summer holidays in Gaspé, now served the timely role of conciliators and calm ultimately prevailed. Captain Donald's Van only superficially damaged, served again. Meanwhile the "Gaspé County" light but fast freighter with limited passenger facilities, continued to flirt with fate by making regular calls to Gaspé. The plodding heavily-laden pulpwood boats leaving Patterson's Jetty opposite Robin's Warehouse, continued without mishap, despite the growing fear German U-Boats might be closing in on Canada. The incessant electrically-activated alarm which rang whenever a ship required the lifting of the bridge's centre span became Donald's main source of concern now, much like the Ghost of Hamlet warning of some inescapable doom.

The escalation of the war in Europe brought more men to the Colours, delaying, for a time at least, the Conscription that Canada feared. After France fell and while Britain awaited the inevitable German invasion in 1940, the threat was electrifying, bringing still more men "to Arms" in unprecedented numbers. And, in Gaspé, a curious thing was happening. While the Bouchards, Arsenaults, Dumaresqs, Sinnetts, Tapps, Pattersons, Norris', Dohertys and Allards from the Gaspé coast flocked to the Colours, and many were sent overseas; the Smiths, Clarkes, Birds, Vautours, Lukemens, McCarthys, Bradleys, Bonners, Blinns, Burtons and Bates right through the alphabet to Kozaks, Scotts, Veyseys and Zavitz poured in to Gaspé's defences from the rest of Canada.

This became a dictum of Canada's Armed Forces, that while inland boys from the Prairies and Ontario joined the Navy, coastal boys from Nova Scotia, New Brunswick and Quebec generally joined the Army and went overseas. In the beginning, New Brunswick boys would provide the main reserves for Gaspé.

But, unlike the early colonizing era, we'd not have the Royal Navy to protect us, as it did against the U.S. Privateers who made life miserable along the Gaspé in the 1700's. This time the enemy would not be our neighbour to the South, but our enemy to the East. Worse, this enemy would not carry the adventure and glamour of huge sheets of white sail upon a summer breeze, but an indescribable horror whose presence would be seen only after a devastating explosion sent yet another unsuspecting ship to the bottom.

the depression years; from communism to naziism

The St. Lawrence Waterway-Great Lakes System makes up the largest body of fresh water in the world. Some 65 trillion gallons cover nearly 100,000 square miles which splits the North American Continent nearly in half. The rivers which flow into this vast water table are of no consequence, but the one which drains the mainly spring-fed and rain-replenished Great Lakes is the mighty St. Lawrence River whose vast maw, beginning at Gaspé on the Gulf of St. Lawrence, mixes with the vast, deep water of the oceans beyond.

Indians sailed on it, and Cartier discovered its tip in 1534—at Gaspé—much as Captain Colin Donald RCN discovered it in 1940—400 years later. Cartier in his day was rebuffed by the St. Lawrence in his quest to discover the passage to China; Canada's military also would be frustrated not only by the Lachine Rapids Canal which however, did make passage to the inland lakes possible, but by what happened when freshwater met saltwater.

Canada in World War 2 would enjoy what Cartier didn't; a unique canal system which allowed the output of Ontario factories and shipyards to feed the vast military system building around Gaspé, as well as feeding war-ravaged Britain. Gaspé would be the fulcrum around which the Quebec City/Sydney/Cape Breton Convoys would turn, before their wild dash across the North Atlantic to Britain; Convoys which would bring treasures of food, clothing, wood products and all the artifacts of war to a war-ravaged Britain facing the murderous onslaught of Germany's "Operation Sea Lion" now in preparation.

France lay in shambles, by June 1940, prostrate under the heel of the most ruthless dictator the world had ever seen, while Canadian boys, from the land Cartier had earlier discovered, now represented the only fighting units intact between Britain and "the Boche." Britain's own regiments were helplessly in disarray after Dunkerque.

In Canada, in 1940, our defence posture wasn't as impressive. From Port Arthur and Fort William, Canada's connecting waterways represented the largest inland-water transportation system in the world, but just to get a ship from the head of the lakes to the St. Lawrence, meant a journey of over 1100 miles, with another 2000 miles to the open sea. While Gaspé offered a well-earned breather in this long passage, the system encompassed canals too shallow and too narrow for the demands soon to be placed upon them. Passage of the Lachine Rapids on the St. Lawrence, for example, had been the focus of successive generations since the early 1800's: Canada finally completed canals both here and at Prescott, Kingston and the Bay of Quinte on Lake Ontario by 1848. Locks were a minimum of 9 feet deep, measuring in length 270 feet by 45 feet wide.

The Lachine locks bypassed the foaming barrier of the Lachine Rapids with a conglomerate numbering five locks. The eleven-mile Cornwall Canal took ships around the Long Sault Rapids on the St. Lawrence near Cornwall, while the Williamsburg Canals, using parts of the St. Lawrence River itself, carried ships around Farrah's Point, Rapide Plat, and Galops, a distance of over 26 miles.

Following the Acts of Confederation in 1867, our fledgling Government decided upon a program for improvement of the canal system—(the locks at Sault Ste. Marie and the Welland Canal were already long enough). Building to a depth of 14 feet, however they left the locks on the lower part of the system the same length and width as before. This meant only relatively short ships could use it, even if the draft was later improved. The Canadian lock at Sault Ste. Marie, for example, was 100 feet longer than the 800 foot Poe Lock on the U.S. side of the system. The Canadian lock was, in its time, the largest lock in the world. Depths were also gradually increased in both the Welland and Sault Ste. Marie locks; the latter was deepened eight inches more than the Poe. Eight inches was important; every inch of increased draft over 21 feet meant an additional 150 tons could be carried. Clearly, an overall plan for an integrated Seaway was needed and this would come about with the St. Lawrence Seaway concept.

The T. Eaton Company sponsored a travelling exhibit about the St. Lawrence Seaway Concept in

1933 and I first heard about it during the unsettled days of the Great Depression, in the same year my hometown of Stratford was gripped with the spectre of Communism. Rapidly forming Trade Unions, grown more militant, found champions in Collins and Minster, two men who appeared from nowhere and set the town at odds with established authority. A contemporary of our schooldays, James Reaney would write about this in later years shocking Stratfordite sensitivities with his play "King Whistle".

In Stratford, it was the Mayor who lost his nerve and read the Riot Act from City Hall steps, which sparked the outbreak. This was not unlike the General Strike in Winnipeg on May 15th, 1919, when irate men returning from the First World War wanted a better deal. Troops and tanks poured in and as school children, we were more frightened than impressed when tank crews had to exit from their steel enclosures following their hurried drive from the RCR barracks in nearby London, because exhaust fumes inside their tanks became unbearable. They were poorly designed tanks, really not much more than Bren Gun carriers.

The show of force, however, was electric. Stratfordites turned on the military and cried "shame" for disturbing working men who only wanted a better deal. The Mayor was driven from office in the next election, while the local Legion members found their own way of dealing with the instigators. Riled at two "outsiders" defaming Stratford's Park system by preaching a foreign doctrine "on our soil," they took Collins and Minster to the Canadian Legion Hall, made them kiss the flag, then drove them to the edge of town with a stern warning never to come back.

One student, I recall, who didn't take this lightly was a newcomer who spoke no English. He and his mother had just recently "escaped" from Nazi Germany to get away from things like troops and tanks rushing through the streets. To find the same thing in Stratford was, to them, incredible. The home they stayed at was Allan Heagy's, a schoolmate of mine from Falstaff School, (Heagy would one day be torpedoed by the very countrymen from which their guests had escaped.) "I don't want my son brought up by Hitler . . . I don't trust that man", was the immigrant mother's reason for fleeing Germany.

The St. Lawrence Seaway, of course, represented peace, much like the League of Nations. My mother, an immigrant herself, arrived in Canada in 1905 after travelling steerage with her parents, three brothers and three sisters, certain that Canada offered the best hope for peace. The hope that the St. Lawrence Seaway was the key to peace was very real to my mother as "Free Trade among all nations" was an integral part of Peace and the Seaway represented "Free Trade". The memories of the First World War still rankled; in that war, she watched helplessly, as first, her two younger brothers volunteered, then her own husband who, despite sergeant's rank and an assured secure posting in nearby London with the RCR's, took down his stripes . . . "so I can accompany young Jim and Ernie". Jim Sugden was only 13 years of age, lying about his birth date so he could join his older brother Ernie, age 19. Ernie was blown up by an enemy shell in France and Jim was repatriated home after his father's urgent request to the military revealing Jim Sugden's real age. My Dad was later wounded in France in 1916, invalided home with multiple wounds, rejoining my mother and two young daughters he'd left behind, and remaining a pensioner for the rest of his life. My mother never in her wildest dreams believed Canadian boys would one day have to die protecting the Seaway, and certainly never believed that her neighbours' son would endure the agony of survival in its cold waters.

Canada entered the war as Prime Minister Mackenzie King would have it believed, somewhat reluctantly, only to guard Canada's rising self-determination. King also had his own peculiar problems not the least of which was his sensitivity to Quebec's historic anathema to fighting Britain's wars. He also never lost an opportunity to insist Canada was a Sovereign State and he liked Britain to realize this. For me at least, this explains how we entered the war on September 10th, 1939, a week after Britain's September 3rd declaration of war against Germany.

The battle upon which Canada's ships would now embark would last sixty-eight months. They would cover some ten million square miles of sea. They would range from the waters of the old world to the waters of the new, from the Cape of Good Hope to the Arctic Circle. But the biggest surprise, and for which we'd be least prepared, would be in our own Gulf and River St. Lawrence.

James Plomer, a banker in Winnipeg in 1937, already advocated greater attention to this lack of preparedness in the St. Lawrence, as indeed would George Allard, a French-Canadian from the little town of Chandler on the Gaspé coast. These men were as disparate in their thinking as station and rank in life could dictate but common was their love of Canada. Plomer, besides being an economist, was a "citizen sailor". He dutifully attended Winnipeg's Naval Barracks (or "Ship" as it was referred to), similar to dozens of designated "ships" now springing up throughout inland Canada. Allard enjoyed a love of the sea naturally as his own grandfather was a man of the sea in the era of wooden ships and iron men and once held a commission under Queen Victoria. Allard as a young man ran away to sea on a Scottish ship, unconcerned over his lack of the English language, sure the crew of the "Scottish Prince" would do him right. They did; his only disappointment being Britain's lack of preparation in the face of Munich in 1938. Allard watching the growing war clouds over Britain, was disturbed one night when he attended the theatre on shore leave, to find a request made from the stage for volunteers for the fledgling

Royal Air Force being greeted with "boos". He was extremely concerned when he learned that the "Royal Sovereign" had powder sufficient for only one salvo from its huge guns. While in the Mediterranean, he watched in disbelief as Royal Navy gunners used vinegar and baking soda to simulate explosions, hoping to scare "Il Duce" now threatening to form the infamous Rome/Berlin Axis.

Plomer, who advocated more boat-practice, even if in whalers in Lake Winnipeg, was appalled at Canada's insistence on continual drill and marching, rather than sailing. "Drill is for soldiers, not sailors," he'd say, and took his turn aboard training cruises whenever possible. He was on one such cruise, just prior to the King and Queen's visit in 1939, on board HMCS "Saguenay", when he wrote to a Captain Colin Donald asking direction on protocol. Plomer knew Donald, a former Royal Navy officer, would "be up on that" but what Plomer didn't know, was that one day he would have to pass judgment on Canada's Gaspé Force, a much more serious tactical judgment than mere protocol.

Canada's Navy was first formed in 1910. The dimensions of the struggle were not fully apparent in the mid-September days of 1939: even less apparent was the future scope of Canada's participation. Until May of 1940, the work of Canadians would be confined to local escort, only taking convoys a few hundred miles from Canada where they could be taken over by more powerful ships.

On September 17th, 1939, 350 miles to the east of Halifax, (Gaspé's Eastern anchor) HMCS "St. Laurent" and HMCS "Saguenay" parted company with a convoy and its escorting cruisers and turned back to base at dusk. They passed HMCS "Fraser" outward-bound with the first "fast" Convoy HXF-1; it was the first Convoy consisting of unarmed merchant ships capable of making over fifteen knots. (The slow SC Convoys, doing four to eight knots, would be left to Gaspé to form up.) Thus, the early sea-war for Canada got started. Not a bad beginning for a country which, with the young King Edward's abdication only three short years earlier left all Canada to wonder about the future of the British Empire.

With his abdication speech, many Canadians wondered what had happened to our "toughness": "You must believe me when I tell you that I have found it impossible to carry the heavy burden of responsibility and to discharge my duties as King as I should wish to do without the help and support of the woman I love", and commentator Lowell Thomas said at the time . . . "Perhaps we should have seen beyond the titillation of an international romance between king and commoner. In truth, it was a portent of things to come; a beginning of the demise of the order the victors had so painfully built on the ruins of the First World War." That same year (1936), the Spanish Civil War erupted with Mussolini completing his conquest of helpless Ethiopia while Hitler re-militarized Germany in defiance of the Versailles Treaty . . . No wonder Mrs. Schmidt had fled Germany with her son, Walter, and come to Stratford. The Communism we purportedly were so afraid of, was now replaced by a greater menace . . . Nazism.

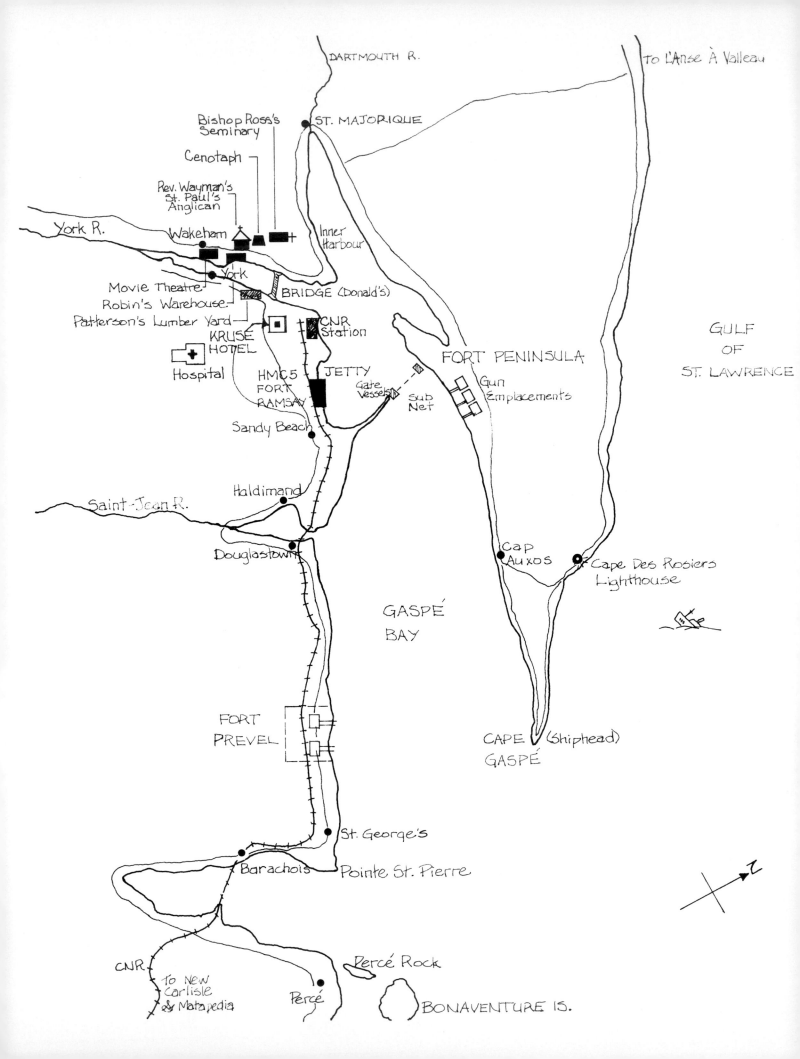

governments in flux: the emergence of the armed forces

Captain Donald was perplexed. He had reason to be. While he had appreciated Plomer writing to him earlier about protocol prior to the King and Queen's Royal tour in 1939 . . . Donald wasn't at all sure the Royal Canadian Navy was going about things in the right way. While the cornucopia of Canada is difficult to assess in the best of times, it's almost impossible in time of war. The resolve of Canada's fighting men was not difficult to assess but the trouble would be on the limitations the government placed on these fighting men, not only in Europe, but in the St. Lawrence, as well. This form of "protocol" seemed to be slowing things down considerably.

The RCN, RCNR and RCNVR, three arms of the Canadian Navy, were all placed on active service as early as September 1st, 1939. Donald noticed the best men were going overseas; mostly "R's" (reservists) and "VR's" (volunteer reservists). While Donald was RCN (Permanent Force), a career officer, if you like, he recognized that the "Naval Reservist" . . . the man who'd already gone to sea, usually on a Merchant ship in peacetime and reverted to commissioned rank upon commencement of hostilities . . . was the backbone of Canada's Navy. The "Volunteer Reservists" came next; those who joined for hostilities only and returned to their civilian jobs when it was all over. These men were indispensable to Canada's defence, and he wasn't at all sure his Permanent Force brothers appreciated this.

Donald was a stickler for putting "the welfare of the men, first", and was always at variance with the officer who was determined to promote himself over another, often at the expense of the lower-deck's welfare.

James Plomer, combining protocol and an astute appreciation for the need to update the Navy was what Canada needed. As a "VR" he was going overseas to become a member of the Tactical Group, forming even now, to counter the growing Nazi sub menace off Britain's shores.

Another was Jeffry Brock, also a Volunteer Reservist who would one day write a damning indictment about politics and war and who would also serve much of his time in England. In his book, "The Dark, Broad Seas" (McClelland and Stewart Limited, Toronto), Brock would write: ". . . I was beginning to believe that bad political and diplomatic leadership had thrust us, all unwillingly and unprepared, into a fight to the finish against people whom we did not know and had not understood. But I had learned, that despite public doubts, a clear call to arms in inspiring terms will quickly rouse the people of any nation, including many of the wishy-washy intellectuals and peacetime conscientious objectors. The most immediate and delighted response, of course, always comes from those who can profit financially."

Career officers like Lt. H. Pullen (RCN) scared the hell out of many a young recruit, determined to make them "disciplined". (Even his own fellow officers held his extreme views in disdain, nicknaming him "Dink" Pullen). Ordinary seamen who felt the wrath of his strict gunnery routine likened him to Hitler, bestowing on Pullen the hated name "Von"; "Von" Pullen became synonymous with all that was anathema to men who had joined to fight for Democracy, while on the other hand politics, epitomized by Prime Minister Mackenzie King, represented the wasteland of indecision.

This thinking was prevalent in Canada in 1940 despite the more pressing fear that Britain might fall. Unfortunately, this was secondary to our penchant for self-recrimination; first because of our doubt, as to whether Hitler really wanted war; second, once satisfied he did, would Hitler actually enslave us all if he had his way? Despite the gravity of this latter possibility, it never seemed to eclipse our delight to politic on anything and everything.

By 1940, it was clear, even to the most faint-hearted that, Canada would stand by Britain even as the U.S. to the south of us vacillated, adding to our own doubts. In Quebec, it was the tractious fighting between Premier Godbout and the Opposition, under Maurice Duplessis, which shared centre stage. The Liberal Godbout followed pretty much the line emanating from the Federal Liberal Prime Minister Mackenzie King, while Duplessis, anxious to regain power in the Provincial Legislature, reiterated hearth and home and not foreign wars as his Province's priority. He even castigated Prime Minister King and other Liberals as "Little Hitlers" who wished to impose their will on a free people, "even if in fact they were anything but warlike."

In the same voice Duplessis was not averse in claiming it was his Union Nationale's perception in matters military which had prevented Anticosti Island from falling into Hitler's hands earlier. "In preventing the Germans from seizing the Island of Anticosti, we prevented Hitler from establishing himself here. Imagine the Germans installed on Anticosti Island. With the protection that J.L. Ralston, Minister of National Defence, has given the Gaspé coast, what would have happened?" Bringing this fact home, Duplessis argued the long overdue plan to get the St. Lawrence Seaway project moving would alienate Quebec, making the transfer Port of Montreal secondary, an unjustifiable expense for a nation strapped with war. Appropriately, the St. Lawrence Conference was still fresh in everyone's mind, even if the incongruity of Canada having to convoy ships in her own inland waters was not taken too seriously in 1940.

The eight million dollars which would be offered in support of deepening the Seaway would at first be denounced by both Ontario and Quebec. Premier Hepburn of Ontario would use this opportunity to speak about Ottawa's initiative as an attempt to augment the B.N.A. Act. However, Prime Minister King would have his way, as was his wont, and by March 18th, 1941, an accord would be signed between Ontario, Quebec and Ottawa, and between Canada and the U.S. The hydro-electric potential of the proposed St. Lawrence Seaway, was an attractive and compelling force for Industrial Ontario and the U.S., not to mention the obvious advantage to shipping. The vast potential of Montreal as an expediting centre for the clothing, shoes, oil, munitions and artifacts of war from Industrial Ontario along with wheat from the West meant that ships would be required with huge holds. This necessitated trans-shipment from the shallow-bottomed Lakers arriving from Ontario to the ocean-going freighters at Montreal waiting to cross the North Atlantic. Soon even this would be minimized, and we would send the frail Lakers into troubled waters for which they weren't designed. They would go all the way across the ocean.

The St. Lawrence River traffic would find Gaspé a valuable fulcrum around which to swing Britain-bound Convoys because they would find relative safety here compared with Halifax, where the dreaded Nazi U-Boat already had been reported offshore.

Contrary to the view held by many in Canada in 1940, it would be the Church in Quebec that would proclaim the need for public vigilance against the Nazi threat to our freedom, not the secular authorities as you might expect. Cardinal Villeneuve opened the churches for public services, even as Bishop Ross in Gaspé admonished his flock to "do your duty . . . debout (standing)". Prayers of support for England's battle against Hitler rose, even while Duplessis, in a rare conciliatory move, joined with Premier Godbout in proclaiming a day's adjournment of the National Assembly in Quebec City to honour England's Patron Saint—St. George—an unusual mood for Quebec.

Duplessis would remind the Provincial Assembly in Quebec . . . "Our adversaries (the Liberals in Ottawa) promised a moderated war, a war of rose-water and gentility. They would stop the war when they felt like it; they would tell Hitler when to cease firing." Nobody, not our Federal Government nor our Provincial governments collectively, nor our veterans of the First World War who dealt so thoroughly with Collins and Minster in far-off Stratford in 1933, could tell Hitler to cease firing. Only cold, naked force by the combined Allied forces could achieve this. Donald and the people of Gaspé knew this now, even as Canada would find it more expedient to not report our losses there, rather than risk a prolonged acrimonious debate over just how bad the Nazi menace had become to Canada.

In human terms, the losses in England, after France fell, now exceeded 17,000 men, women and children injured or killed by September 1940, with October's casualties threatening to go even higher as Britain fought it out in heroic proportions in the "Battle of Britain". Every enemy plane downed was tagged like some coveted trophy, and newspapers in Canada carried box scores of the tally at each day's end, displaying Nazi aircraft downed much like the baseball scores.

The Royal Navy prudently remained aloof from bombarding hundreds of landing barges in marshalling yards on the occupied coast of Europe, remaining instead in Scapa Flo. The wisdom of this move would be proven a year hence when HMS "Prince of Wales" and HMS "Repulse" would both be sunk in the South Pacific because they ignored the potential of superior Japanese land-based air power. With the fall of France, Hitler achieved air superiority. By remaining in Scapa Flo and using the air defences available, Britain denied the Germans the opportunity to prove American Billy Mitchell's contention, that aeroplanes in sufficient number could sink a capital ship.

Meanwhile in Gaspé, the roar of an approaching aircraft jolted Donald out of his ruminations on the war situation. The aircraft seemed to reach a crescendo of sound, then suddenly stop. Captain Donald called all hands to the jetty. It was the surveillance aircraft he had asked for earlier, suprisingly delivered when he had all but despaired of help.

The sound suddenly stopped and the answer lay with the aircraft unceremoniously upended in the harbour, obviously too light an aircraft for the heaving waters of Gaspé Harbour. What he really needed

Surveillance aircraft assigned in 1940 to Gaspé. The plane however flipped over on approach and was rescued by tackle gear normally used for hauling fish onto jetty. Capt. Colin Donald may be seen with hands on hips.

—*Peter Donald*

were PBY's, huge amphibious planes better able to withstand these waters. But it would be two years before they came in force; for now, this was the best Canada could do.

He hailed all available hands to quarters and in minutes, the jetty winch, normally used for hauling fish into Robin's Warehouse, now seved "to fish" the disabled plane from the water. After it was all over, there was little doubt Captain Donald needed a respite.

The opportunity came with Col. Samson's arrival. Earlier, Samson had been invited by local sportsmen to take in some fishing, which he had entered into with typical Army despatch. To everyone's surprise, Samson caught a 24 pound salmon, reportedly one of the biggest yet. In an expansive mood, Samson invited everyone of any consequence in Gaspé to the Battery Park Hotel. It was the biggest social gather-

ing in months, according to Donald's 15 year-old son, Peter, and all watched the guests arrive with great anticipation. Peter would act as bellhop for the occasion.

Halfway through the dinner, Mr. Henry Berchevais the manager, instructed Peter to advance to the Head Table and deliver a telegram. Usually, a telegram meant something of unusual gravity. What could it mean? Not wishing to appear indifferent to the guests looking on in apt anticipation, Samson did the polite thing and read it aloud. He read . . . "From the Swift Canadian Company STOP Please remit payment in full for one 24 pound salmon STOP Signed Swift Canadian Company".

Stealing Samson's thunder, the junior officers had gotten one back on the Colonel. Everyone enjoyed their first good laugh in months; for some, it would be their last.

Battery Park Hotel, Gaspé 1942.

—*Ian Tate*

politics at home and at sea

In 1940, the feast of the Sacred Heart fell on the thirty-first of May, in the midst of "Dunkerque." The Quebec Premier, now Adelard Godbout, joined in a massive demonstration for the deliverance of the Imperial and Allied cause, presided over by Cardinal Villeneuve himself. He declared that for Canada, victory was an issue as critical as life itself and that the vastness of the Atlantic Ocean should deceive no one into a false sense of security. George Allard had already been telling this to his own folks back home in Chandler in the Gaspé after returning disenchanted from Europe. Retribution was at hand, or, as the Cardinal put it . . . "Armageddon".

Army officers in Gaspé, with little knowledge of how they fitted into the overall strategy of events in Europe, even now shaping the world, were nevertheless sure that the immunity of North American waters would not long continue. As for the Army buried in paperwork, envious of their seagoing brothers, they fought their days through a multitude of conflicting demands, grasping for the thin outline of the struggle which awaited them. They didn't know one of their higher officers had already proposed using Canadian soldiers to help defend Hong Kong—half a globe away.

Gaspé's Bishop Ross, echoing Cardinal Villeneuve's call "to stand", raised patriotic fervour and with it increased recruiting throughout Bonaventure County and Gaspé. Patriots such as Major George Sams and Lieut. Price accordingly, now roamed the shore gaining recruits for the Royal Canadian Rifles. These in turn would join with the Royal Winnipeg Rifles to bolster seaward defences; not for Gaspé but for defences in the Carribean. At least, that's what they'd been led to understand. This idea drew a skeptical response from Major Sams. As an old Army man from World War One, he was used to this sort of thing. He remembered that it was "Canada's Finest" in 1917 who, himself included, once paraded in their underwear after being torpedoed off England. They lost all their clothes when the ship went down and only had what was on their backs. It was the same type of skeptical response which registered now with Sams.

He also remembered when his own father rounded up over 700 horses destined for the cavalry overseas in the same war. They had swum ashore at Gaspé after being shipwrecked off Cape Gaspé. The official account said the weather had caused the ship to go down. Major Sams wasn't so sure. He was convinced it had been torpedoed although no record of German submarines operating in the Gulf of St. Lawrence had ever been recorded in the First World War. Sams believed, like Allard that the submarines would come again.

There were two types of Convoys leaving Canada now; the "HX" or fast Convoys out of Halifax, and the "SC" or slow Convoys from Gaspé. The latter originated from Quebec City, sailing to Sydney in Cape Breton before the hazardous voyage overseas. These included Lakers loading at Gaspé before taking pulpwood upriver to Major McCormick's newspaper empire while Lakers coming downriver carried cargoes to Goose Bay, Newfoundland or Sydney, from transshipping points in Montreal or Quebec City. Some lakers would take cargoes all the way to Britain, bearing ominous letters "WNA" above a waterline normally marked with Roman Numerals for the more calmer waters of the Great Lakes. "WNA" denoted their destination (Winter North Atlantic) and all that it meant in hardship and suffering. For the crews, defended mainly by D.E.M.S. gunners, (DEMS meant Defensively Equipped Merchant Ships) . . . this was their Armageddon.

The single code word, "Funnel", sent to all shipping just prior to the outbreak of the war, had initiated this movement of ships and now every ship in Canadian waters sailed under the aegis of the Admiralty. The next signal "Winston's Back" gave everyone an added lift.

The character and first main theatre of the naval war had been fairly well marked out and included the sweeping of enemy trade from the seas. Largely anticipated by the German merchantmen, they had already abandoned their voyages and dashed for neutral ports. The work of sealing them in or of

The "Pasteur," converted to a troop transport and still with its characteristic large funnel, prepares to leave Halifax for overseas. —*Maritime Museum of the Atlantic N-10-894*

intercepting them if they made a run for it was a measure of our resolve. A little known story concerns the "Pasteur", a French luxury liner of 15,000 tons, and how it came into our control.

The "Pasteur", whose keel was laid in France in the Depression Years, was incomplete when war broke out. Two slender funnels, originally planned to grace its top deck, were hastily changed to one large funnel, just so it could be launched and the huge broad funnel became a characteristic of this steamship.

The vessel was now in New York and the impending fall of France by May of 1940, meant it might yet capitulate in New York if it could not get to France. Already, the Mauretania in New York had been fitted out with deck guns and bunks, making it a useful troop transport for the Allies.

Churchill's foresight saved the Queen Elizabeth, still incomplete in 1939, by personally intervening as First Sea Lord and preventing her from being scrapped in order to obtain much needed metal. Two months after the war began, the "Q.E." was rushed to completion, and raced to sanctuary in the U.S. with some of the dockyard mateys still on board. Even in the First World War, the "Vaterland", a superb German-built ship, was taken over by the

U.S. and successfully used as a troopship. Why not the "Pasteur"? It wouldn't do to let her slip through our hands like the "Bremen". She made good her escape at the outbreak of World War Two as a result of the crew painting over the "Bremen's" gaudy peacetime colours and exchanging them for North-Atlantic gray. Adding insult to injury, the crew sang "Deutschland Uber Alles" even as the vessel slipped quietly out of New York harbour, and gave the Nazi salute as they sailed for Germany past the Statue of Liberty. The U.S. as a neutral couldn't touch the "Bremen" nor could they touch the "Pasteur".

"I can't speak French, you'll have to go". The words were those of Lt. Cmdr. J.N. Smith, C.O. of the examination vessel HMCS "Andrée Dupré" sailing just outside Halifax harbour's Boom Defence. While late of the Royal Navy, Smith considered himself a Canadian, although now would be the first, and only time, he encountered animosity between French-Canadian and English Canadian serving in the same fleet.

The lonely posting to the examination vessel by Halifax authorities, accentuated Smith's isolation compounded by the possible loss of "Pasteur". And it made him angry —almost as much as when the report came to him that his signalman on the bridge

34

Naval Boarding Party in dory, preparing to inspect incoming ships off Halifax. Shown are (left to right): Lt. Jacques Trepanier, SkipperLt. Georges Allard, Able Seaman Donaldson.

— *Cassidy's Photos, Gaspé.*

awaiting word on "Pasteur" (now rumoured to have left New York) had, instead, received word France had fallen. Smith had left Skipper Lieutenant Allard on duty with the signalman with instructions to keep an eye on the horizon, between scheduled signals from the Dockyard.

Allard, although just in the Military, already was showing promise of learning Navy ways. Most men like him from the Reserve already had Coasting Certificates in the Merchant Marine and, on the strength of these, had been brought into the Navy.

There were actually three Navies in 1940. First, there was the Royal Canadian Navy, the RCN or elite, whose officers had joined the force as cadets, been in the Royal Navy as "snotties", then, with their first stripe, a solid gold band, returned to Canada more British than their English cousins. Second was the Royal Canadian Naval Volunteer Reserve, to which I, and hundreds like me from inland cities of Canada, would soon belong, had no knowledge of the sea, recruited mostly from high schools or, as in my case, trained by technical courses most of which were home study. The Depression wasn't kind to young men of my generation seeking training in a trade, and technical schools, such as Beal Technical School

in London, Ontario were few and far between. Despite this sober fact, seventy-five percent of new recruits would come from Quebec, Ontario and the Prairies, where inland "ships", really a barracks somewhere in the core of the town or city, provided basic training. This training was short of ideal with the heavy emphasis on marching and drill rather than seamanship. The RCNR (Royal Canadian Naval Reserve) on the other hand, represented the opposite extreme. Most of its men had Deepsea Master's Certificates and had commanded large merchant ships. While the RCNVR was marked with officers wearing a wavy gold band (wavy-navy), the Reserves wore a thin criss-crossed stripe consisting of a series of links—as in a chain. The difference between the three was obvious as often shown by the condescending attitude of the solid-striped officers of the "RCN", who acted more like members of an exclusive club than sailors. It was once summed up with the wry observation that . . . "the RCN(R) are sailors trying to be gentlemen; the RCN(VR) are gentlemen trying to be sailors; and the RCN were neither but trying to be both."

It was a VR trying to be a sailor who accosted Allard now.

"You G . . . D . . . Frenchman", he hollered after reading the signal that "France had capitulated", taking his telescope from his eye and threatening to throw it at Allard. Allard had no time for theatrics. As a seasoned Merchantman and with the British Merchant Service, he had his watch-keeper's Certificate and by now, several years at sea. This was just a job, albeit a tough job, to be done. Not a world of fantasy wherein there were no limits to the roles that new recruits imagined of officers who appeared too often as "Little Nelsons."

Allard was too concerned about the Submarine menace, both here, and along the coastline of his own hometown at Chandler. If subs were coming, and he believed they were, he preferred to defend his home shoreline if there was a choice. That is what made the signalman's outburst so inept. This was a prime example of insubordination: Allard, although suffering the same isolation as Smith, wasn't that homesick for his native shore in Gaspé that he couldn't do his duty now. This was a most serious breach of Naval Regulations—a rating threatening an officer on watch. ". . . Tenshun", Allard snapped; "You are on charge . . . report to First Lieutenant's report tomorrow morning."

That had been yesterday and Smith already had been briefed—not only on Allard's charge, but the fact that even at this moment "Pasteur" was heading for Halifax for replenishment before making a break for France. Apart from the gnawing frustration of "why can't they get along" (he didn't like having English-Canadian pitted against French-Canadian) "Pasteur" might appear at any moment on the horizon, its broad single funnel a dead give-away.

Twenty-four-hours had passed since laying his charge but Allard's resolve had not softened, although his consternation as to whether a small town boy from Chandler could make his charge stick before an ex-Royal Navy man was in question. His trust in "British Fair Play", which had never wavered in all the time he had spent in the British Merchant Marine, remained.

Lt. Cmdr. Smith took his place before the tribunal on the bridge of HMCS "Andrée Dupré" while a stiff breeze sprang up, warning of a storm to come. Smith was not a big man, but what he lacked in build was more than made up in a strong face and steady eye. He looked at Allard, then the First Lieutenant, then to the signalman, his eye finally resting on the First Lieutenant:

"First Lieutenant, what is your comment on Allard's charges as read?" At first, he was taken aback by his response. "I find Allard has been too severe with regard to the Signalman's gesture". Smith was almost moved to reprimand the officer's inordinate response, but turning now to Allard asked." What is your pleasure?"

"I want the charge to remain as read", Allard responded, his broken English betraying his French background. Without a moment's hesitation, Smith responded: "Granted", at the same time turning to the signalman announcing "14 days stoppage of leave"; "Dismissed".

It was only moments after the defaulter departed the bridge, when Smith turned to Allard and the First Lieutenant. Smith spoke; "I want to remind you that Allard's Oath of Allegiance to His Majesty the King is the same one we have been given ourselves, English-Canadian and French-Canadian alike; I insist all officers on the bridge be treated with the respect due their station". Smith then turned to Allard and, recognizing his own particular situation, reminded him that the Monarchy represents an unbroken line through the Governors-General, of a system of Government going back to Champlain; the fact that it was an English King was incidental. "Allard, if you had not reported this incident, and I later heard of it and you took no action, I would have had you discharged from my ship and crew." Allard, for his part, satisfied British "Fair Play" had been exercised prepared to go below. Smith interjected. "Oh, Allard, hold on a minute, will you?" Allard paused. "Word's out that 'Pasteur' is heading this way and I'm determined to have it."

What followed should not be minimized because of its brevity. It wasn't anything like the Gunnery courses ashore in Halifax with "Von" Pullen mouthing bravado orders; nor was it comparable to the all-too-often organized disorder of new entry ratings scrambling for position while the 45 pound practice shell was rammed home. Rather, everything was done quietly and in a seamanlike manner, much as they'd been doing ever since both Smith and Allard had joined "André Dupré" some months ago. During that time, they jumped regularly into the dory, whether on a dark and blustering night or, as today, in the scorching sun of June with the storm not yet upon them. After a wet pull to the heaving side of a Merchantman, balanced athwartships, they'd valiantly leap for the swaying rope ladder reluctantly dropped from the huge ship's side, followed by the interminable climb topside. There, they'd examine the ship's papers and deck log, speak to the captain who wanted nothing so much as to get inside Halifax's protected harbour, only happy when the submarine net closed behind them. (At one point, Hitler had wanted to mine Halifax waters, only thinking better of it when he realized U.S. ships might be sunk as well. He didn't want to risk bringing neutral America into the war; the "Athenia's" sinking by Kapitänleutnant Fritz-Ludwig Lemp in the U-30 September 3rd, 1939, had been enough. One hundred and twenty men, women and children went down with her to a watery grave. The Lusitania in the First World War was still fresh in Hitler's mind and that sinking brought the U.S. into the war.)

"When 'Pasteur' comes into sight, we're going aboard". Allard, appreciating Smith's determination in the face of earlier uncertainty, instinctively knew what he had to do. "You can speak French . . . you

The Gate Vessel "Andrée Dupré on station at the entrance to Halifax Harbour. Note the half-section of the Submarine Gate is "open" indicated by the two "balls" posted at the masthead of the Gate vessel's yardarm. York Redoubt Herring Cove may be seen on the point of land in the background. —PAC 134327

Halifax Harbour's "Eastern Passage" off which the "Louis Pasteur" was captured in 1940. Note sub net in foreground. —PAC 134328

talk to the Captain . . . and persuade him to jump in on our side" said Smith. Allard, buoyed by his own Captain's obvious determination, and still glowing with the fact he'd backed him earlier, responded generously. The huge "Pasteur" appeared on the horizon, came onward toward the examination vessel and finally stopped. Accompanied by two crew members who went aboard, Allard, failing at first to prevail successfully on the Purser who greeted them, gave the reasons, in impeccable French, why they should surrender "Pasteur". It wasn't until Allard gave a recital of the guns he could bring to bear if they didn't, that the possibility of being blown out of the water from guns at both York Redoubt and McNabs Island opposite the Harbour mouth, made them recant. Slowly, the sub gate, which stretched between York Redoubt and Maugher's Beach on the opposite shore, winched open and "Pasteur" majestically slid through, as Allard put it, "in the name of the Crown". The winches thumped as they drew the gate shut again, the moveable section now fast against outside intruders. "Pasteur" was ours.

Paradoxically, while Canada's Navy went quietly about its work, unheralded and, in most cases unsung, the Communist menace which so many feared in the depths of the Great Depression was now replaced by the more urgent and real Nazi menace.

On induction into the Navy, a recruiting Chief Petty Officer attaches the man's name and number below a frame surrounding the new entry's face while two seamen in the foreground compile statistical data. A Pay Book was issued denoting: Rank for pay purposes; "T" designating "Temperance"—therefore no Rum Tot; Religion;—R.C., C of E or OD (Roman Catholic, Church of England, or Other Denomination).

—PA 134349

"d.e.m.s."; and the emergence of the secret "r.d.f." for defence

Halifax in 1940 was like the scriptural version of our Lord's reference to the narrow portal through which few entered, "the straight and narrow gate"; no one 'came or went' in the Navy except through Halifax. This was also true of the Air Force and Army and thousands from inland Canada 'would enter' before going overseas. A few would be held back to man Canada's guns at York Redoubt at Chebucto Head on the west side of Halifax Harbour or at Eastern Passage on the Dartmouth side, hard by McNabs Island. Between this island which dominated the harbour, and Eastern Passage lay a narrow strip of water: the entrance to Halifax Harbour and the passage through which Canadians would go to war. Today a new breed of Canadians came to fight the Germans across the sea: young men like Jack Whiteside and Bruce Ferguson, who left hearth, home and Sunday School in Ontario, and exchanged their sheltered life for the adventure of wartime Halifax, where guns would be placed under their control for the first time and they would be ordered to shoot; guns like those at York Redoubt.

While men like Whiteside and Ferguson chose the Army, a role closer to landlocked Ontario, other young men like Allan Heagy, Lloyd "Dutch" Davey and myself chose the Navy, for no other reason than that the Navy offered electronics training and the chance for a commission. It certainly wasn't because we'd had experience paddling a canoe on the Avon River in Stratford, and not because, unknown to us at the time, all three of us would eventually be posted to Gaspé.

Ferguson, affectionately named "Fergie" by his Army mates, was a teetotalling Presbyterian who possessed as little love of the sea as he did for guns. He would stay ashore, even if the most unkind thing officialdom did, was to put him in charge of the bar in the Officer's Mess. Officers, often frustrated by the menial task of firing the big guns at inconsequential drogues drawn by seaward tugs off Halifax, insisted on him having a drink when off duty, keeping him at the bar past closing hours while they pondered the meaning of war. "Fergie" preferred the 'straight and narrow', not touching a drop, although at one time he wondered at his sobriety when he watched huge telephone poles being placed on every hilltop and vantage point on the road to remote Herring Cove west of York Redoubt. He later learned the real guns were in bunkers below; these were decoys and, from the sea, they looked for all the world like 16-inch mammoth guns, sure to frighten the prying eye of the enemy now believed to be offshore. He didn't dare ask just what the 'bedspring-like affair was being erected facing the sea. It was Canada's first "RDF" and intensely secret.

Camouflage was the big thing, and ships, now assembling in Bedford Basin, the large anchorage a few miles directly inland from Halifax Harbour, were painted in gaudy zig-zag shades of black and gray to fool the enemy. The Royal Navy had held the seas since 1749 and the Royal Canadian Navy was its legitimate offspring. While our Navy was actually born in 1910, it only reached maturity under the tutoring of the RN. Even at this date battleships like HMS "Renown" and "Repulse" called regularly at Halifax to shepherd troop convoys to England, in ships like the SS "Aquitania"; "Empress of Britain"; "Mauretania" and the CNS "Lady Hawkins" and "Queen of Bermuda." Bedford Basin on which Halifax Harbour based its fame had been used as a haven by the Micmac Indians and as a sanctuary from the sea.

It was once the home of the Duke of Kent, where, in grander times, the sounds of martial music wafted over its calm waters and quietly spoke of the Duke's love for Julie St. Laurent, the beautiful lady from Quebec whose life with the Duke brought English and French blood together like no other. Today, over the same waters French and English Canadians now united to oppose a common enemy. For 15 years, there was a Royal household here. The Prince's regal home stood atop the sloping well-kept grounds, fronted by a rotunda flying the Royal Standard and from which the Royal Marines in 1797 played superb band music, while the fleet of that day lay at anchor below. The Duke of Kent was recalled to England;

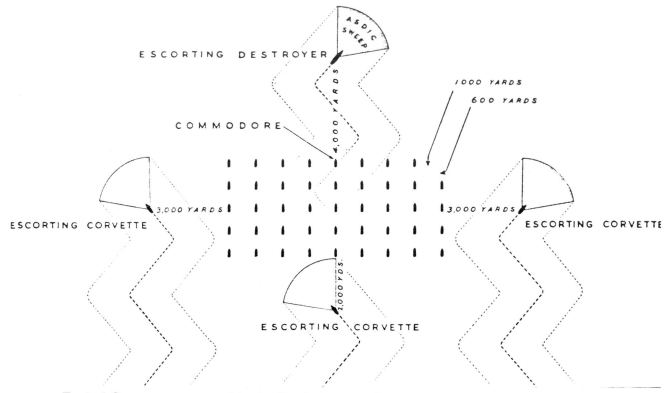

Typical Convoy pattern used in the North Atlantic. Convoys usually were smaller in the St. Lawrence.
                                                                    —Author

the glitter of the parties that took place on the spacious lawns bright with the colour of uniforms, accentuated by daring gowns of the ladies would have to be left behind. Also left behind was the first telegraph system in the New World which the Duke had laboriously fashioned between Prince's Lodge and the Citadel Hill fortress atop the hill overlooking Halifax Harbour. Now, a century and a half later sailors, newly trained in the art of Aldis lamp, challenged all incoming ships. The Duke had reluctantly left to return home on Royal orders to wed a *blue blood* German Princess to preserve the Royal Line, leaving behind a heart-broken Julie. Ironically, the one he wed was from the same line of people who now threatened our freedom and our lives.

The military tradition however remained and so did the spell of romance. More than one sailor, including myself, met his bride in Halifax. Overall, Citadel Hill towered above Halifax's waterfront and the huge clock which the Duke had installed in the tower ticked away the hours. Below, rust-covered freighters crawled slowly out to sea to meet their fate, sailing bravely in "line ahead" dictated by the Convoy Commodores echoing the discipline that the Duke of Kent had shown earlier on his obedient return to England. Now, sleek destroyers, like annoy-

ing terriers, snapped at the rusty merchantmen, occasionally sending forth a "Whoo- Whoo-Whoop" with the siren rising in steady crescendo with each blast. It appeared that they believed that the bleating somehow would frighten waiting U-boats now suspected to be offshore. Stories now circulated that Sambro Light served unknowingly as a beacon for submerged subs; of strange-looking seamen attending local theatres undetected among the hundreds of merchant seamen who now inundated Halifax; preposterous stories, none proven true. But, it focussed on the enemy, and that was good. Even the diminutive Birney trams, synonymous with Halifax as were the cable cars with San Francisco, were eyed with apprehension lest enemy agents should climb aboard. It was remembered that in 1917 during the "other war", an explosion in Bedford Basin had devastated the city of Halifax and it was feared that the agents, travelling north on the streetcar could repeat the occurrence and do incalculable damage. The Birney car barns, as a precautionary move, were now sand-bagged with a guard posted, just in case.

Men in uniform now poured into Halifax and helped to double the population, sending it from 50,000 to over 100,000 nearly overnight. The recruits regarded the uniform as merely an appendage to

normal every-day-life, moving freely with the civilians as if uniforms were the style-of-the-day. To do otherwise, of course was to court arrest by the Provost, no matter if you were in Halifax or any other part of Canada. Only a few tried, like Bob Dick of Toronto, who, before leaving on the Halifax draft, doffed his Navy uniform in favour of "civvies". His fianceé asked why? Bob replied "Joan, I don't want you falling only for the uniform; I want you to love me, for myself . . . not the uniform." Bob entered the "straight and narrow" at Halifax, after proposing and being duly accepted, leaving his bride of two weeks back home. There was no room in crowded Halifax. (Dick was a coder with the RCNVR, and coders would be indispensable to this new "secret war") and where Bob Dick was going, there'd be no room for brides. Those fortunate enough to receive shore posting for the duration, as "Fergie" eventually enjoyed after leaving the big guns at York Redoubt, would court and marry local girls. Hundreds of sailors would eventually fall under the romantic spell of Halifax and marry, even as did I. Most of us, however, didn't enjoy a shore posting, and got "a draft" to sea. Still others, like those brought out of retirement after serving in the First World War, had raised their families and it really didn't matter if they stayed ashore or went to sea. This latter group, formed the nucleus of the "Citizen's Navy": Canada's Volunteer Reserves (RCN VR's).

By July of 1939, in the midst of a sweltering Ottawa summer, the Director of Naval Intelligence had arrived from England. By established custom, and fortunately for Canada, it was a Royal Navy officer who took over. The first Chief of Naval Staff was a Canadian, Rear Admiral Percy Nelles and the former Naval Reserve HMCS "Carleton" became our first "Naval Service Headquarters" (N.S.H.Q.). The Honourable Angus L. MacDonald became our Naval Minister, while Sir Eldon Manisty, who had managed convoys in the First World War, had been quietly brought out of retirement, sent on a tour of the world, including Canada, and this world overview resulted in his writing of a handbook called "A Preparation for War." By late 1939, the contents of the book had been thoroughly perused and Ottawa was made "NSHQ". Actually, in August of 1939, Naval Service Headquarters first consisted of the second and third floors of a commercial building above a delicatessen on Queen Street. Crew complement numbered eleven all told, including Chief of Naval Staff Rear Admiral Percy Nelles and Deputy Chief of Naval Staff Captain Leonard W. Murray. They subsequently moved their quarters into HMCS "Carleton", ultimately to be renamed HMCS "Bytown." The letters "NSHQ" would become synonymous with all signals regarding our defence of coastal waters, including Gaspé. In the North American perview, Ottawa became the most important headquarters in North America, including control over the adjacent waters of the United States (even if that country was not officially in the war). This added to the delicacy of the situation, for the U.S. nation's capabilities would need mobilizing if the British war effort was to reach its full potential and Canadian control of American waters was delicate indeed. Not so well publicized was the Naval Intelligence Service which, together with the R.C.M.P. under Commissioner C.W. Harvison, would provide essential spy surveillance.

Everything about the Navy now exemplified crises.

Naval Reserve building in Ottawa (formerly HMCS "Carlton") renamed HMCS "Bytown" in honour of Col. By, Ottawa's Founder. —PAC 134336

Men who helped guide our Navy's early planning. L to r, Arnold Heeney, Lt. Col, K.S. Maclachlan, V/Adm. P. Nelles, Major Power, Col. Ralston, Angus L. MacDonald.

—PAC 134339

An early model of the "Corvette" being viewed by the Navy Minister and Rear Admiral Nelles. L to r: Rear Admiral Percy Nelles, Navy Minister Angus L. MacDonald, unnamed person.
—PAC 134335

Plotting Room NSHQ, Ottawa, where the fortunes of Canada's Navy were displayed on huge maps.
—PAC PA134337

"On duty" Halifax.   *— Ian Tate*

"On shore leave" Halifax 1942.   *— Ian Tate*

All the activity of "ships", plus Halifax's rapid growth, was masterminded from the little known, unpretentious and inland "ship at HMCS "Bytown." This, in turn, was supported by equally little known and unpretentious "ships" in all cities of inland Canada which managed to keep "Volunteer Reserves" active, often in the face of frustrating indifference through lack of funds. Unhappily, we had ignored our ship building program, to our peril, and now the acid test was upon us.

At this stage, the "Permanent Force" or RCN were "Kings" and the Reservists too often were regarded by the RCN permanent force as inferior. The Navy's new Naval Minister, A.L. MacDonald, a Maritimer familiar with the ways of the sea, believed a "citizen's Navy", backed by adequate ships, could do the job. Supported by men of Canada's industry, MacDonald set about building a force which eventually would become the third largest of the Allied Navies. The ratio of increase in Canada's fledgling Navy, compared with how it stood in 1910 at its inception, now would be fantastic. From the Depression-ridden years of the thirties, when we could boast only 137 officers and 1546 ratings (all ranks), to September 1939, our Navy would swell to 397 officers and 2,776 ratings. (By war's end in 1945, the Royal Canadian Navy would number 562 ships, including auxiliary patrol craft such as HMCS "Oracle" and HMCS "Venning" at Gaspé. These two ships and early armed yachts like HMCS "Raccoon", "Beaver", "French", "Husky", "Otter", "Reindeer", "Sans Peur", and "Vision" would constitute Canada's initial inshore defence. Later, armed merchant cruisers like HMCS "Prince Robert" and "Prince David" and a host of minesweepers, motor torpedo boats, troop-carrying landing craft, Fairmiles, corvettes, frigates, destroyers, two aircraft carriers and two "full-fledged" cruisers would represent the crescendo of ships now on the way.) Our initial overseas commitments would be handled by six destroyers for the present.

Prime Minister King's insistence on protecting Canadians from the harsh realities of war understandably sowed doubt as well. Wartime censorship would further accentuate this problem. Our familiar "two solitudes" between French and English Canadians, feared by some in higher circles to be uniquely Canadian, was paralleled by differences between the U.S.A. and Canada over Newfoundland jurisdiction. A large U.S. naval base was nearing completion at Argentia in Newfoundland and authority in the western Atlantic was delegated to the American Admiral based there. The Canadians, with the British and other ships they controlled, were now placed under an Admiral whose country was not a belligerent. Fortunately, Admiral Bristol of the U.S. and newly appointed Canadian Admiral Murray based at St. John's, Newfoundland were diplomats as well as realists, and relations between the two not only moved along smoothly but improved with time. In the case of Anglo-French Canadian relations, I only heard of one instance worth recording when Major LeBlanc changed his name to become Major "White" at Fort Prevel, below Gaspé. Relationships at Gaspé under Captain Donald, remained good—and they would get even better.

For the rating, we had 'our own' doubts. This was mainly because of having to wear a uniform at first associated with what most mother's insisted every three-year-old boy wear in childhood. The idea seemed somehow a retrograde step. However, the extreme comfort of baggy bell-bottom trousers and a hastily donned pullover (compared with the khaki battledress of the Army or the tight fitting pants and tunic of the Air Force) won the day. The casual manner in which the Navy suit obviously caught the fair maiden's eye, also helped.

For many, enlistment was an improvement over the austere Depression-filled years from which we emerged, where lack of money often meant lack of everything including dates. The Navy provided both money and dates. Compared with the lackadaisical days of "civvy street" where our inalienable right in a Democracy was to 'sound off'—without retribution, the sober realization that this ended with the Navy's strict insistence on obedience, was exemplified with induction before a battery of clerks and a Chief Petty Officer. A paybook was issued containing your non-substantive rating and your religious affiliation; RC for Roman Catholic; C of E for Anglican and OD for other denominations. Standing before a framed square, we were photographed, complete with service number. It was only now that the resentment began to diminish, when you realized you now were about to fight for the very democracy that was being restricted. Everything evened out, somehow, as young men "exercised Democracy" within the limits of their own uniform. We were the "lower deck" and there were compensations therein compared, for example, with our officers. The Sub-Lieutenants drew more sympathy from the ranks, than fear; their's was the lowest rank on the immense totem pole of officer seniority. Not yet a Lieutenant, they neither enjoyed the immense prestige which commissioned rank conferred, nor the tremendous influence a Chief Petty Officer commanded, even if the latter also was "of the lower deck" himself. "Lower deck" was a term going back before Nelson, an apt term, considering a ship was divided topside and lower: the neat division conferring rank and status accordingly. The "quarterdeck", or the after-end of a ship, was the most luxurious and contained officer's quarters and their messing facilities. All was duplicated ashore in the sense that officers still enjoyed a premium on quarters in spacious barracks (as for example, Nelson Barracks on Gottingen Street in Halifax) with elaborate messing facilities and with meals served by waiters. Ratings, on the other hand, lived under the grandstand (formerly the Halifax Race Track off Windsor Street, hastily converted for sleeping quarters) and messed in the

Officer's Billets, Nelson Barracks. —*Ian Tate*

(interior) —*Ian Tate*

45

former Agricultural Building on the same grounds. This was given the impressive name of HMCS "Stadacona (II)"; HMCS "Stadacona I" was the temporary group of wooden "blocks" containing nothing more than picnic tables, over which iron pipes were installed to which you slung your hammock. "Stad 1" built of clapboard and unpretentious in a setting of four huge blocks of buildings overlooking Halifax Harbour, was considered to be "more Navy" than were the red brick, but more substantial, buildings of "Stad 2". It was here at "Stad 2", a more pastoral, and therefore less warlike atmosphere, that the Signal ratings were trained; the setting being more conducive to thinking and study than was the more swashbuckling atmosphere of "Stad 1" on the Harbour.

The "Sig's" penchant for reading signals was evident everywhere. On every building corner on the grounds, lights twinkled far into the night as the ominous dot-dot-dash of the flashing light meant a signal was being sent, (in practice only,) and anyone who cared could read it. The dedication of the sailors was amazing, considering that the tram for "the bright lights of downtown" went right by the door. It was not unusual to see groups of blue-clad sailors standing around with signal board in hand, reading the mysterious flashings, which, to their trained eye, now meant something. We would receive our initial "R.D.F." training at this base and our induction to all the mysteries that this new art portended.

The letters "R.D.F." stood for "Range and Direction Finding", a byproduct of signals to be sure, but signals which were transmitted in pulse form at a pre-determined rate. They were "read" by a high frequency radio receiver which received the miniscule high frequency pulsed transmissions returning much like the echo from a mountain when you throw your voice. The time interval between transmission and receiving was carefully monitored by a sensitive cathode ray tube and calibrated with time. Thus, this time interval became a measure of distance, an incalculable aid in determining the range of a ship or airplane. The direction the antenna pointed (much like a TV aerial of today) gave the location of the plane or ship. Huge antennae on the south coast of England could locate German airplanes even before they left the coast of France, allowing the despatch of the few Spitfires and Hurricanes available for maximum strike.

Wireless facilities for communication with ships at sea were greatly expanded in order to handle signal traffic. One station in one month totalled 180,000 cypher groups. Small ships for the coastal patrols were somehow found, many not more than fishermen's tugs, equipped, armed and finally sent to sea. Zones along both coasts were organized for the control of navigational warnings, and a communications system was set up, whereby lighthouses in any area could be extinguished on the approach of enemy ships or submarines. A cryptic message often followed the Marine Weather Forecast for fishermen, or preceded it, and it meant the enemy was in the area and the lighthouses, accordingly, doused their light. Even CHNS Halifax, the only radio station which could be heard locally, transmitted its own particular code, actually the first four notes of Beethoven's Fifth Symphony. This spelled "V" for Victory. This lone radio station added to our sense of isolation, particularly when we were aware of the flood of Canadian and American stations which crowded our radio receivers in Ontario. This commercial broadcast station wasn't to be improved until the summer of 1942 when CBA Maritimes began broadcasting to the whole region with their powerful station, a 50 kilowatt voice destined to cover all of the Maritimes. In hindsight, this station was not necessarily a good thing, as it absorbed much-needed funds which could have been put to use developing better electronics for our ships, including improved RDF.

In reality, "this war" was rapidly leaving behind old concepts of warfare: of blind obedience to duty in the face of a foe. It was really a war of the minds. Whichever side could produce the greatest thinkers would win this war. Abuse of rank and the continual exercise of authority for authority's sake, would have little bearing on the outcome of "this" war. And those of the lower deck who couldn't abide the heavy hand of rank and all that that inferred, sought other avenues of service, while still in the military milieu.

To illustrate the determination of some sailors to gain a little authority, the following story is not unusual: upon arriving in Halifax and seeing the austerity of the amenities, the chance to be a Captain of anything was jumped at. Picture the young seaman's letter home to his parents, announcing he'd been made "Captain of the Heads". You can imagine his chagrin when he learned that the Leading Hand had merely given him the job of cleaning out the washrooms (in Navy terminology, these were the "Heads").

More than one sailor balked at officialdom, and found their natural outlet in "DEMS", the most hazardous and thankless job in the Navy: novices who stood along the inland lakes of Ontario dreaming of far-distant ports whenever a lake-boat sailed by, like Jack Cooke, Jack Kelly, Bob Dowson all of Oakville and, nearer the sea, John Ritcey of Moncton, all joined DEMS. One of the most unlikely candidates was Kingsley Ferguson, while a commissioned rank with Sub-Lieutenant rating, he nevertheless sought more freedom within the service and found it in "DEMS". Typical posters which went up in barracks now helped encourage this desire to 'get where the action was'. These men would become the "indispensables"; men who would set a record of glum, silent, wonderful endurance. Typical of their group was Joe Vautour who, soon to be torpedoed

COULD YOU

Destroy Every Messerschmidt Sighted?

VISIT THE NEAREST D.E.M.S. TRAINING CENTRE

The address and full particulars of the days and times for attendance can be obtained from the Superintendent of the Mercantile Marine Office or the D.E.M.S. Inspecting Officer.

THE SCHOOL IS RUN SPECIALLY FOR YOUR INSTRUCTION—WHERE YOU ARE TAUGHT BY SPECIALLY TRAINED INSTRUCTORS.

Every Merchant Navy Officer and Man should qualify. The Course lasts TWO DAYS.

FIRST DAY—Eye Shooting with the aid of Cinema Screen. Stripping and maintenance of all A-A weapons.

Merchant Navy! It is Your DUTY to Learn to defend your Ship.

SECOND DAY—Visit the range. Fire your guns at dive-bombers and fast-attack aircraft. Snap shooting at clay pigeons and parachute balloons. See and operate your newest weapons. 10s. prize and certificate valid for 4 months.

Spare TWO DAYS and qualify as an A-A Gunner. All this at YOUR Gunnery School.

COME ALONG AND SEE THAT YOUR SHIPMATES COME TOO.

Advertising Poster used to attract recruits to DEMS (Defensively Equipped Merchant Ship).

Typical poster of Wartime Canada.

— Canadian War Museum

repeatedly in oilers in the North Atlantic, found consolation in Kipling's poem . . .

"We have fed our sea for a thousand years
and she calls us, still unfed
Though there's never a wave of all her waves
But marks our gallant dead;
We have strived our best the weeds unrest,
To the shark and the shearing gull
If blood be the price of Admiralty,
Lord God, we have paid in full:

(Rudyard Kipling, an officer of the Royal Navy, penned those lines long before the 1939 debacle but in a rare prophetic mood, aptly described Canada's own, soon to begin trial.)

Even before Captain Donald had his twenty Navy men in place at Gaspé, or Col. Samson began installing guns along a peaceful shore, or indeed Mr. Goldie erected the first barracks at "Fort Ramsay", Canada's capital city Ottawa, had become a flurry of activity. As early as mid-1939, on the eve of the War, Ottawa became the most important control centre in the world. Here, giant maps appeared on the walls on which trained girls (the forerunner of the WAVES) shifted meaningful dots across the huge surfaces; each dot representing a ship movement off Halifax and in the Gulf of St. Lawrence. The exercise would continue over the next five years.

Halifax marked the terminal for departing fast "HX" Convoys. "The narrow gate" had expanded to become the major Eastern Canadian Port while Gaspé and Sydney would shepherd the slow "SC" convoys. And now it would be Gaspé upon which all our attention would be focussed. We never for a moment thought we wouldn't make it. Even after the fall of France, our conviction didn't waver. For most, this was rooted in the belief in an unshakeable moral and intellectual certainty that Britain could not lose. This in turn was founded on schoolboy learning which taught that we were at the centre of an enormous Empire and the life of the Empire was actually an all-pervading presence. The possibility of enemy submarines in the Gulf of St. Lawrence, let alone the St. Lawrence River, the backyard of our Naval defence, was too remote to take seriously. Yet, trained mariners like Allard believed it would happen and Gaspé's fears grew each month.

The seriousness of the Atlantic war touched Gaspé in a unique way: after labouring so long and hard to provide a meaningful defence of Gaspé, Donald at last was getting his wish to go to sea. Earlier in September 1940, the British exchanged naval and air bases for 50 old American destroyers. This was the famous "Destroyer Deal" which led to unpleasant comments regarding America's becoming a hostile neutral at Raeder's next conference with Hitler. Erich Raeder was a Grand Admiral of the Imperial German Navy. For Britain, however, the destroyers could do little more than cushion the shock of the first large sustained convoy battles in the Western

Approaches in September and October. In three nights in mid-October, eight submarines sank thirty-eight ships from three convoys.

Captain Colin Donald was drafted from Gaspé to command Flotilla Leader HMCS "Annapolis", one of the seven over-age U.S. destroyers that Canada received as part of the "Destroyer Deal" with the U.S. Donald had realized his wish for an active sea posting. But Frank William Kelly, stoker with the U.S. Navy and crew member delivering the destroyer to Canada, couldn't get off the vessel too soon. The boilers required constant monitoring after more than twenty years of idleness; they had been "moth-balled" in a U.S. Navy Yard since 1919 after the end of World War One. The fear they might blow at any time made watch-keeping a nightmare. Frank Kelly was finally transferred to the U.S. tender which accompanied the destroyers, leaving his particular "four-stacker" at Halifax on Sept. 9th, 1940 and returning to the U.S.

Any inconvenience, experienced by Canadians having to adjust to ships entirely different to our destroyers and Corvettes now coming off the ways, was offset by the generosity of the American "delivery" crews. In the case of the "four-stackers", every square inch of storage space was crammed with a variety of provisions which were now only a memory in England. In the mess decks, instead of the usual austere fittings, there were bunks instead of hammocks; there were typewriters, radios and coffee-making machines instead of the spartan fare to which our Navy was becoming accustomed.

There were drawbacks, however. The "four-stackers" had a narrow beam and shallow draft which made them difficult to handle in rough weather; and their progress through heavy seas was a fight which would test the mettle of Capt. Donald far beyond anything in Gaspé. As Joseph Schull was to write; "Their steering gear was flimsy and cranky; and they were to remain, to the end of their not inglorious careers, seagoing purgatories which those who would sail in them would remember with mingled horror and affection."

Three of the U.S. "four-stacker" destroyers Canada received from the Americans, as a result of an arrangement between Britain and America in 1940.
—Halifax, N.S. PAC 104338

seaward defence—without the royal navy

The Royal Navy did not come to Gaspé and neither did any of the "four-stackers." They would all go 'overseas'. As compensation, if that's the right word—a British trawler came for a brief stay. This was the same type that Churchill eventually would make available to the Americans when fourteen would arrive off their eastern coast in 1942. For now, one trawler was better than none. A year earlier, "Bras D'Or", a converted lightship and somewhat similar in size and appearance to a trawler, had technically captured the Italian ship "Capo Noli" as it was trying to escape from the Gulf of St. Lawrence on the eve of Italy's declaration of war. That was in June 1940 and served as a sign that we could fight. Unfortunately HMCS "Bras D'Or" was a precursor of things to come. It later foundered with the loss of all hands during a violent storm in the St. Lawrence, in October of that same year.

Our side now had a Navy with at least 50 destroyers, even if overage. Capt. Donald was leaving behind the interminable "ringing bells" as the bridge at Gaspé opened or closed as well as the tedious inspections by "Oracle". No longer would he have to watch ill-fated ships bravely contributing to our fight for freedom, facing perilous odds as they headed into the North Atlantic. Capt. Donald departed from Gaspé knowing that, at least he had instituted proceedings to construct a submarine net and the construction was already underway under the direction of Chief Petty Officer Percy Roberts. Roberts, a First World War veteran, would be aided by Lieut. Paul Belanger, and Skipper Lieut. George Allard, both trained in anti-submarine net installations. A little more than a year earlier, Korvettenkapitän Gunther Prien had entered the anchorage of the Royal Navy at Scapa Flo in Northern Scotland, bypassing the net and sinking the battleship HMS "Royal Oak". Later Prien, in U 47, helped decimate Convoy SC-7 off Ireland. This Convoy had departed from Gaspé in October 1940. Canada didn't want U-boats in Gaspé Harbour and thus the anti-submarine net was of vital importance.

In the face of all these possibilities, Army, Navy and Air Force detachments had placed our primitive shore and air defences on a war footing, including a Boom Defence. Failure to prepare a Boom Defence in neighbouring Newfoundland would result in SS "Lord Strathcona" and SS "Saganaga" being sunk right in the harbour of Wabano. While provision had already been made to build examination vessels, the "Oracle" would not be re-inforced for another year at which time the patrol vessel HMCS "Venning" would be available.

Detection, warning and signal facilities had to be greatly expanded, in addition to procuring enough men to operate the equipment. A re-assessment of requirements long known, but unfulfilled, was being made. This would continue for months to come by signals, letters and telegrams urgently requesting materials which did not exist. In this respect, manpower would be the most difficult problem with material coming next. Both would, however, be subject to attrition by the enemy, illustrated vividly for me watching a year later, from the same bridge Donald had watched from, as men and ships went down to the sea from Gaspé. Many would not make their destination overseas.

One Convoy, loaded with tanks, trucks and guns was lost just off Shiphead on Cape Gaspé at the harbour's outer fringe. Many of the ships in this particular convoy were "Lakers". The "Trevisa" was typical; narrow beam, shallow draft and not over two hundred and fifty feet in length, she was flat-bottomed and, in a heavy swell, rolled unmercifully. Canada had hoped to use such ships as a "trump card" in making up deficiencies when our ocean-going ships were being sunk. They were anything but "Trump"!!

The Nazi submarines were now attacking with new methods which were ruinously effective. They no longer lay in wait submerged but, instead, rode surfaced and awash during the day, paralleling a convoy's course at binocular range at night, coming in from the dark side of the horizon to launch their torpedoes with deadly accuracy before making off at high speed on the surface. The "Wolf Pack" was developing rapidly and it was this approach which

One type of British trawler loaned to Gaspé by the Royal Navy. Single 12-pounder may be seen on bow.
—J.A. Cook

W.W. war veteran CPO Percy Roberts. When Canada needed experts, Roberts supervised installation of the submarine nets at Gaspé in 1942.
— G. Boutilier

Making up Anti-Submarine nets at boom defence, Gaspé.
—PAC PA-134334

decimated Convoy SC-7 in October 1940. Captain Colin Donald had a personal interest in that convoy; he helped supervise loading part of the convoy of thirty-five ships carrying mundane but vital cargoes of timber, grain, steel, scrap iron and ore. Ships lost in SC-7 added to the final miserable statistics for the month of October which recorded the highest tonnage sunk by U-Boats since the war began—a total of 352,407 tons. Sixty-three merchant ships were lost with almost a third from convoy SC-7. The U-Boat Commanders called it the "Happy Time", and the SS "Trevisa" was torpedoed by U-124, 600 miles off Ireland in what was called the "Bloody Foreland". Despite these losses, the ships continued to sail, carrying food and fuel to help replenish the dwindling supplies in the British Isles.

Others carried wood products from the Gaspé to help build much needed huts and barracks to house the growing Army of men now pouring in to help save Britain. Many of the men came from the Gaspé, the results of Bishop Ross's ecclesiastical arm.

Mgr. François-Xavier Ross, Bishop of Gaspé, 1923-45.
— Georges Allard

Bishop Ross, true to his calling, eschewed war and found it especially difficult to countenance a war which purportedly served the "British Empire" and not Canada. While he supported the war against Naziism and Communism, he questioned Canada "declaring war" in the Empire's defence, feeling it was the politician's end we were serving and not Canada's welfare. Ross is quoted in Jules Bélanger's "Histoire de la Gaspésie" . . . "I can no longer accept the idea, however expressed, that in the face of this menace (Communist and Naziism) we must encourage the government to drain the country and to unman our shoreline in order to defend the English Empire on every world continent; that is the objective that motivates our leaders. As I submit to the law, I avoid saying anything that would impede the action of government; but I do not wish to intervene on political fronts, or talk too much, so as to approve officially, in the name of the Church and religion, the course government takes . . . " The above was written 8th April 1942, thirty-four days before the first ship was sunk by the enemy off our coast in May 1942.

Bishop Ross's secular counterpart was Major George Sams whose duty was to organize the Reserves, now being formed into an Active force from the many volunteers coming to the colours.

When war broke out, Sams was "called up" and took the Reserve Battery to Quebec City, where they had volunteered to complete the two batteries already there, the 57th and the 94th. The Quebec Battery was actually his old Reserve unit which he had left in 1921, following the First World War. Asked to recruit another Battery, he returned to Gaspé and organized the 82nd Anti-Tank Battery which eventually would go all through North Africa, Italy and Europe. He took the Battery to Petawawa as a training officer in 1941 and it was while there that he casually noticed two guns (one, a huge 10 inch) on the railway siding ominously marked—"Gaspé". It was the first time that anyone at Petawawa knew of Canada's determination to defend our shore. At the same time, the Royal Rifles under Lieut. Jack Price, a long time Gaspesian, was recruited, including young men like Phil Doddridge and nearly 200 others mainly from neighbouring Bonaventure and Gaspé Countries, for Canada's defence. (45 from these two counties alone would subsequently be killed in action or die in the Japanese Prison Camps of wounds or disease.)

When Sams returned from Quebec with orders to report to a Lieut. Col. LeBlanc, he was surprised to learn there was no "LeBlanc". "That's strange", said Sams to his mentor, "I was specifically ordered to report to Lieut. Col. LeBlanc". "Well, there's no one here by that name" was the terse reply. The sensitivity of the French-Canadian to his English-Canadian brother was obvious to Major Sams and he drew the only conclusion. It turned out that he was to have reported to a Lieutenant-Colonel all right, but to a Lieutenant-Colonel White the Anglisized version of the name. LeBlanc felt, rightly or wrongly, that the Anglisized name would gain acceptance more readily from his English-speaking counterparts who were now flooding the "Defended Port of Gaspé". The war wasn't all taking place overseas.

The Royal Rifles under Jack Price went first to the Carribean; the next posting was yet to be revealed, but it was certain by now they would not remain home to defend Canada's coast. Their convoy of one escorting warship, actually a converted CNS passenger boat, was waiting on the west coast, armed with vintage six-inch guns built in 1898. The accompanying passenger liner "Awatea", borrowed from New Zealand, was also waiting. It would soon take the two thousand men to a foreign shore for their appointment with destiny; and I would be one of the crew of the escort ship, HMCS "Prince Robert".

For now, the shortage of warships for convoy work in the Atlantic was pressing. Every conceivable ship was commandeered in order to act as a stopgap, until corvettes in sufficient numbers could be built to relieve our already over-burdened fleet of six

This once peaceful pastoral scene was converted to a naval base. —PAC/PA-105386

The huge task of preparing Gaspé. —PAC 105385

Defence buildings and Gaspé Bay at Sandy Beach. —PAC/PA-105384

Located next to Boom Defence; Jetty at HMCS "Fort Ramsay". —L. Leblanc/PAC/PA/134338

New buildings take shape at HMCS. "Fort Ramsay"; note ships at jetty in background.

—*K.G. Fosberry PAC/PA-134323*

HMCS "Raccoon" prepared for war October 1941, later sunk in the St. Lawrence by German submarine Sept. 7, 1942   *Dr. W.A.B. Douglas, Directorate of History/DND*

destroyers. The bulk of the fifty overage U.S. destroyers already had gone to shore up Britain's coastal defences, leaving only seven here to be worked into fighting ships. Proceedings of questionable international legality were now entered into with citizens of the U.S. bringing once-posh yachts under the Admiralty flag. Conversions to Armed Yachts followed, going ahead at a steady pace in our Eastern Shipyards. The result was a phalanx of new "warships" ready to enter the fray, and the "Halonia" —now the HMCS "Raccoon"—became one of these. Lieut. G.N. Smith left the Boom Defence and the "Andreé Dupré" at Halifax to take an independent command; (this time of "HMCS Raccoon") something he'd wanted ever since he joined the Canadian Navy.

Meanwhile, the Church in Quebec rallied to oppose the forces of evil while men like T.D. Bouchard, Federal Member of Parliament from St. Hyacinthe, reminded them that it wasn't just the Communists to be opposed but the far greater menace of Naziism. Earlier, Bouchard had opposed Duplessis's "Padlock Law" closing down any building known to be used for composition or dissemination of Communist Propaganda; now, Bouchard urged everyone to recognize the greater Nazi threat and fight the war at its roots. They gladly chose Britain's fight for freedom over Mussollini's and Hitler's dream of world enslavement and domination.

In my hometown of Stratford, not a decade after witnessing this pristine city's General Strike of 1933, everyone recognized the Communist threat to be a pale shadow of the real danger, Naziism. The same hungry men who once walked our streets now flocked to the colours to face this far greater threat, most joining the Army or Air Force; a few like myself, though inland and miles from the sea, chose the Navy.

A little more than a year after hostilities began, there were some nineteen thousand men in all branches of the Navy. They served in the destroyers and converted CNS passenger liners, the latter now named HMCS "Prince Robert", "Prince Henry" and "Prince David". Each of these ships carried over 250 men protected by four six-inch guns hastily drawn from World War One Naval stores and built in 1898. Such was the measure of our desperation that even yachts and patrol vessels, little more than fishing boats, largely comprised our initial Navy. These vessels were supported by shore bases such as at Gaspé; bases which now stretched from Esquimalt (HMCS "Naden") on the West Coat to Halifax on the east coast (HMCS "Stadacona").

Some of our men were now on loan to the Royal Navy, while by 1941, twelve thousand looked back less than a year to their day of enrolment. Nearly seventy percent had come from Ontario, Quebec and the Prairie Provinces—hundreds of miles from the sea. We were all volunteers, and our health gave little cause for concern to the medical examination boards which found few physically defective. Most were merely youngsters who somehow survived the "Hungry Thirties". In London at HMCS "Prevost" where I joined, one of these was Gordon Gee, who, as we stood before the M.O. "au natural", talked incessantly; I predicted one day Gee would be paid for talking. Today, he's the effervescent "Weatherman" on CBC's Metro Morning Show.

Ontario, Canada's largest industrialized province, now began turning out ships in increasing numbers. Between the years 1940-44, 80 Fairmiles, type "B" class boats, fabricated from plywood, would be built in eleven Canadian boatyards, seven of which were located on the Great Lakes in centres like Orillia, Gravenhurst, Penetang, Midland and Honey Harbour. Fourteen would be built on the west coast and seven at Weymouth, Nova Scotia. Larger, all-steel ships such as Corvettes would roll off the ways at the shipyards in Collingwood at an unbelievable pace with up to four being launched at one time. Fairmiles numbered ML 050 through ML 0129, would become the backbone of Gaspé's defence.

While the signing of the "Lend Lease" Bill in the winter of 1940-41 brought a ray of hope to our worsening Convoy situation, the circle of German U-Boats was spreading ever outward—with some audacious Nazi Submarine Commanders even threatening "neutral" American shipping on the high seas. In October 1940 a mere eight U-Boats sunk more of our shipping than the U.S. could build under the cumbersome arrangement as our "Arsenal of Democracy". Hitler, piqued at Britain's refusal "to make a deal" and capitulate, and before the failure of Germany's "Operation Sea Lion", now announced that "every ship, with or without a convoy, which appears before our torpedo tubes is going to be torpedoed." Some 63 Allied ships totalling over 350,000 tons would go to the bottom before winter.

For its part, the U.S. Navy had already instituted neutrality patrols, a 400 mile neutral zone westward from Land's End at Britain's western tip. Beyond this zone, merchant ships travelled the best they could, with capital ships of the Royal Navy assisting 'overworked' destroyers and 'novice' corvettes still not quite used to their new challenge. Meanwhile German surface raiders brought an additional threat.

The "Admiral Scheer" had scattered several convoys, decimating ships, in one instance only being stopped by the brave action of HMS "Jervis Bay", a converted passenger ship. Captain Fogarty Fegan, RN, on November 4th 1940, sacrificed his ship, doing uneven battle with the superior firepower of the "Admiral Scheer", allowing the rest of the convoy to escape while his ship 'went down firing all guns". From mid-Atlantic westward to Canada, our six destroyers gave valiantly of their time, overworked but game, making the turn-around with little fanfare and continuing until either sunk or replaced by equally valiant, though less pretentious corvettes. The need for a miracle became more urgent. Our losses now were disagreeably high. This was necessarily a military secret, but as a result the gasoline supply in Canada slowly shrunk and civilian use was restricted. Items like galvanized pails for fishermen and other simple household articles dwindled because the precious metals needed for their manufacture were now needed for war. The war was quickly coming to Canada.

the disciplines of science

There was a saying about Canadian-built "R.D.F."; it performed best when "switched off", but it was typically Canadian to make it work, even after example upon example proved that it didn't.

While the University of Toronto concentrated on turning out commissioned ranks for the new "R.D.F." early in the war, Canada realized it would also need technicians to operate and maintain it. Before the war was three months old, officers, like John Robarts, were being recruited and trained in Canada for the Royal Navy's "secret weapon". Before "R.D.F.", U-boats had been able to rise to the surface at night and attack Allied shipping with no fear of reprisal. Once on the surface, they could not be located by ASDIC but only with binoculars. In the concealing night, they were thus able to sneak up on Convoys, fire their torpedoes, and then steal away. By installing "R.D.F." on escort ships, U-boats no longer could enjoy such freedom of attack. "R.D.F." could "see" in fair weather or foul, enabling escort ships to effect kills. It was an effective countermeasure to the growing number of U-boats, and Canada bent every effort to maximize it, even if some officers still believed discipline alone was sufficient to win the day. Nineteen officers went to the U.K. as early as May of 1940 and within a month, all but six of them were at sea.

For a time, thirty out of the forty "R.D.F." officers in the Royal Navy were Canadians. Throughout the war about one hundred and twenty-five Canadians would serve in some of the RN's largest ships in the most responsible "R.D.F." appointments.

But, as Canada's corvette Navy expanded, it became obvious that we would have to train additional men to operate our own "R.D.F.", and we would have to build it as well. The University of Western Ontario agreed to a training course. Accordingly, fifty students, not yet having completed their Grade Twelve, were recruited from classrooms in Stratford, St. Thomas and London. Our neglect of Physics in the high school training of the day meant pressurized "crash-courses" were necessary to bring the students up to minimum standards in electronics. When Dr. R.C. Dearle, Dr. G. Woonton and Pro-fessor R. Allen, together with Doctors Hutton, Durnford and Laird, along with lab instructors like John Murray and Ross Love, began interminable lectures on vacuum tubes and math, it was perhaps natural that frustration set in to dim our hopes. One student actually "took to the bottle" during class, and literally had to be "poured from the classroom", resulting in a dishonourable discharge for him, and an introduction to Naval discipline, for the rest of our fifty ratings.

By May of 1941, HMS "Hood" had been sunk by gunfire from the German Battleship "Bismark" and we wondered aloud in class what had gone wrong. Our professors already had preached the gospel of our Allies ascendancy in "R.D.F."; using the successful use of "R.D.F." at the battle of Cape Matapan only a month earlier as an example. The Royal Navy had sunk three Italian cruisers and two destroyers at Matapan, following on the heels of Admiral Cunningham's success earlier on November 11th, 1940 at Taranto when he had smashed the Italian Fleet. Both engagements relied upon "R.D.F." to spot the enemy at night. In March of 1941, the German U-Boat ace Schepke commanding U-100 had been located in the dark of night at a range of over a mile by the British destroyer HMS "Vanoc". The "Vanoc" was one of the first escorts to be equipped with "R.D.F."

We had been smug about our supremacy in "R.D.F.", only learning later that the Germans actually enjoyed a form of "Range and Direction Finding' (R.D.F.) capability themselves with their "Seetakt" radar instrument. Perhaps it was their "R.D.F." that was partially responsible for the accuracy of "Bismark's" fire power that dismissed "Hood" so quickly. Operating on as little as .8 meters, it could have been actually superior to the Allies 1.5 meter wavelength, typified at the time by the Model SW 1C Canadian "R.D.F." British research had advanced well beyond this, and into the microwave era, successfully entering centimeter and far shorter wavelengths with little fanfare. This British advancement was as incredible as was the most recent word in 1941 that the atom had been smashed and that

Lt. John Robarts as a young naval officer, 1942.

—Author

The first trainees recruited specifically for the new secret "R.D.F." (Range and Direction Finder) later called "Radar". Recruits are in "summer attire" awaiting inspection outside the Physics Buildings of the University of Western Ontario at London, Ontario. (Note: one sailor still in the usual "Navy Blue" just returned from "shore leave". He was too late to change into the rig-of-the-day and was appropriately disciplined later).

—London, May 1941

Relief from the heavy program of studies finds four ratings relaxing on campus. Pictured in front of the University of Western Ontario are l to r: "Ordinary Seamen" Allan Heagy, Andy Devine, Alfred Searle and James Essex. May 1941, London.

—Tom Dent

Three graduates of the University of Western Ontario "R.D.F." course in Halifax, entrain for the opposite coast on draft to the auxiliary cruiser HMCS "Prince Robert" and the first ship on the West Coast to have the new "R.D.F." installed. L to r: J. Essex, B. Louckes, S. Miles.

Einstein already had written President Roosevelt, alerting the leader that this new phenomena would lead to the construction of an atom bomb.

Allied with our "R.D.F." was another electronic device, less complicated than "Range and Direction Finding", it was nicknamed "Huff-Duff". "High Frequency Direction Finder" ("Huff-Duff") offered bearings but no ranging capability. It worked on the same principle as ordinary shore-based direction finding stations, except much higher in frequency; so high, in fact, "Huff-Duff" could literally "listen in" on German U-Boats calling for directions from Doenitz's shore-based control centres in German-occupied France. The "Bismark's" radiating Seetakt "R.D.F." instrument had tipped off the Royal Navy as to the "Bismark's" exact location, enabling an accurate "fix" by triangulation of several "Huff-Duff" stations and helping to seal "Bismark's" fate. Leslie Claxton would be slated to be trained on "Huff-Duff", having been chosen from wireless communication ("sparks") trainees from our parent "ship", HMCS "Prevost" in downtown London, Ontario. Both "Huff-Duff" and "R.D.F." operators would wear the same "wireless" badge on our tunics and we were told that this was necessary should any of us ever be captured by the Germans. We were instructed to give only name, service number and rank hoping to delude the enemy into thinking we were simply wireless operators and thereby protecting our advanced knowledge.

At this point, any thought of other than victory was unthinkable. Our churches were behind us, and although of varying faiths, we essentially were already, or rapidly became, ecumenists. This was not difficult for me as my father had already given me an appropriate example. Dad, a staunch Anglican, had been invited by Father Egan in neighbouring St. Joseph's Roman Catholic Church to play "Ave Maria". War wounds from the First World War had blunted Dad's ability to sing in his own St. James' choir, something he'd been taught to do as a boy chorister in England.

Dad emigrated to Canada in 1905 and the fact that he'd play this holiest of songs on the violin was understandable as it was part of his training in England. What wasn't so easy to understand to we kids of our generation was that this was a "mickey" church—a term used freely by Public School kids. Dad played his violin well on that occasion, so well, in fact, that Father Egan invited him after the service for a whiskey sour in the privacy of his own study. A new regard for our RC brethren now emerged for me.

I recall I wasn't so sure of Allan Heagy but I'd live to see the day he'd not only bravely face the enemy but, along with his Canadian compatriots under attack, would survive. Heagy lived just down the street from me, went to the same Falstaff School where we played school-league hockey together and listened regularly to Miss Mary Stewart regale us about the British Empire "upon which the sun never

set". He could recite the twelve tribes of Israel at an early age and true to his Germanic background shared the pride of "Hindenburg's" twelfth flight to the United States after the largest airship in the world had instituted trans-Atlantic passenger service. His happy look however when "Hindenburg" crashed in a fiery ball that May of 1937 wasn't so difficult to fathom; Heagy was first of all a Canadian. Rumors had persisted that "Hindenburg" had been late in arriving in New Jersey because it had taken time to fly up the St. Lawrence River photographing the Gulf. This was not altogether unbelievable considering another airship, the "Graf Zeppelin", already was suspected of espionage by taking classified pictures including our own Naval dockyard at Halifax while on so-called "goodwill" tours. Churchill reportedly ordered all experimental "R.D.F." stations on the south coast of England "switched off", when "Graf Zeppelin" flew a goodwill tour over Dover prior to the war, in order to deny them monitoring our secret "R.D.F." frequencies. (It was later shown that the British frequencies were much too high for prevailing German receivers, therefore undetectable.)

Our own fifty "R.D.F." candidates came from all walks of life, from the son of a coal merchant like Allan Heagy in Stratford, a working-man's son Tom Dent from Woodstock, to a minister's son like Dennis Bright from London. I remember Bright well for he was chosen over the usual strict Naval limitations. Despite thick eyeglasses, he was accepted because he could work a slide rule like no other. He exuded solutions all over his youthful face whenever he smiled.

We were a motley crew; at one extreme we had diminutive but doughty Bob Shales, who appeared better suited to the officer classes of the University of Toronto as he arrived in a chauffeur-driven automobile. On the other extreme was huge Lloyd "Dutch" Davey, who once knocked me flat in a school-league hockey game making me look foolish as I tried my first bodycheck. Within a year, most of our original "R.D.F." would have sailed nearly every ocean. No one would have guessed it possible at this time. At first, our "R.D.F." class consisted of reading critical radio journals without much comprehension.

Gradually, working day and night, our grasp of electronics grew. Any earlier sensitivities that we might have felt about fighting a war, because of our Christian heritage evaporated in our first taste of victory: HMS "Hood" had been avenged by May 27th, 1941 and "Bismark" lay at the bottom of the sea; a victim of superior sea-power . . . and science. British "R.D.F." had been vindicated.

I recall how earlier our own Rector of St. James Church had argued the Christian calling by "fighting for the right". Our generation was the second in a little over twenty years to don the uniform and leave home. Our Rector, the Rev. F.G. Lightbourn, had himself been a vet of the First World War. He served when each man was issued a rifle.

In marked contrast, Jim Sugden, who had already served in World War One at the age of thirteen, found that after Dunkerque, Canada could not even supply a gun, but only a club. That was all they had been given in 1940 to defend the south coast of England from attack which luckily, didn't come.

Separated by an ocean upon which I expected to sail, on the eve of Dunkerque I was confirmed. It was early in 1940. In an age that was often uptight about authority and wanted to reject questions of faith for the challenge of reason, both our Rector and Dennis Bright's father, also an Anglican Rector in the Diocese of Huron, preached a larger view of philosophy that could do justice to both scientific knowledge and religious experience. Confirmation usually came at age twelve but, unlike Bright, I'd procrastinated and now I was nineteen. Living with the likelihood of war ever since the failure of the League of Nations, I only agreed to be confirmed now because my older sister, Helen, who sang regularly in the choir had insisted. The dictum "there are no atheists in foxholes" now proved a stronger argument than any anticipated embarrassment in approaching our Bishop Seager in a lineup of twelve year-olds! This embarrassment was happily overcome when my older brother, George, agreed to join me. A Sgt. Whitehead showed up in the same line, dressed in the full battledress of the local Perth Regiment. George was twenty; Whitehead nearer forty. As Dr. Samuel Johnson had written in books which were in my father's library at home . . . "the good and evil of eternity are too ponderous for the wings of wit; the mind sinks under them in passive helplessness, content with calm belief and humble adoration." In this sense, our generation "fighting the good fight" was content to leave the sorting out to the Ecclesiastics; ours was but to do or die, and we went off to war; my brother to Italy and I to the East Coast preparing for the Atlantic.

However, it wasn't to be exactly this way. When we arrived in Halifax by the summer of 1941, it proved as anticlimatic as had our sudden earlier departure from London, cutting short our studies. No ships were ready; instead, we were put to work digging postholes for the new RCN Naval Hospital being built next door to our barracks (HMCS "Stadacona"). Soon the hospital would receive our own dead and dying, while officialdom pondered what to do: tell Canada or remain silent.

While still in London in our "Ivy Halls of Learning," it became apparent that all was not well between the University and the Navy. When it became necessary for punishment for an earlier misdemeanor perpetrated by the one rating drinking in class, an officer, whom we had never seen before, addressed us peremptorily . . . "Now I've got you scared, we'll keep you that way". This was followed with endless route marches all over London and drill, drill, drill.

While the University carried the candle for an echelon of recruits who should have commanded respect,—after all, we were helping forge a new weapon which could be decisive, the officer persisted with drill. Endless drill somehow wasn't compatible with books and lab sessions; teachers wondered why we came to class tired.

Canada by this time faced the prospect of "spreading itself too thin", and took on more than it could handle for a nation of only twelve million. This was true especially in manpower, where pressure was being exerted to send the Royal Rifles of Gaspé and the Winnipeg Grenadiers to Hong Kong, even as no less a person than Winston Churchill argued there was not the slightest chance of holding Hong Kong for long or of relieving it if attacked. No one at the centre of government had realistically judged all the details. Men like C.D. Howe argued that Canada could make a strong industrial base and remain Britain's closest ally. Canada would actually man a large proportion of Britain's airplanes fighting the Luftwaffe; would take care of Convoys in the western Atlantic, as well as put seven army divisions in the field in Europe. Military and industrial ambitions expanded, but our power of decision as to who to send where, waned.

This was the reason that discipline, executed by the heavy hand of officers who believed that numbers alone could make up for Canada's poorly trained manpower, hoped to smooth over the inherent fear felt by a government not prepared for war. In much the same way, our determination to "go our own way", by developing a uniquely Canadian-built "R.D.F.", benefitted only the Canadian Industrial producers. About forty out of every one thousand Canadians would serve; unbelievable if one reflected on the "Hungry Thirties" when the only discipline was the soup-line for single men and a bag of potatoes for married men.

Dennis Bright should have gotten a shore posting as an instructor upon arrival in Halifax; instead, we all were subject to more drill under an officer pantheon which included Gunnery Officers wearing horrible black gaiters just below the knee causing their pants to appear like baggy plus fours. They left an indelible mark on raw recruits, typified by one who described them succinctly as . . . "Bull-shit and 'Gaiters'."

The only way out of the Halifax dilemma was to get a draft to a ship, preferably a Corvette, where the less "Pusser Routine" was far easier to take, even if the discomfort at sea was not. Commodore "Daddy" Woodward proffered his own solution; join DEMS and go to sea on a merchantman where there was no military routine at all. Of course, the danger was an important deterrent and I never envied the DEMS their lot, even if by joining DEMS, you automatically avoided constant drill. DEMS personnel received a wage of $75 to $100 per month plus a war-risk bonus of $44.50 and sailed on poorly armed merchantships. "This isn't Democracy", Gerry Gray complained to me during an extra heavy drill session under the hot August sun. It was only one month after our arrival, and Halifax's Navy Parade Square was rapidly becoming an object of hate. "I'm going to write a letter to the newspaper," Gerry heatedly exclaimed after one particularly grueling session. Of course, he never did, so far as I'm aware, but what happened subsequently left me to wonder.

An unannounced visit one day found Canada's Naval Minister Angus L. MacDonald touring the Dockyard. During a brief rest, he casually glanced from the window and spotted a rating carrying a sandbag pack while carrying a rifle spread-eagled above his head. He'd also been ordered to run "on the double" in the hot sun. MacDonald, understandably angered, ordered the exercise stopped much to the consternation of the attending Gunnery Officer.

Even officers themselves weren't spared the strictures of the Parade Square. Men like Kingsley Ferguson, for example, following in the vanguard of Robarts and other promising young officers who had already gone to Britain for advanced training, stopped short because he couldn't stomach Navy-style discipline. To him, it seemed patterned more after "Captain Bligh" than common sense. Woodward succeeded in getting a posting for Ferguson to train merchant ship gunnery crews in Newfoundland.

At least sixteen battleships, twenty-three fleet and escort carriers and thirty-seven cruisers of the Royal Navy received some two hundred and fifty Canadians from the University of Toronto "R.D.F." training. Our class of forty-nine were sent to corvettes with the exception of myself and two others. We got a draft to HMCS "Prince Robert", actually an auxiliary cruiser stationed on the West Coast and the most "pusser" ship in the Navy. More drill!! This was the first Canadian warship to be "R.D.F." equipped on the West Coast, and despite the "pusser" handicap, we enjoyed some degree of pride in this posting: "Prince Robert" would also be the only escort for the New Zealand ship "Awatea" preparing to take some two thousand barely trained men to Hong Kong. As they boarded in Vancouver, we could see the flash badges plainly marked "Royal Rifles" and "Winnipeg Grenadiers" which included about one-hundred and eighty from Gaspé and Bonaventure Counties.

Dennis Bright, from our class, was posted to HMCS "Windflower"; already a veteran of the North Atlantic. When "Windflower" first went overseas in 1940 carrying a wooden gun, it was greeted by HMS Rodney, who's skipper reportedly signalled . . . "My God! Since when are we clubbing the enemy to death?" It was about this time that we hoped America would come into the war. When this momentous news did come, I remember the date, not for the horrific event and what followed but because it

HMCS "Prince Robert", sole escort to the passenger liner "Awatea", which convoyed the Canadian Garrison to Hong Kong. Photo taken at Esquimalt, B.C. —PAC 116834

marked the second loss in our tight little original fifty "R.D.F."; and death was far more final than the dishonourable discharge of that earlier rating in London.

"Windflower" was off Newfoundland when it happened. Seven successive convoys westward bound from England already had been dispersed by gales which drove merchantmen apart, making watch-keeping difficult. The fogs of the Grand Banks added to their hardships and Model SW1C "R.D.F.", with its characteristic blank half-mile profile on the green trace of the oscilloscope which meant nothing under a half-mile could be spotted, could offer little help. "Windflower" fell victim.

The freighter "Zypenburg" was lost to the radar operators on "Windflower" in the torrents of sea and fog. Undetected, it swept down on "Windflower", slicing across the diminutive Corvette as the boilers blew. Within ten minutes, "Windflower" was sinking, the starboard lifeboat thrown overboard by the explosion. Live steam, mixing with the interminable fog, made visibility impossible for the men remaining on board even though they managed to get the port lifeboat away, together with one Carley float. The once-proud "Windflower's" stern went under first, then her forepart heaved up perilously close to the men already swimming. Suddenly, looking up, the men spotted Dennis Bright, wandering around the deck without his glasses, arms outstretched and feeling his way. They called out to him to jump, but he couldn't hear above the din. He vanished with the ship.

It was December the seventh, 1941; Pearl Harbour day, and the U.S. was in the war.

Raising the White Ensign marks the official opening of HMCS "Fort Ramsay" as Canada prepares to defend herself at home.
— C. Scott

"pauchenslag"; canada's trial begins

"Pauchenslag", or "Drum Beat", was the signal for all out U-boat warfare, as Carl Doenitz's great attack upon North American shipping began in 1942. From his headquarters in France, Doenitz stopped the submarine campaign in the Mediterranean and Bay of Biscay with this signal in favour of defeating the Allies by completely cutting the lines of supply to Britain. By Christmas of 1941, the German submarine fleet had only one sub remaining active in waters off Newfoundland; the bulk of them having earlier been sent to support Rommel in North Africa by blockading Allied shipping in the Mediterranean. Now, things were about to change. Germany declared war on the United States on December 11th, 1941 following Pearl Harbour, and President Roosevelt ended U.S. neutrality in the European War. Italy echoed the German declaration and the U.S. replied by declaring war on both on the same day.

By January of 1942, the Nazi subs fanned out in groups and headed for the Eastern Seaboard of the U.S. and Canada. For Canada, a nation of only twelve million, this was going to be the big test. The "Docnitz Dagger" was pointed at the vast shipping lanes off the East Coast from south of Florida up to New York and Maine, and including the Eastern Canadian Seaboard. Here, the vast maw of the Gulf of St. Lawrence beckoned: from the ports of Quebec and Montreal and along the St. Lawrence, the artifacts of war and supplies moved along a vast waterway through Gaspé for final convoy muster at Sydney before the perilous journey to Britain. Plans earlier had been made at the St. Lawrence Conference of 1940 to provide a St. Lawrence Escort Force but it somehow hadn't materialized. Considering what our military disposition had been in 1939 when war began, at the beginning of 1942, Canada hadn't much to look back on militarily. For us, this was the "Eve of Battle"; yet, Canada hadn't been properly prepared, even if Gaspé's HMCS "Fort Ramsay" would be officially opened May 1st, 1942.

In the closing days of August 1939, the Chief of Naval Staff was instructed to provide for the seaward defence of Canada in view of "a state of anticipated war". Almost a year later in Ottawa, two soldiers at Army HQ sat playing checkers while C.P. Stacey, having received his "call to arms" when teaching in the U.S., returned to Canada to find Gen. H.D.G. Crearer "apparently planning the defence of the Maritime provinces with the aid of an Esso road map."

Canada was slow to realize that this was a formidable assignment. Half of the continent that was to be defended had a great swath of ocean penetrating its very vitals with the St. Lawrence River, a deep-gashed seaway which would bear with wide impartiality the ships of enemy or friend. About one fifth of Canada's wealth was fed by it, with ocean freighters and the ubiquitous vital and vulnerable "lakers" sailing everywhere on this indivisible sea. No one seemed to fully recognize this area as being a major problem. By early 1942, our six fairly modern destroyers had already been reduced in number by action in the Atlantic, while our defence of the river and the Gulf of St. Lawrence at this time rested on one Bangor Class minesweeper, HMCS "Medicine Hat", and two Fairmiles. The Fairmiles were actually gasoline-powered motor launches of 112 feet in length, and the two on hand were the vanguard of Canada's first half-dozen Fairmiles to come down the St. Lawrence headed up by Lieutenants Norm Simpson and Bill Grand, both of Toronto. These two would be the aegis of the bulk of our Fairmiles to navigate the long inland waterway, involving the Welland Canal and the tricky smaller canals on the St. Lawrence. Often, the Fairmiles would require "standing to" while the larger ships of commerce passed. The Fairmiles, then would be tossed about like corks; an upsetting harbinger of things to come in the Gulf. Corvettes and minesweepers would endure the same thing, except that the sheer bulk of the Corvettes would be their saving grace in riding the swells.

While all this was going on, Commander "Daddy" Woodward was scurrying around trying to locate enough seamen in Halifax to ship out on our merchantmen for DEMS. How to find them? Perhaps they

Launching of the Corvette, HMCS "Charlottetown". Fitting-out commenced at Kingston, Ontario, Sept. 13th, 1942.

—*PAC 135901*

could be found among those men facing military discipline or men being "run" as the Navy called it. "See who's being 'run' today, and bring me that man", Woodward would charge Petty Officer Anderson who already had several recruits in mind. One included a Jack Kelly, representative of our youth of Canada and an example of our fighting sea arm to come.

Kelly was just seventeen when he joined up at HMCS "Star", the volunteer Naval Reserve Base at Hamilton which served the area of Oakville, Kelly's hometown. Kelly's ideal had been a particularly gifted Naval officer, Lieutenant Sennet, who made a name for himself in the torpedo school at Halifax. But there the parallel ended. When Kelly fell under the harsh commands of Gunnery Officers such as Lt. Hugh Pullen, his love affair with the Navy ended. "Kelly was staring into space when I found him, mumbling something about 'looking at three years behind bars', Anderson related, so I decided to bring him to you." Typically, Woodward listened attentively. Kelly, it transpired, had made the fatal mistake of striking an officer when he charged Kelly with getting out of bed too slowly. "I talked to him . . . and . . . assured him I would get in touch with you," Anderson paused, not quite sure he'd done the right thing. "You will see him sir"? There

was no hesitancy on Woodward's part. "Why? A rating is not allowed to strike an officer", interjected Woodward, an old Royal Navy man himself and wise to the ways of K.R. & A.I. (King's Rules and Admiralty Instructions) "Bring the lad to me". Kelly was "sentenced" to three days confined to barracks, not a life sentence as expected, and became one of the best DEMS men around. "You tell young 'Nelson' in there you're going to work for me," Woodward had said, and that's all there was to it. Kelly would go on to serve twenty months on a host of freighters, as well as the all-French speaking ice-breaker "Ernest Lapointe." Kelly got on famously, helping to clear the St. Lawrence of ice during freezeup. In contrast "R.D.F." personnel couldn't get out of Navy discipline and into "DEMS". When I tried to get out of the Navy and into the Air Force, I was told . . . "The government's spent too much money on you; you can't leave." Thus paid as a seaman but wearing a wireless badge, my masquerade continued.

Not only acquiring the men to run them, but building the ships was an equally traumatic experience for Canada. Shipbuilding on the Great Lakes of Ontario and the St. Lawrence River now became the focus of attention. HMCS "Arrowhead", one of the first corvettes to be built in Canada, already had been through WUPS (work-ups) off Halifax and

Fairmiles in "line formation" head for Gaspé, 1942

— *Gavin Clark*

HMCS "Charlottetown" was already launched by September 12th, 1941 at Kingston, Ontario with the actual fitting out of that ship commencing on the thirteenth, a date that was to have dire forebodings for the crew later on. The ships HMCS "Hepatica"; "Vegreville"; "Weyburn" and "Trail" would eventually converge on the Gulf, as well as Fairmiles Q 063, Q 064 and Q 065. Further Fairmiles would mainly come from shipbuilders in Ontario. Contrary to common belief, Ontario, although almost land-locked, is a nautical province with salt water at its northern boundary (James and Hudson Bays) and a string of freshwater lakes making up its southern boundary and it has a Naval heritage that goes back to the war of 1812. Small wonder, therefore, that Ontario would provide many of the ships for the coming conflict. Too bad much-needed accommodation for the men who'd sail them hadn't fared as well.

The deteriorating barrack situation at Halifax unhappily typified the Navy's Maritime Command. HMCS "Stadacona 1", Halifax's land-based Naval establishment, consisted mainly of so-called "temporary" wooden barrack blocks fronting on Barrington Street overlooking the Naval Dockyard. Many had burned down early in the war, and the excess of men spilled over into remaining buildings, increasing the load on this already overloaded facility. When our "R.D.F." group arrived in late July 1941, we necessarily were pushed over into equally "temporary" grounds at "Stadacona 2," actually the Halifax Agricultural grounds where we slept below the grandstand pending assignment to ships. It was from here we travelled by open truck seven miles to Herring Cove, relieved from the burden of digging postholes at "Stad 1," and took up our "R.D.F." studies again. It was at the Cove we saw our first operational 'R.D.F.'—the "bed-spring" Fergie had earlier seen at York Redoubt. It was here we also saw the guns which earlier had threatened "Pasteur" into capitulating; actually huge telephone poles mounted on stone pillars and nothing more. The real guns were hidden in concrete bunkers below. To subs now known to be lurking offshore, they looked menacing enough from a distance and provided a succesful ruse.

The "bed-spring" was actually an intricate array of transmitting and receiving antennae which fed a small, darkened room in an equally small wooden hut resembling a fisherman's lair. Because of our numbers, only a few at a time were allowed inside to work the machine. The others stood around, until one man hit upon the idea of skinny-dipping in the secluded cove. So while we watched the thin green trace on the face of the six inch cathode-ray tube delineate freighters approaching Halifax Harbour, (some as far distant as eighteen miles this side of the Sambro Light) our exuberance for this newly discovered "art" was offset by the longing to be jumping in the cool waters of the Atlantic. When we returned to "Stad 1," after the exhilaration of the outdoors, we

recognized the problem which would face Commodore Murray when he returned from Newfoundland's earlier appointment. By Sept. 9, 1942, (Murray would subsequently take over all of the Atlantic Coast including Gaspé as C.O.A.C. [Commanding Officer Atlantic Command]) Halifax's so-called temporary buildings would lead Murray to say later . . . "that lack of accommodation presented a major problem; that his officers and himself looked forward to the day when the majority of HMCS 'Stadacona' ratings will be housed and amused in this establishment without recourse to the dubious recreation which the Port of Halifax provided." However, failure to address this now would bring dire consequences for Murray, later.

The "dubious recreation," of course, was the slum area just down the street from the barracks, which housed bawdy houses on a grand scale . . . the same Barrington Street every sailor had to traverse on his way to the movie theatres downtown. It was only by sheer energy and hard work that the people of Halifax had this problem corrected: a change which the Naval Authorities too often appeared to view with disdain. But for these people, many young God-fearing men, strapped by authority and lacking necessary training might easily have been deprived of the few remaining niceties of life in a world now gone sour.

To partly compensate for this, a welcome relief came in late 1941 when a Canteen, the "North-End Canteen", was built adjacent to the barracks. It was here that homesick sailors could go for a home-cooked meal; a welcome change from horrible barracks food which the Navy passed off as nutrition. Before the year was out, the young ladies of Halifax's local Simpson department store would come to the canteen (Canada's own 'Stage Door Canteen') to entertain at Saturday night dances. In late September 1941, it was here I met a sprightly redhead with the familiar name "Burgess". It was a name I'd been familiar with since studying radio which used "Burgess Batteries"; no relation, of course. It was as good an introduction as I could think of, however, and we got along famously, until my draft to the West Coast came through and I decided to forget her. My apprenticeship to war, however, brought love's remembrance, and Halifax wasn't forgotten. When I would return a year later, Esther Burgess would visit me in my next "R.D.F." posting, as my fiancée.

Such was our defence posture in late 1941; sailors pouring into Halifax to be billeted in poor quarters while waiting for a posting to sea. Others waiting anxiously for a corvette or minesweeper which never came, because they were iced-in upriver beyond the St. Lawrence. After Pearl Harbour, the authorities focussed on the West Coast for a possible attack, while ignoring our own peril on the East Coast. George Allard kept up pressure on authorities to consider the problem of the St. Lawrence while

One of many Lake boats employed by Canada for deep-sea operation. Shown is the "Donald Stewart" later torpedoed by the enemy in the Gulf of St. Lawrence in Sept. 1942.

cooling his heels on "Andrée Dupré" until he was finally granted a transfer to "Fort Ramsay." Paul Belanger was another Naval officer who wished to leave Halifax for Gaspé, sure that's where the action would come.

Already, reports of indiscriminate sinkings off the U.S. were reaching Canada. At the outbreak of war, Canada had only 38 oceangoing merchant ships totalling less than 250,000 tons. U-Boats in their best months could sink more tonnage in a fortnight. Canada would build 456 merchant ships before the war was over, but in the meantime, merchant seamen had to go to sea in whatever could be found. This included Great Lake "Canalers" or "Lakers" like the C.S.L. "Fernie" on which George Mundy was a crewman. She was sailing out of Windsor when Pearl Harbour was announced over the ship's radio. After delivering its cargo at the Lakehead, Mundy left the ship to join the Air Force and later bomb enemy targets in Germany. Another ship "Donald Stewart" sailing in the opposite direction would enter the St. Lawrence and eventually saltwater. One of her crew was Bill Keith, just sixteen, an oiler who had to be content to continue working until old enough to "join up". His job as seaman was forcibly interrupted when his mother found out he was on "Donald Stewart." "That ship's sailing into saltwater," Mrs. Keith protested, literally removing young Bill from the ship, kicking and screaming. "No it's not," Keith protested, "it's only a freshwater ship." "Well, I hear it's going to saltwater and you're not going on it," she hollered, "ships are being torpedoed out there" (meaning the Gulf). Her intuition was to prove surprisingly accurate. Bill Keith reluctantly licked his wounds at home before running away and joining another ship leaving Montreal in early 1942.

The blow which fell on December seventh was so startling in its magnitude that we almost forgot the Atlantic War. The loss of the HMS "Prince of Wales" off Malaya, together with HMS "Repulse," removed a symbol of the free world. Off Argentia, Newfoundland, in August 1941, not a year earlier, HMS "Prince of Wales" had hosted Winston Churchill and Franklin Roosevelt.

The memory of that ship's company lustily singing "Eternal Father Strong To Save" as the two leaders departed in high hopes now seemed in ashes. Jingoism, and all that stands for, may have brought us into this war, but a genuine recognition of the evil threatening the world was our strength. The public perhaps saw us more as rowdy types sometimes seen in a supercilious vein, yet the once brash and noisy kids they curiously eschewed in peacetime were now defending their very freedom in the skies over Britain, or as soldiers preparing for the big scrap to come, or as sailors manning the very escorts necessary to bring more men in even greater numbers needed to eventually storm fortress Europe—and win.

All along the coast from south of Newfoundland to Cape Hatteras, the blow fell. During the nineteen

Two RC prelates accompany Brigadier Blais of the Canadian Army and two newspaper reporters as they tour the Museum at Rimouski, Quebec before moving on to report on military fortifications at Gaspé in early 1942. L to r: Chan. Alphonse Fortin, Brigadier Blais, Mgr. Georges Dionne P.D., a young French-speaking reporter, unnamed but believed to be Rene Levesque, Jack Brayley representing Canadian Press.
—J. Brayley

remaining days of January 1942, thirty-nine ships of nearly 250,000 tons were sunk; sixteen of them much-needed tankers. Most sinkings were close inshore, the German U-Boats scornfully aware that there were no convoys in operation. The attack was a deadly one. During the sickening months to follow, watchers from Boston to Key West would see two hundred ships go down within ten miles of shore with no retribution. The "Second Happy Time" for the Nazi sub had commenced. In February, the attack spread southward to include the Caribbean, striking oil traffic at the source. Twenty-three more tankers went down and the total shipping losses for January and February came to 144 ships or nearly 800,000 tons. The Convoy was the answer, but the U.S. had few ships to spare after Pearl Harbour and little know-how in actual Convoy work. Churchill offered several deep-sea draggers to serve as escort ships which the U.S. reluctantly accepted.

A Diversion Room was set up in naval headquarters with four experienced officers maintaining a round-the-clock watch over the movement of independent ships and the reported positions of submarines. These were meticulously plotted and intercepted transmissions monitored. Whenever approaching ships reached a suspected sub infested area, it was signalled an alteration course; the educated guesses during the next six months undoubtedly saved many, but the first attack on Canada was a complete surprise.

Canada had already thought it prudent to assure Canadians there was no cause for alarm; that our Maritime coast had been properly prepared and that effective countermeasures were in place. The report didn't say that in Gaspé, this consisted of tin plates hanging from string along suspected coastal coves to act as "sounders" should the enemy try to get ashore: Nor that there was as yet no effective "R.D.F." installed in the St. Lawrence basin. Nor that needed warships just weren't there. To allay our fears, Canada enlisted the newspapers to catalogue shore fortifications which did exist and to this end, CP (Canadian Press) provided two reporters, one a little-known French-speaking reporter named René Levesque, and the other CP bureau reporter out of New Brunswick, named Jack Brayley. They were to be accompanied by Brigadier Blais from Quebec City, a former executive with Johns-Manville. Accordingly,

The telltale wake of the periscope.

Brayley set out to " . . . tell Canadians how Canada intended to protect them."

The protection hinged mainly on HMCS "Fort Ramsay" officially opened on May First, 1942 amidst much fanfare of raising the White Ensign and Morning Divisions. This was impressive considering that it was hardly a year since Canada first achieved considerable independence of Command, when the British Admiralty, with the concurrence of Ottawa, put the Newfoundland Escort Force under Commodore Murray on June 15th, 1941.

March saw the attack swing back north, concentrating the attack between Charleston and New York, where, off the hump of Cape Hatteras the seas became a graveyard with as many as six ships going down in a single night. Between March 20th and May 28th, 1942, the Gulf of St. Lawrence gaped invitingly, despite the still present ice in the water. Naval officers began to consider just what might be done about the prospect of attack in the St. Lawrence when the ice moved out.

Even while our side was thinking, an unwelcome "guest" arrived in the form of Submarine U-553. Lieutenant-Commander Thurmann of U-553 already had had a series of frustrating experiences crossing the Atlantic. The St. Lawrence looked as good a place as any to lick his wounds before returning to Germany. He cleared his base at St. Nazaire, France in April and, avoiding Halifax-Boston shipping, had stolen into the Gulf unnoticed. By the night of the 10th of May, he was lying on the surface off Anticosti, enjoying the moonlit calm and speculating on his next move. Joseph Ferguson, in his lighthouse, built in 1858, on the point at Cape des Rosiers, considered turning in. He and neighbour Philip Dunn, manager of the local fishery had had a weary day trying to ascertain why fishermen's nets had been torn. One fisherman was laughed at by his mates after swearing he saw a "stove-pipe" sticking up out of the water. "Sacre Bleu!!" Ferguson, sure that he'd seen the wake of a periscope earlier in the day, had phoned his report in to Gaspé. He had difficulty making his French understood and went so far as to mount a special watch with his "glass", but came up with nothing. Finally, he went to bed and then, it happened.

An hour before midnight, of May 11th, 1942 Thurmann surfaced. In the waters just off the Cape, he spotted the ship "Nicoya." It was of British Registry, built in 1929 and was 5,400 gross tons. He let go the first torpedo (the first to be fired in anger in waters of Canada's "True North Strong and Free"). It struck home. The second which he let go was hardly necessary, but equally telling. The SS "Nicoya" began sinking almost immediately while sending up smoke and flames against the night sky off Gaspé. The pyrotechnics of the annual Odd Fellows Club celebrations at the old "Fort Ramsay" wharf were nothing compared with this.

Not satisfied, two hours and forty-five minutes later a little to the northeast, in the early morning of May 12th, 1942, Thurmann sent another torpedo home. This time it was the Dutch freighter "Leto" and it sank almost immediately. Satisfied, he headed back down the Gulf, careful to maintain radio silence even against Grossadmiral Doenitz's dictum that all actions be reported to headquarters. He took the next ten days to crawl along the bottom and emerge into the Atlantic undetected. Thus, the first two blows against Canada went unanswered. Although witnessed by the people of Gaspé and the Press, Jack Brayley, feared that a British United Press reporter who'd just joined their party would "scoop" him if he didn't tell the story himself. Yet, Brayley recognized that for him, Canadian Censorship applied. He had a plan . . . Canada just *had* to know!

survivors reach gaspé as the st. lawrence shuts down to shipping

Setting up the defence of a country is often more difficult for those at the top than facing up to the fact that an attack is imminent or actually underway. Mobilizing a nation whose hallmark had always been the pursuit of peace is difficult, but failing to take proper steps in the first place can weaken a nation's resolve and compromise its will to fight. With Canada, our old penchant for Regionalism vs Centralism brought a surprising response from a Prime Minister known to hold the view that the fear we avoid is often more important than what actually happened. In our case, it was apparently far easier just to close the place down than to do as Jack Brayley did in trying to tell the Canadian people what happened, or as Leslie Claxton did in helping with our defence. For the ordinary Canadian, or for that matter, any ordinary newspaperman or naval rating, nothing proved easy when the attack came.

At Harbour Grace in Newfoundland, where the flat-topped hill overlooked the Harbour below, Claxton was wrestling with a thousand different signals as they tumbled into his earphones in his "Huff-Duff" listening post. Even if Doenitz did have only twenty-two submarines ready to throw into the fray, the submarine signals reporting back to headquarters in Brest provided the warning we sorely needed. The "Huff-Duff" would do its part, even if nothing could be done about it. For many of us of Claxton's generation, Harbour Grace had been the focus of high school controversy. It was the British Empire's Alcock and Brown who first flew the Atlantic in 1919 from the same Harbour Grace long before Lindbergh did it from the U.S. in 1927. Canada's "place in the sun", as illustrated by their flight, was neglected in history similar to the neglect of defence we were now experiencing.

For Canada's infant Navy, the turn-around point at sea had been moving farther and farther east until Canadian Corvettes now provided the sole convoy escort over seven hundred miles distant from Halifax and Newfoundland. The loss earlier of two of Canada's destroyers, HMCS "Fraser" and HMCS "Margaree" and two patrol vessels, HMCS "Bras D'or" and HMCS "Otter", had happily been offset by seventy corvettes becoming operational. In addition to the submarine menace and the increasing distance of patrol, another natural enemy was the weather. But steps were already under way to correct this problem.

Weather had become almost as important as defence and both the enemy and ourselves coveted the rewards which accurate forecasts provided. Accordingly, Germany had already earmarked Martin Bay near Cape Chidley in neighbouring Labrador for a clandestine weather station which they would install the following year in 1943. In the meantime, the R.C.A.F.'s Bill Shields pushed ahead plans for a weather station of our own, on a treeless, windswept island off Newfoundland's coast. Bill McLachlan, along with seventy other men of the Air Force soon felt the privations of their location but "felt it was worth it knowing it was a job needing to be done". The warm Gulf Stream meeting the cold Arctic air at Newfoundland provides almost constant fog which in winter clings to every stanchion and deck-head of our ships. This raised the incessant fear that the ship might "turn turtle" due to the huge Atlantic swells and the accumulated fog-produced ice topside. This problem had to be feared almost as much as the U-boat.

The politicians could not, as Duplessis said earlier, shut down the war nor would the seas; nor the weather. As the considerable force of U-Boats approached North America, the Germans, too, had to know the weather for best penetration of our Convoys as heavy seas could reduce the submarines speed above water from sixteen knots to less than half. With the increase of submarine launching to the incredible rate of two a month, expected to reach three by year's end, the German Navy was understandably optimistic. They were now using two new types: a 500 ton boat having a cruising range of 11,000 miles and a 700 tonner with an incredible range of 15,000 miles, more than halfway around the world and easily within reach of Canada. They could carry sufficient fuel, to put them well up

Hardships above deck—a sailor secures depth charges during a storm.
G.A. Milne/PAC/PA-134326

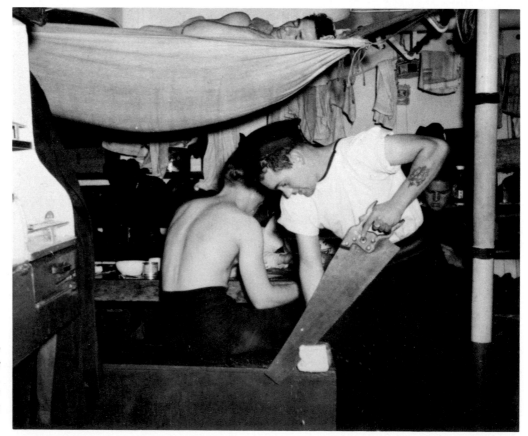

Hardship below deck—a sailor cuts stale bread with a saw.
-- W.H. Pugsley/
PAC/PA-134351

Photo taken from "Canada's Atlantic War."

— *W.H. Pugsley*

Iced-up ships pose an additional hazard.   —*PAC/PA 134331*

Frightening profile of a German U-boat.   *McRae:PAC/PA-134332*

into the St. Lawrence River, a fact considered purely hypothetical until the first attack. Worse, they carried 21 torpedoes, each with a telling range of some 15,000 yards travelling at a speed of 40 knots: a death weapon difficult to avoid. Torpedoes could be fired from the surface or from a depth of up to 200 feet. Submarines, together with increased aircraft operating off the coast of occupied France, made possible the sinking of an estimated 750,000 tons of Allied shipping per month. Already, total sinkings were estimated at 400,000 tons per month. With Britain capable of producing replacements of only some 200,000 tons per month, by sinking 750,000 tons and maintained this rate for a year Britain would be clearly out of the war. (Anglo-American ship-building wasn't even expected to reach 500,000 tons per month until mid-1942). Already, 471 ships totalling some 2 million tons had been lost to submarines during the first full year of the war and as many more were lost to mines, aircraft and surface raiders. Canada's "Armageddon" was upon us.

Canada had to act with alacrity because the U.S., of necessity, now had to withdraw ships made available earlier in the North Atlantic under their controlled Neutrality Policy. When the USS "Kelley" and the USS "Reuben James" had both been torpedoed (the latter just off Halifax), all pretenses were finished and all Allied ships, including the American, became fair game. This created complications for American shore authorities in Newfoundland, as the U.S. had few warships remaining to protect their own shipping on the East Coast after Pearl Harbour.

Canada's Captain Murray, now Commodore, would next be promoted to Rear-Admiral and by September 1942 would be Commanding Officer Atlantic Command. For now, the ascendancy of Canada's Navy had reached its zenith. We now had thirteen destroyers, including seven U.S. Lend-Lease four-stackers, and some seventy corvettes.

The Canadian Navy now formed the main Western Escort Force (W.E.F.) which stretched to a point 45 degrees west longitude or some 700 miles from Halifax and Newfoundland. Together with the Western Local Escort Force (WLEF), the new arrangement led eventually to our ships being extended right to the U.K. This became the famous "Newfie to Derry" run, where, with luck, some crews stayed over in Londonderry instead of holing up in Iceland, giving them a few days with the smiling green of the Foyle rather than the crags of Iceland.

Murray was satisfied that no ships could be spared from this pressing Atlantic need just to come to the seemingly inconsequential relief of the St. Lawrence. After all, the St. Lawrence was really "small potatoes" compared with the millions of tons of Allied shipping needing Convoy protection to save Britain and the Free World. Even so, the St. Lawrence Conference of 1940, which originally had entertained the idea of the Royal Navy coming, had been re-convened by March of 1942 to consider overland

All submerged speeds 6-7 Kts

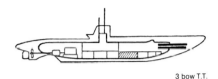

Type II (250 tons)

| North Sea Boats | Speed on Surface 11 Kts |
| 50 built | 6 Torpedoes |

3 bow T.T.

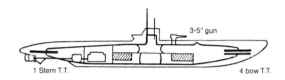

Type VII (500 tons)

Standard Atlantic Boats	Surface Speed 16 Kts
Nearly 700 built	14 Torpedoes
actual tonnage 769	

1 Stern T.T.   4 bow T.T.   3·5" gun

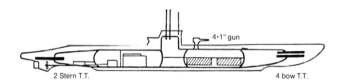

Type IX (750 tons)

Long Range Boats	Surface Speed 17 Kts
Over 150 built	19 Torpedoes
actual tonnage 1051	

2 Stern T.T.   4 bow T.T.   4·1" gun

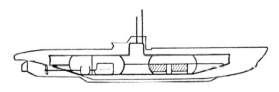

Type XIV (U-tanker)

Supply U-boats	No Torpedo Tubes
10 built	635 tons fuel to replenish
1688 tons	up to a dozen other
	U-boats

Scale in feet

0   100

GERMAN U-BOATS, 1939-45

Under the direction of Lt. Paul Belanger, the "Venning" puts to sea to help search for survivors of the SS "Nicoya", sunk May 11th, 1942.

— Ian Tate

DEPARTMENT OF TRANSPORT—MINISTÈRE DES TRANSPORTS
SIGNAL SERVICE—SERVICE DES SIGNAUX
DAILY REPORT—RAPPORT QUOTIDIEN

912
2-40

STATION ___Fame Point Q___ DATE ___May 12___ 19___

INWARDS NAME OF VESSEL — ENTRÉES NOM DU NAVIRE	TIME HEURE	OUTWARDS NAME OF VESSEL — SORTIES NOM DU NAVIRE	TIME HEURE	WEATHER			TEMPS	
				FOG OR SMOKE			**BRUME OU FUMÉE**	
					COMMENCED COMMENCÉ	CLEARED ÉCLAIRCIT	TOTAL	
G. Montcalm	21⁵⁵	Tug Manoir towing						
Aeroplane	3 30⁵	dredge	10 20ᵃ	LIGHT LÉGÈRE				
Aeroplane going SW	3 43⁵	Steamer	85⁵					
Aeroplane going N.	3 5⁵	Aeroplane	83⁵	HEAVY FORTE				
Aeroplane	7⁵							
Patrol boat	5 3⁵			DENSE ÉPAISSE				
Aeroplane	8⁵							
				RAIN OR HAIL			**PLUIE OU GRÊLE**	
					COMMENCED COMMENCÉ	CLEARED ÉCLAIRCIT	TOTAL	
				LIGHT LÉGÈRE				
Nicoya				HEAVY FORTE				
Steamer Nicoyla torpedoed at								
Chlorydorme 49 survivors landed at				**SNOW OR SLEET**			**NEIGE OU VERGLAS**	
L'anse au Valleau some landed					COMMENCED COMMENCÉ	CLEARED ÉCLAIRCIT	TOTAL	
at chlorydorme				LIGHT LÉGÈRE				
				HEAVY FORTE				
				BLINDING AVEUGLANT				
				WIND - VENT N W				
				LOW WATER			HIGH WATER	

Lighthouse Keeper's Log for May 12th, 1942 showing sinking of SS "Nicoya" the previous night;
"49 survivors landed at Anse Au Valleau, some landed at Chlorydorme."

Rescuers head down the roadway enroute to Anse Au Valleau. The men arrived by truck, only to find the late snow blocked further passage so they carried in the medical supplies. The party consisted of Cmdr. Armit RCN(R); Capt. Keaons, Army M.D.; a Naval SBA (sick-bay attendant); an Army SBA; Naval truck driver; Mr. Fournier, a volunteer from Gaspé; Cos'n Sam Booth.

—Ian Tate

Survivors of the SS "Nicoya" and "Leto" arrive offshore in separate boats. Surviving lifeboats from the ships may be seen in foreground.

—Ian Tate

Cmdr. Armit (left of centre) with survivors from the S.S. "Nicoya". Unidentified fisherman in left foreground is one of many unsung heroes.

—Ian Tate

Generous fishermen provided horse-drawn carts to aid in the evacuation of survivors.

—Ian Tate

routing of river cargo from the St. Lawrence, in the event that the worst happened. No one foresaw it coming so soon. When the attack came, Brayley's task wasn't easy either: he had to report the first sinkings in the St. Lawrence to the people of Canada. What had been a routine assignment turned into a nightmare. True to the spirit of a free press, Brayley felt Canadians should know what happened, and cut short his visit and prepared his typewriter. His until-now-relaxed attitude had received a severe jolt earlier when Brig. Blais related the story of the three spies who supposedly had been living in an abandoned house in Barachois. Located just below Gaspé, on the Bay of Chaleur shore, with a clear view of our shipping, the canned goods found in the abandoned house were mute evidence that they had been there. The sinkings tended to confirm this story. An invitation from Father LeBlanc at Cloridorme on the North Shore near the Light at Cape des Rosiers (the same light from which Ferguson saw the first sub) would have to wait. He dashed off the story that two ships had been sunk in the Gulf of St. Lawrence, and waited.

For the new Base at HMCS "Fort Ramsay," the effect of the sinkings was electric. Submarine gates and nets, only recently installed, were now put on alert while HMCS "Venning", Gaspé's newest Examination vessel, was prepared for sea. "Venning" had been on chocks all winter pending the breakup of ice in the harbour and was not expected to go out until month's end. Now, all was activity as Lt. Belanger echoed Commander Armit's order to "prepare to put to sea."

This was an old story to P.O. Gilbert Boutilier. He had already "put to sea" months earlier when he successfully brought two Gate vessels safely down from Sydney. Facing a gale in the Northumberland Straits which literally stopped his entourage, his tug poured on full steam for over 24 hours battling the wind and waves. He'd finally made Gaspé with less than two inches of fuel in his tanks. Once in Gaspé, it was just a case of posting watches and making the five-man crews of each vessel "feel at home". C.P.O. Percy Roberts oversaw installation of the huge mesh submarine gate, not realizing its need would be immediate. With the sinkings, the customary 'Harbour routine' enjoyed earlier reverted to 'action stations' as watches were doubled and switched to 'four hours on and four off'. An attack was expected anytime.

Meanwhile sparse reports were coming into "Fort Ramsay" from Anse Au Valleau where 39 survivors from the S.S. "Nicoya" were coming ashore. A rescue party was already threading their way along the narrow gravel road leading to the North Shore but to gain access to the remote location meant 'walking-in' medical supplies over roads still covered with patches of snow. Cmdr. Armit himself took over supervising rescue operations in boats readily provided by area fishermen. Even their two-wheeled carts were pressed into service carrying injured away from the shore.

For Ian Tate, newly arrived Sub/Lieutenant from "sheltered" Toronto, this was just the sort of thing he'd been looking for. Frustrated by stilted barrack routine since leaving home, he'd managed to make life interesting by pursuing his hobby of photography. Admittedly, this "free enterprise" was frowned on by the authorities but everyone did it and hardly a ship put to sea without its own "unofficial" photographer who, incidentally, provided some of our best action pictures of the war. It was also a known fact that many sailors profited from pictures taken clandestinely and passed on to newspapers who eagerly sought them and paid well. However, Tate lovingly put his photos into huge albums thus providing an accurate folio of the events which followed. When the newspapers proclaimed Jack Brayley's story, they indicated not two, but only one ship torpedoed. Recognizing the heavy hand of the censor he realized that he was lucky to have gotten that much information out. Before he had left for Gaspé, he'd made arrangements with Forbes Rhude, bureau chief in Montreal, that if he ran into anything spectacular, he would use a code to get the information across.

Ian Tate, the unofficial photographer of HMCS "Fort Ramsay" relaxes in the Officer's Mess between alerts.
—*Ian Tate*

Accordingly, a 'laundry list' went out purportedly requesting his wardrobe be replaced. It consisted of "socks" to represent U-Boats; "shirts"—torpedoes; "shorts"—freighters, etc. to be translated accordingly. This would have comical repercussions, later.

Canada's first sinkings not only set "Venning" into action, but our entire escort force of one Bangor class minesweeper, HMCS "Medicine Hat" and two Fairmiles, Q063 and Q083. While not in the immediate Gaspé area at the time, they would eventually be joined by five more Bangor minesweepers then operating off Newfoundland, with the Western Local Escort Force (WLEF). For now, "Venning" was the best we could get. Belanger called down to Clark in the engine room to valiantly squeeze out the last ounce of energy from the wheezing engine while five seamen clung nervously topside as Skipper Lukeman manoeuvered around ice floes still in the harbour. "Venning" had no depth charges and not even a machine gun to protect them. If they did see a sub, they did not even have a radio to report their quarry. Canada was going to war, in a motorboat.

Thursday: Cloudy

THE Ottawa Evening JOURNAL

HOME EDITION

VOL. LVII.—No. 131. OTTAWA, WEDNESDAY, MAY 13, 1942—TWENTY-FOUR PAGES. PRICE THREE CENTS

SHIP SUNK IN ST. LAWRENCE ON MERCY TRIP

Carried Survivors From Vessel Attacked Earlier

Believed Picked Up Elsewhere Than in St. Lawrence

A ST. LAWRENCE RIVER PORT, May 13.—(CP)—Nearly half of the more than four score survivors of a vessel torpedoed on Monday in the St. Lawrence river were reported to The Canadian Press today to have come from a vessel other than the one sunk by the first enemy submarine ever to invade these inland waters.

Reports from various sources have indicated that either 87 or 88 survivors of the torpedoed ship announced in Ottawa yesterday by Navy Minister Macdonald have reached land. Forty-one survivors are said to have been members of the vessel gun crew.

Germans Claim 40,000 Russians Captured

CANADA'S GAS RATIONS ARE REDUCED

Motorists Reduced to Category 'A'

Oil Controller Orders Drastic Cut

A general and drastic cut of gasoline rations has been ordered by Oil Controller G. R. Cottrelle.

Cracking down on the waste of gasoline burned in non-essential driving, the Oil Controller has directed reductions to Category "A" in the ration ratings of all but an excepted few motorists.

Happy Over Release From Italian Prison Camp

The joy of being home again shows clearly on the faces of these British soldiers who were exchanged for Italian prisoners at Smyrna, Turkey. Nine hundred and nineteen Italian wounded, sick and protected personnel were exchanged for 129 British soldiers, including South Africans, New Zealanders and Australians.

Soviets Report Furious Air Battles

But Claim 'No Substantial Changes' On Front

LONDON, May 13.—(CP)—

Canadian Makes Heroic Parachute Attack in France

VICHY, May 13—(BUP)—A lone Canadian parachutist who landed near Langon last night with a radio transmitter and demolition material, killed seven German soldiers in a rifle battle and then, with his last bullet, killed himself, officials revealed.

Martinique Grave Issue Says Vichy

Reply Made To Demands by United States

VICHY, May 13.—(AP)—The Vichy government announced tonight that it had sent a reply to a United States note concerning Martinique which "has given rise to grave questions."

King's Stable Wins Rare Double

NEWMARKET, England, May 13.—(CP)—The King's stable completed a rare double at Newmarket today when a filly, Sun Chariot won the 1,000 guineas stake after the Royal colt Big Game took the 2,000 guineas classic yesterday.

Jap Drive Now 80 Miles Inside China

British Troops Are Retreating Into India

LONDON, May 13—(CP)—The reinforced Japanese are striking northeastward in China's Yunnan province toward Paoshan, 100 miles by air from the Burma border and 180 miles as the Burma Road winds, the Chinese reported today.

Japs Prepare New Thrust

MELBOURNE, May 13—(AP)—A Japanese invasion fleet is assembling off island bases northeast of Australia awaiting naval reinforcements for a new offensive thrust, despatches from Allied advanced bases indicated today.

Claim Gort Hit By Bomb Splinter

LONDON, May 13—(CP)—Rome radio claimed today that a bomb splinter pierced the left arm of Lord Gort, new Governor and Commander-in-Chief of Malta.

Thrown From Buggy And Drowned

BROOKS, Alta., May 13—

Pope Appeals For Second Front That of Family

VATICAN CITY, May 13.—(Vatican broadcast recorded by BUP at New York)—Pope Pius called upon the rulers of nations today to rally for preservation of the family in peaceful existence and warned them that the future of the world will be on their consciences.

Invite 16 Nations To Parley Here

An enlargement of the Air Training Conference which has been called to meet in Ottawa May 18 to include representatives of as many as 16 nations, instead of the eight nations invited in the first instance has been decided upon.

Gallant Exploit At Madagascar Port

LONDON, May 13.—(CP)—An official source said today that the fall of the Madagascar port of Antsirane was precipitated by the "extremely gallant exploit" of a British destroyer which through the narrow, mined entrance to Diego Suarez Bay under fire of French batteries.

13 Nazi Troop 'Planes Downed Off North Africa

CAIRO, Egypt, May 13.—(CP)—Thirteen Junkers 52's, the German troop-carrying planes, and two of their Messerschmitt escorts were shot down yesterday into the sea off North Africa.

35 Canadians At Hong Kong War Prisoners

By The Canadian Press

Names of 34 officers and one Civilian Auxiliary Service man were reported as unofficially listed prisoners of war in an Army casualty list today.

Sir Gerald Campbell Relinquishing Post

LONDON, May 13.—(CP)—The Press Association said today that Sir Gerald Campbell is relinquishing his post of Director-General of British Information Services.

Elephants Dispute Right-of-Way Mosquitoes Raid Burma Evacuees

Reporter Tells of Difficult Trip Over World's Worst Road to India

By DARRELL BERRIGAN, British United Press correspondent who covered the Burma campaign, has arrived in Calcutta after a difficult trip over mountain trails.

CALCUTTA, May 16—(Delayed)—(BUP)—Elephants disputed the right-of-way, tigers and thieves-overrun roamed the wilds around us, but the only thing that really attacked us were the swarms of mosquitoes that abound in the malarial swamp of Assam.

54 Death Toll In Mine Explosion

MORGANTOWN, W.Va., May 13.—(BUP)—Rescue crews reached the bodies of 33 men in the Christopher Coal Co. Mine No. 3 today raising to 54 the death toll of an explosion which ripped through the mine late yesterday.

Enticing Items

From Today's Want Ads

Asks Injunction Against Churchill

LONDON, May 13—(BUP)—W. R. Hipwell, one of two Independent candidates in a Salisbury byelection to Parliament.

Stevens Tells Church Take Down Dollar Sign Replace it With Cross

VANCOUVER, May 13—(BUP)—A former Federal Cabinet Minister today advised the Church to take down the dollar sign and replace it with the sign of the Cross.

THE WEATHER

SOME PEOPLE BLOW BUBBLES WHILE OTHERS JUST BLOW!!

FORECASTS

The Ottawa Evening Journal headlines announcing "ship sunk in St. Lawrence…" No further reports of ship sinkings off Gaspé were permitted.

—Canadian War Museum

our lack of defence

The only official word given the public was now offered by our House of Commons. On the afternoon of May 12th, the Minister of the Navy, Hon. Angus MacDonald, rose slowly to address the hushed House. He said only *one ship* had been sunk off Gaspé and that *NO FUTURE SINKINGS* would be reported! Sasseville Roy, the M.P. for Gaspé, suggested that sinkings not be revealed for fear of what the news might do back home to an unsuspecting public. For MacDonald and the House, it was agreed that "for fear of giving the enemy information of value to him", they would remain silent. For Prime Minister Mackenzie King, these sinkings, completely unexpected, had brought the war too close to Canada for his liking.

The submarine attacks swung back and forth between Charleston and New York, and with the coming of spring, moved northward to concentrate along the Canadian and Newfoundland coast. Their instructions were to risk no damage which would put them out of action thousands of miles from home and every torpedo had to count. When torpedoes were exhausted, gunfire was to be their last resort. Off American waters, they operated in such numbers and with such little risk (the Americans were still demurring on Convoys) that they sometimes were reported operating with running lights for fear of collision among themselves. Understandably, the authorities were frightened even while the public basked in indifference.

The organization of the Boston-Halifax Convoys was the first palliative, although they left our own Western Local Escort Force (WLEF) painfully short. HMS "Mansfield" was an example of "reverse Lend-Lease," with the former USS four-stacker destroyer, first loaned to the Royal Navy, returning to help protect the U.S. coast. HMS "Mansfield" was still serving on the Halifax-Boston run when Mel Perkes, who hailed from Dundas, Ontario, and had never been to sea, joined her in 1943. Canadians were now serving on Royal Navy Ships. The BX and XB Convoys formed up in Buzzard's Bay south of Cape Cod for the voyage to Halifax. This convoy

system was so successful that by late March '42, this area was subtracted from the "U-Boats' Paradise", and the "Happy Time" moved north. The gaping maw of the Gulf of St. Lawrence beckoned, but we would not know this, as the newspapers would not be permitted to tell the story.

Not unnaturally, the sinking of the "Nicoya" and "Leto" in the Gulf on May 12th was upsetting for Canada, especially for people bordering the river, who found the meagre report from Parliament, unsatisfactory. All the people in the neighbourhood of Gaspé knew however that not one but two ships had been sunk. They'd seen the survivors brought ashore and had heard their cries. The identity of the ships was even known to them—so why all the secrecy? It was difficult to see why the news should be withheld from an anxious country. For people like Mrs. Kruse, all she could do was to "turn to" and help with the injured and needy; something that she and the Gaspé people were destined to do for the remainder of the war.

Evidence of Canada's determination to keep secret what was happening within our own borders now became apparent by our lack of press reports. The silent treatment seemed the best; a course which hardly could be faulted in time of war. The sub which sank "Nicoya" and "Leto" hadn't yet wirelessed home. It was possible that if it awaited radio reports from our side of the sinkings, among other things, they could tell them the time of the torpedoings and thus indicate the best conditions for future attacks in the area. If we reported the number of ships sunk, it would verify the submarines' own tally. If we listed the position of the attack, it would enable German authorities to calculate the distance the U-boat travelled and therefore its possible present fuel position. They could estimate the volume of shipping to better gauge future operations; weather conditions prevailing when the ships were sunk and any statement as to whether or not the ships were prepared for attack which would help to inform the German Admiralty whether the U-boat had likely sustained damage itself. Worse, it was feared that if the names of the survivors of the Dutch ship were given, for example, the Gestapo could attack the morale of relatives or friends back home.

Actually, Canada hadn't had an enemy within its borders since 1812; she was unsure just how citizens might react about an enemy, as Allard put it, "now right in our own house." Perhaps if we said nothing, the threat might just go away.

Two wrongs don't make a right and Canada's stifling of the news of our reverses in the East, which just preceded our amplifying the news of a similar although far less compelling attack on our West coast at about the same time, were both done for political ends. The West coast shelling of Estevan Lighthouse by a lone Japanese submarine brought headlines, ostensibly to make Canada's subsequent action in removing Japanese-Canadians from sensitive coastal areas in British Columbia less distasteful to Canadians, while further sinkings in the Gulf, notably around Gaspé and in the St. Lawrence River itself, were effectively squelched in order to ward off any further criticism of the Government's conduct in the war.

As a sailor just returning home myself from the Pacific, the cavorting of the Government and the press at the time seemed somehow amusing. The fact our own ship "Prince Robert" had only just escaped the horrors of Hong Kong, while some of our own Canadian boys were captured by a malicious and determined enemy, said much about our military unpreparedness. Why didn't we just admit it all and let the chips "fall where they may." Perhaps we might have developed a backbone forged on the anvil of war.

Perhaps Gaspé itself provided the seed which eventually blossomed into the celebrated and soon to be revealed differences between Ralston and King, epitomized by the "Conscription Crisis" which culminated in the two protaganist's final split. For Jack Brayley, it had been a source of pride that he had been originally picked by Ralston himself to go to Gaspé. Imposition of strict censorship ended all this. "Ralston trusted me," Brayley said, "and knew me to be fair." Ralston expected unbiased and open reports on the condition of Gaspé's preparedness, although he never quite expected ship sinkings. He looked for simple, colourful descriptions of Canada's Army and military general preparedness along the Gaspé coast. Now, all the news desk in Montreal got back from Brayley was a laundry list; . . . "socks, shirts and ties" as the enemy pressed home their attack.

Meanwhile, by the late Spring of 1942, the House of Commons was wrestling with the new problem of how to pacify the Canadian people over our severe losses in Hong Kong. It also became a convenient way to divert attention from the growing problem of Gaspé and the debate shifted to accommodate Hon. George Drew's insistence on a proper hearing over Hong Kong. By the early summer of 1942, the Duff Royal Commission was being set up but was claimed by Drew to be "a political whitewash." The Duff

Report, 228 pages in length, was still not available for public consumption in 1978 and was classified "Secret"; nor is it for private study, according to a book by Cpt. Grant S. Garneau entitled "The Battle of Hong Kong." As it became essentially tied in with the Conscription issue, the ensuing controversy became one of the real thorns in the side of the Liberal Administration throughout the war and for a considerable period thereafter. The Royal Rifles had had a fair percentage of its officers and men drawn from the Eastern Townships and the Gaspé. The issue became similar to what was shaping up in the St. Lawrence and Gaspé; men being sent to do impossible tasks, against a determined enemy, for which we had few weapons and little or no defence.

"Hell, no, we had no guns—not even in Canada," observed Bill Keith, describing how he went down the St. Lawrence in the early summer of 1942. After eluding his mother, following his earlier removal from the S.S. "Donald Stewart," he decided to leave home for good. Keith got to Montreal and succeeded in boarding the S.S. "Shurwater," being taken on as a stoker. Ignoring the fact that he had just turned sixteen, he was determined this time that his mother wouldn't stop him. Neither did his determination waver when "Shurwater" slipped Montreal for downriver and hatch-covers floated by, providing mute evidence that his mother perhaps had been right . . . "They're sinking Canadian Lakers in salt-water." Already, the bright colours of the Upper Lake ship had been camouflaged to battleship gray ready for the inevitable brush with the enemy. He recalled practicing "jumping off ship": no mean feat for a husky kid of 185 pounds burdened with a heavy life jacket. He faithfully shovelled, as Keith described it, "Sydney Shit," a powdery black coal more like tar, while sailing all the way down the St. Lawrence leaving a tell-tale trail of smoke. According to Keith, "Lewis machine guns were all we had for defence; Lakers can't stand the concussion of a large gun on the stern anyway, without falling apart." His one consolation was that his mother didn't know where he was. Keith's ship was one of the last heading for saltwater before the river was closed to all but local traffic.

By this time, I was returning by train from the West Coast to Halifax, stopping off at London, Ontario where "HMCS Prevost," my old "ship" was going full out recruiting still more sailors for our rapidly expanding Navy. Pressure pervaded everything at "Prevost" and, curious about the University, I wondered now if anymore "R.D.F." ratings were being trained. Apart from expressing regret over the loss of Dennis Bright, Dr. Woonton who coupled this loss with the fact no new "R.D.F." ratings were going through, did suggest that new and bigger developments "were in the works." The only hope was that this might mean our Navy was swinging over to British-built type 271 "R.D.F.", but this remained unanswered. We later learned that our class of '41

Stoking coal ("Canada's Atlantic War")   — W.H. Pugsley

would continue to shoulder the training of any new operators of the Canadian SW1C . . . not an enviable task.

Did Woonton know something we didn't? The science of war was moving now at an unprecedented rate, and three "R.D.F." ratings labouriously watchkeeping with a single SW1C whose antenna rotation depended on a "Chevy" steering wheel, could hardly be expected to have kept abreast of world events. In the world of "R.D.F.", my interest, the British already had conducted secret tests as early as 1940, quietly determining the efficacy of the first Magnetron, originally invented by John Randall and Harry Boot in November of 1939. We were amazed to learn later that British type 271 Radar could actually detect a submarine's periscope within a half-mile, and conning towers at greater distances than that. According to Brian Johnston, who did research for the British Broadcasting Corporation after the war . . . "It is impossible to exaggerate the importance of Randall and Boot's work; it lifted Radar from an electronic stone age to the present day. The lead it gave to the Allies during World War Two was incalculable. The Germans were certainly never able to catch up in the field where it was to confer the greatest advantage . . . the prototype Cavity Magnetron cost an estimated 200 Pounds; had it cost 2 million Pounds, it would still have been a bargain."

By shortening the operating wavelength of the Radar, they were able to do away with the cumbersome "Yagi" aerials such as we had on our corvettes. Shorter wavelengths meant equally shorter aerials down to the size of your little finger and made it possible to bring the aerial in out of the elements and house the whole thing, including the operator's 'shack', within the confines of a neat cabin which could be put almost anywhere. By comparison, on "Prince Robert" our SW1C employed a "used" Chevrolet steering wheel to rotate the cumbersome conduit running up the ship's mast at the top of which was mounted the "Yagi" antenna (named after a Japanese Physicist). The coaxial cable running through the centre of the conduit, had to be "purged" regularly and, while a gas bottle was provided for this nearby, the pet-cock which released the gas vapour was located at the top of the mast. This necessitated a frequent climb to the top and in a rough sea, it was a nearly impossible task. On HMCS "Prince Robert," our mast was almost ninety feet high.

Another limitation of the SW1C, besides having poor sensitivity and therefore a limited range, was the broad beam of the "Yagi" which made bearing discrimination of more than one target virtually impossible. Also, the huge "ground pulse" emitted with each burst of the transmitted wave left a "dead spot" on the trace, up to a half-mile immediately before the ship and meant that nothing could be detected in the immediate vicinity. In convoys, this was just where the warning was needed most. That

A Corvette HMCS "Battleford" braves heavy seas while shepherding a convoy: Note triangular-shaped "SWIC" aerial atop mast—difficult to service and often in error. —PAC 115381

An "R.D.F." SWIC antenna at the top of a ship's mast: HMCS "Spikenard"

—Marcom, Halifax, N.S.

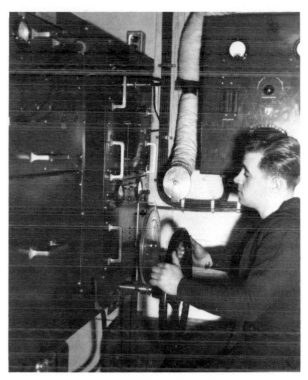

An "R.D.F." operator grasps the "used" Chevrolet steering wheel to rotate the huge length of conduit piping which connects the "R.D.F." apparatus in the cabin below to the masthead antenna above...an exacting task.

—PAC 105667

British-Built 271 Radar is seen here mounted on top of the bridge of HMCS "Sea Cliff". It is housed in a weather-proof plexi-glass "lighthouse", insurance against inclement weather. The compact aerial operated at much-higher frequency and thus shorter wavelength, providing a more penetrating beam with NO back-echoes. This improved Radar only came into wide use in the Canadian Navy in late 1943.

—J. Ritcey

half-mile might have been crucial to Bright's ship, and failure had lost us not only Bright, but HMCS "Windflower." It was a demoralizing experience for us all. It was the nadir of our experience; SW1C proven inadequate, while Type 271 offered so much promise, but was not available to Canada's Navy.

In the meantime, the common grief shared by the Hong Kong losses spilled right across Canada where men had been drawn from every part; from Winnipeg in the west, through to Stratford at its centre, to Gaspé in the east; hardly a family went untouched. Mrs. Rachel Kruse in distant Gaspé knew the cost, for she'd known many of the boys on a first name basis. Though Canadian policy on newspaper censorship was driving us apart by compartmentalizing Canadians, the common grief of Hong Kong united us.

While near-panic developed on the West Coast in both Canada and the U.S. with ill-founded rumours sweeping British Columbia after Pearl Harbour, we never expected that Canadian-Japanese residents would bear the brunt of the panic and be removed from the coast to inland locations. Much of the fear stemmed from the U.S. Pacific shore. The U.S. Army at Seattle had erroneously reported on December 11th, 1941, that the main Japanese Fleet was only 154 miles west of San Francisco. This was entirely believable after the devastation of Pearl Harbour on the 7th. About the same time, a Jap sub had fired on a California oil refinery and was greeted by 1,440 rounds against an imaginary air raid. When 6 months later, on June 7th, 1942, Japanese troops occupied the Aleutian Islands of Kiska and Attu, the "fat was in the fire," accentuated also by the shelling of the lighthouse at Estevan Point, B.C. at the same time. It brought headlines in all Canada's papers but still nothing was said about the threat to Gaspé.

When I did return to the "straight and narrow" after a period of just six months absence, it seemed more like a Biblical admonition . . . "even that which you had would be taken from you." The "Battle of the Atlantic," now occupying our attention, meant corvettes which might have gone to help in Gaspé were just not available. Our rust-splattered corvettes now took a quick turn-around (with no time for 'paint ship' routine) to the Atlantic, with limited capability of the SW1C, and poor ASDIC as well. Although both were indispensable, unfortunately, they provided a false sense of security. It was almost another two years before a really dependable ASDIC would be available, having vastly improved bearing and range capabilities and the ability to determine the depth of the ubiquitous U-boat as well. It would be about the same time-span before improved "R.D.F."

With the SW1C "R.D.F.", only one target could be read at a time. Targets showed up as a 'pip' on a thin green trace of an oscilloscope; the bearing of the target could be read from the direction of the antenna, which in the early sets did not rotate. Hence, the range was determined from the position of the pip on the 'scope, but with a fixed antenna, the whole ship needed turning, either port or starboard, to get a bearing. Some corvettes, like HMCS "Arrowhead", had the fixed "bed-spring" type antenna; corvettes with "Yagi" rotatables were considered privileged.

The SW1C aboard HMCS "Medicine Hat", when false echoes appeared, almost piled Ben Ackerman and the crew up on Newfoundland's rocky cliffs during a severe fog. Before the year was out SW1C wouldn't fare any better aboard Q083 at Gaspé either.

"R.D.F." also would see another year pass before needless accidents were eliminated.

Our corvettes reflected this situation as they bravely went forth to do battle sounding their plaintive "whoo-whoo whoop" prior to leaving, making up in bravado what they lacked in science. Perhaps this was why it was sometimes said that a collection of matelots is akin to a court—all unduly serious, yet hiding a penchant to break out into a smile when danger threatens. Had we known just how close danger was threatening, perhaps we wouldn't have been smiling. But the truth of it was that we didn't know Canada was being attacked, and I remained one of the few to find out even though I learned it by accident. The newspapers hadn't told us.

The "East Coast Port," the jargon newspapers used to denote Halifax without actually saying the name, was now secrecy personified; no one was to talk ships and discussion of troop movements was understandably taboo. In our own "R.D.F." school, the simple word 'secret' stamped on all our handbooks meant just that. That's why I was surprised when a lieutenant, one of our recent returnees from the U.K., where he had gone following graduation from the University of Toronto, to learn "R.D.F.", burst out with a "put that handbook away." A fellow officer, in his rush for noon-hour break, apparently had left the 'secret' document on the desk among the SW1C handbooks. The lieutenant was indicating that the document should be returned to the special Safety Vault. The so-called important papers locker actually had once been a corvette's ammunition locker from one of the same corvettes which now steamed valiantly to meet the enemy in the Atlantic. The pictures I saw left me numb. The officer clearly didn't want me, nor any of us in the class, to share what he apparently considered privileged information and for officers ONLY. But it affected not only all of us, but all Canadians as well. The handbook contained pictures clearly showing a Nazi sub right in Canada's Gulf of St. Lawrence. We certainly weren't supposed to know.

For the moment, I was more concerned over his command which, I confess, left the strong impression that our group already was relegated to the nuts-and-bolts arm of "R.D.F." while his genre would go on to perpetuate the 'rank' system, regardless of qualifications. While the officer's one trip to the U.K. apparently was grounds for his criticism of us technically, "I have studied Radar type 271," it was no grounds for his obvious lack of manners. Most of our class which graduated from the University of Western Ontario, by now had months to our credit on the North Atlantic, albeit with SW1C; and three of us had already been halfway around the world operating it. But we hadn't 271 experience, through no fault of our own. Only two of our group would receive commissions; the one, who had earlier driven up to the campus in the chauffeur-driven car while the other because (we suspect) he had been employed at Labatt's who apparently saw fit to sponsor one of their own. Heagy, Davey and myself and two score like us would all remain "seamen" R.D.F. for the present. The evolution of the 'Scientific War' had apparently passed us, and Canada, by. There was no point in arguing this; I didn't wish to end up "doubling on the Parade Square."

Even the secret "R.D.F." was now removed from our lexicon of terms, while the vintage ASDIC was threatened with the ascendancy of U.S. "Sonar". ASDIC had been the abbreviation for "Allied Submarine Detecting Investigation Committee", in World War One. Included among the august board members were two Canadians; Aubrey Fessenden and John McLennan. Fessenden hailed from Quebec where he was born in an Anglican Manse and lived for a time at Fergus, Ontario, not far from my old hometown of Stratford. McLennan lived just down the street from Falstaff School, the same school both Al Heagy and I would subsequently attend and both men worked in English Laboratories during the First World War where ASDIC was developed. I'm sure they never believed for one moment that their work was destined to help defend our shores. Even in the development of "R.D.F." and earlier radio research, much of the latter done by Fessenden who had developed radio before Marconi. By World War Two, the evolution of Robert Watson Watt's "R.D.F." in England, culminating in the Magnetron, saw Sir Henry Tizard sent to the U.S. to share its secret. The entrepreneurial 'Yanks' had the name changed now to "Radar" which we were ordered to use 'forthwith.'

As for the pictures 'clandestinely viewed', they were now returned to the "ammunition-locker" even if the memory remained. They revealed a Nazi submarine, photographed right off Anticosti Island, surfacing in daylight and already underway.

The last straw in a series of frustrations for me now arrived. I learned from the Draft Office that I was "on draft" again. This time it was not west to the Pacific but up the shore to Gaspé. No more Pacific, with those endless watches while longing for Halifax; no more visits to the Capitol Theatre with my favourite girl, either. Now, all had that would change. Even if I'd happily taken up with Esther again, figuring on a shore posting for the duration, I was going to Gaspé. However, this time I didn't leave without slipping a ring on her finger. I wasn't going to lose everything.

NOIC's home (Naval Officer in Charge) at HMCS "Fort Ramsay". Note: newly seeded front lawn, watched by rating. Cmdr. German on verandah.
—Ian Tate

Marine slips and workshops at HMCS "Fort Ramsay". —PAC 105383

gaspé fights back

Canadian Naval Planners had anticipated an attack on shipping in the St. Lawrence as early as 1941 and within a month of the initial onslaught, Canada had taken action.

The creaking railway train, snaking slowly along the 200 mile Gaspé shore proved to be no match for shipping by boat and slowly the convoys began to return. Some comfort to Gaspesians was found in knowing that our Naval Planners hadn't been without some preparation at Gaspé itself.

HMCS "Vegreville" and HMCS "Burlington" had slipped down the St. Lawrence earlier, and before 1941 was over, had wintered in Nova Scotia where fitting-out had been completed.

Within days after Thurmann in U-553 had struck, "Vegreville", with "Burlington", were on their way back to Gaspé, arriving on the 21st of May for ammunitioning. HMCS "Medicine Hat" had already departed WLEF headquarters in St. Johns, Nfld. together with two Fairmiles, and had already begun sweeping the Gulf. They were our sole defence, at the time of the attack, for hundreds of square miles of water.

Meanwhile in far away Brest, Doenitz anticipated easy pickings attacking shipping along America's East Coast. He had already been rewarded beyond his wildest expectations, but the trawlers Churchill had freed to help the U.S. defend herself, together with America's beefed-up aircraft surveillance using blimps, frustrated the German's initial success.

Doenitz's entries in his diary show his mounting concern. With an actual decline in sinkings by May of 1942 along the U.S. East Coast, he noted two of his submarine raiders had been sunk and two more badly damaged. This was contrary to his orders that submarines were to countenance no attacks, however daring, which might threaten a submarine and crew. Everything had to be easy. At one point, the Nazis even used spies to covertly forward reports on their sinkings, landing eight men successfully on Long Island, June 28th, 1942, but all were captured by the FBI. This feat, involving only one spy, would be repeated just south of Gaspé, at New Carlisle, later in 1942 and would nearly succeed.

Doenitz wrote: "I nevertheless had a feeling that conditions off the coast of Canada at the estuary of the St. Lawrence might well be more favourable and, in spite of the recent negative results in U.S. coastal waters, I sent two new boats to the Gulf of St. Lawrence". Thurmann's exploit in U-553 had thus provided two new disciples; U-132 and U-517. Of these two, the U-517, captained by Paul Hartwig would prove to be the deadliest. U-165 and U-69 would follow but neither would equal Hartwig's record of sinking nine Allied ships and killing scores of men.

Canada's initial defence was plagued by hard luck. HMCS "Medicine Hat" which was in the best position to catch Thurmann escaping, had to put in to Gaspé for fresh water. When storage tanks were topped up, water from a recently drilled well which was contaminated left the crew sick, with a loss of precious days. When they did put to sea again, their Skipper, an old China coaster named Bevan, did get "an echo", but it was at 2200 hours in the dark of night. The "R.D.F." was operating poorly, plagued by "echoes" from nearby mountains leaving no sensitivity for close in objects. In addition, the RCN was still short of Radar operators, meaning that telegrapher Ben Ackerman, with a commercial radio operator's licence only, had to help fill the gap. He even helped the ASDIC with their underwater sweep. Ackerman knew that the "echo" they received at 2200 hours was bona fide as it had a "good Doppler" much like a railway signal bell changing pitch as a train races by a crossing. It indicated a moving submersible. They ran two depth charge patterns and waited. The echoes ceased and they continued sweeping an upriver course. The next morning, a freighter, outward bound from Montreal, reported debris and an oil slick sighted, and "Medicine Hat" was given a "probable."

Doenitz had long suspected that cargoes for Britain were being routed through the Gulf of St. Lawrence and out the Straits of Belle Isle to Greenland and Iceland, in addition to Convoys serving the burgeoning U.S. Air Force Base now mushrooming at Goose

Sub/Lt. Gavin Clark of Toronto, age 19 reveals the extreme youthfulness of typical Fairmile Captain. Here he is shown during a stopover while patrolling the St. Lawrence and Gulf at a port in Labrador. A member of the W.R.C.N.S. (Wren) was writing a story about the Navy's role in sub-hunting, and together with dogs belonging to a local resident, posed for this photo.

— Gavin Clark

Bay, Labrador. And he was right. He called the move of submarines into the St. Lawrence "a particularly lucky one" and Gaspé became the focus in the summer and autumn of 1942 for his attacks.

Meanwhile, Ontario shipyards continued to pump out the 112 foot long wooden Fairmiles in ever increasing numbers. Powered by twin V-12 engines using high octane gasoline, they had to be handled like kittens, with the danger of a spark always present which could blow the whole ship to "Kingdom Come". The novice crews, many just seventeen year-olds, were usually under an equally novice "Skipper". As an example, Gavin Clark at nineteen, was the youngest Skipper to arrive with his Fairmile at Gaspé between May and December of 1942.

Eng./Lieut. Phillips arrived to survey the engineering for the whole base. He would stay for the duration. My job was to help outfit Radar on newly arrived Fairmiles under Petty Officer Don Clark,—not "Knobby" Clark of the "Venning",—formerly with RCA's bustling Montreal electronics plant. Of course, it was an impossible task and we never did complete all ships by winter. One crew member of Q064, who inadvertently included the Radar aerial in a photograph he snapped to send home, was severely reprimanded. O/S George Munger remained chastened the rest of the war regarding pictures, but he never changed his mind about what we all knew, that Canadian-built SW1C was one secret that we should have given to the Germans. Our immediate task was formidable; two men were expected to outfit a whole fleet of Fairmiles with Radar equipment which even the most uninformed knew, was obsolete.

What wasn't obsolete was Clark's recently developed hi-fi amplifier and record player. This would prove to be more practical in maintaining morale than the SW1C Radar protecting our ships.

As I departed Halifax, my Drafting Officer's parting remarks were no less inauspicious: "Just ask at the Gaspé Railway Station for Mrs. Kruse," he had said unconcernedly, "she runs the Kruse Hotel and she'll find you quarters". This was the most unusual draft I'd experienced in my short year with the RCN, which by now included drafts to all of Canada and the Orient. Navy men were more accustomed to barracks and ships than hotels.

Our train out of Halifax was the now-familiar "Ocean Limited". After an overnight stay at Campbellton, the train shunted us to neighbouring Matapedia, Quebec. Nestled among the hills near the Restigouche River, it was the demarcation point between New Brunswick and Quebec. Matapedia was the "switch point" where the "Ocean Limited" went on to Montreal while we boarded the "Bullet" to take the rickety, snail-like route along the Bay of Chaleur to Gaspé.

Even as we were enroute, events were shaping officer candidates for ships rapidly coming off the ways in Canada's "make-do" Navy. Armed Patrol

Another youthful skipper, Lt. Bill Murray of Halifax, guides his Fairmile, the Q093, on patrol.

An example of censorship (note censor's direction to "crop RDF"). George Munger, seaman aboard the Q064 was hauled before the Captain for photographing similar picture. — PAC/PA-134340

vessels, typified by HMCS "Raccoon" were already patrolling in the Gulf. We felt some familiarity with this "ship," only recently outfitted at Dalhousie by the International Paper Company. The C.O. for this new venture was a familiar figure, J.N. Smith, late of the "Andrée Dupreé." With typical swashbuckling manner, he acquired new officers and the best trained men available. One of these was Russ McConnell of Montreal. Trained at the Naval College at Royal Roads in Esquimalt, McConnell would initiate his seatime with "Raccoon". For Russ, it would be his first, and last, tour of duty at sea.

Meanwhile, Clark and I arrived late at Gaspé (the "Bullet" never did run on schedule) but we were welcomed by the girls who operated the telegraph office and they directed us to Mrs. Kruse's Hotel across the street.

Mrs. Kruse immediately made us welcome, "Just help yourself if you need a snack; the kitchen's free." In the weeks ahead, she would prove to be a no-nonsense lady. Although only five feet tall, she had an intense dislike for braggards and those who didn't pull their weight. It was matched only by Clark's dislike for the same traits, which contrasted with "Knobby" Clark's devil-may-care attitude, now a boarder of The Kruse Hotel, also.

When she learned that a shortage of quarters existed for the men of "Fort Ramsay", she offered her home to fill the gap. Accordingly, she added more tables and chairs in her spacious dining room, while retaining only a bedroom for herself and an additional room for her newly married son, George. He and his wife, Bertha, a registered nurse from Percé, had just started an insurance business in Gaspé. Skipper/Lieutenant Cassivi had asked George to assist in setting up Cassivi's office in the growing Boom Defence Base but George politely declined. Cassivi's cryptic words . . . "You'll always be here to help out" slowly came back to George as he now watched his mother valiantly rearranging her home. The only room sacrosanct was the parlour which contained her late husbands' piano. Since her husband Alfred had died in 1936, the piano had seen little use until a sailor had arrived recently while on shore leave. He had walked all the way from the Naval Base by way of the railway track and had arrived thirsty. With no local fountain to quench his thirst, he had enquired from the girls at the telegraph office and had been directed by them to Kruse Hotel.

Since the sailor's real talent was music, after Mrs. Kruse had offered refreshment, the matelot was encouraged to play the piano. He was a superb pianist and it was not long before the tunes of Cole Porter and Gershwin began to pour forth. The music from Kruse Hotel now became competition for the Bach and Beethoven emenating from the Seminary of Bishop Ross as well as the jukebox noise from Patterson's Cafe. The only noise of Gaspé which remained silent was that of the bells on the lift section of Donald's Bridge. With the going of the ice and the opening of the river, it began to ring again and joined the cacophony of sound.

When Clark and I had arrived at Mrs. Kruse's home we were welcomed and met her sons; Walter, an auto dealer; Earl, a hardware merchant; Reginald, a machinist; George, the insurance agent and Carl, who was the projectionist at the Kruse Movie Theatre. The theatre was opposite the Church of England at the end of Gaspé's main street. There was no clash between church and movie house, and when Walter approached the Rev. Wayman with an idea to help the sailors, it was received with enthusiasm. Following "Evensong", it was agreed that sailors who attended the church service would be allowed into the theatre first, before the rest of the audience, thus guaranteeing both a seat and a premier location.

Since Mrs. Kruse had been instrumental in bringing the theatre to Gaspé after her husband had established himself as a successful businessman, she had continued to bring in modern movies together with views of the outside world through "Movietone News". Thus it was that Gaspesians were able to see Ribbentrop of Germany signing a non-aggression pact with Russia and Hitler doing his 'jig' before the Eiffel Tower. There were no news reports on the sinkings in the St. Lawrence; censorship had seen to that. The people of Gaspé didn't have to go to the movies to see the action that was all around them. They had only go to to the edge of the river and see the debris.

Perhaps because of all of this, the young sailor-pianist's departure was all the more poignant.

"I promise I'll drop a line if I get safely to England", he'd said when he left.

"If you don't hear from me", he added . . . "why, then you'll know I got it".

Mrs. Kruse never did hear from the sailor. In neighbouring Dalhousie just downshore from Gaspé, Lillian England would also wait, together with a whole town, for word that 'their boys' had survived.

They would also wait in vain.

Lillian England had been engaged in helping establish radio station CKNB in Campbellton. Sixteen miles away at Dalhousie N.B., the giant International Paper Company had offered its services when HMCS "Raccoon" needed a refit and neither Pictou nor Halifax could handle it. The Government accepted the Paper Company's offer and sailors from Vancouver Island to Newfoundland now poured into the small community of Dalhousie, a town of 3500. It was here that Russ McConnell joined "Raccoon". Mrs. England, enlisting the aid of the IODE and the Women's Naval League, began a successful fund-raising campaign. Together with volunteer help from the four officers and 34 men of "Raccoon", they thoroughly cleaned up the Chinese Café and within days, it boasted a stage. The Paper Company provided carpenters and material to build a mockup of

Percé Rock with Bonaventure Island in the background, the childhood home of Mrs. Rachel Kruse, proprietor of the Kruse Hotel. —Ian Tate

Gaspé, looking north. "Donald's Bridge" in the background clearly outlines the 'lift' portion between the iron trusses. The bridge joined the Town of Gaspé and Gaspé Harbour across the York River. Right of centre and halfway up the picture is IIMCS "Fort Ramsay" while directly to right of bridge ramp may be seen the white-painted Kruse Hotel. —Ian Tate

their ship and in the "Navy Show" which followed, the sailors sang "Lights in the Night", a ballad about the loneliness at sea. The townspeople gathered for the first, and only, "Navy Show" to hit town.

The song would prove horribly prophetic. HMCS "Raccoon" would shortly disappear in a brilliant flash of "light in the night", as one of Doenitz' submarines pressed home its attack, deep in Canada. And no Canadian would know and Lillian England could only guess.

Youthful crew of Q064.
— George Munger

Fairmiles Q064 and Q083 dock at Rimouski, Quebec in Sept. 1942. — Ian Tate

testing the waters

The first "Convoy" to sail upriver from Sydney N.S. since Thurmann's initial attack of May 11 in U-553 was SS "Connector" accompanied by a single mine-sweeper, the HMCS "Drummondville". The "slow-convoys" had proved out so well that authorities had hesitated to stop them. Despite the adverse effect of winter gales on the faithful canallers or diminutive freighters, the name of the game was perseverence. We couldn't let the fear of submarines stop us. Thus Sydney continued to provide convoys, on which depended our accustomed well-being and our future hopes and a good quarter of all our exports going through the St. Lawrence. To take stock by the railway during the winter was difficult enough but the prospect of having to depend on the trains during the summer months was too much.

Shipping had to be resumed and the SS "Connector" now tested the waters of chance between that "East Coast Port" and Quebec City. Commander "Daddy" Woodward waited in a back room at C.O.A.C. headquarters for word that the river was safe again.

Word finally came, "Connector" had made it and Woodward was not surprised. To him, "Connector's" feat was understandable, she moved at 10 ½ knots; most convoys would go at 4 to 7 knots, a painfully slow speed. If only they were all like the "Gaspé County", the fast coastal freighter which continued to run despite the scare, it would be different. River traffic would move slowly and Woodward knew, so he dared not be too optimistic: "two swallows don't make a summer". Accordingly, he made every effort to make every Merchant ship a "Defensively Equipped Merchant Ship" . . . even if Woodward knew some would inevitably go out armed only with a Lewis gun or a smoke-float: the latter at least providing the modicum of security of a smoke screen. Four to seven knots made such ships horribly vulnerable and Woodward loved his men enough to give them what he could in the way of defence, even if Canada could provide nothing better.

That's why young Bob Dowson of Ottawa found himself at twenty years of age, agreeably free of RCN "pusser routine" and into the responsible job of arming merchant ships. He had opted for DEMS, where Woodward's obvious respect for his men was the main attraction. As Dowson put it . . . "We respected him, too."

Woodward now controlled the armament of most ships including the slow SC's out of Montreal. Often, it would only be a Lewis gun, but these were adapted for use so they could be handled like a Thompson machine gun. They came with six or eight ammunition pans supplied in a box . . . . all that Canada could give.

Jack Cook, formerly of Oakville, joined Dowson in Montreal. He too was unable to abide the "straight and narrow" in Halifax. They would eventually sail in separate ships from the Port of Montreal in convoys serving the growing U.S. Air Base at Goose Bay. Since that new port facility could only handle four or five ships at one time, convoys necessarily became numerous through the Straits of Belle Isle, the shortest course. Unfortunately, Doenitz in far off Brest knew this as well and he had prepared his trump card with U-517 already on the way. Unsuspecting, the "Donald Stewart" from which Bill Keith had been forcibly removed earlier by his mother, was already leaving Toronto for Goose Bay loaded with high octane aviation fuel in 45 gallon drums together with bulk concrete to be used on the runway construction. The river was thus being reopened despite the fear of submarines and despite what authorities considered inadequate escorts. The Battle of the Atlantic had taken an ugly turn and river escorts were required to bolster the depleted corvette ranks. Ultimately the availability of more ships and the ascendancy of British type 271 Radar would even the scales and give us a fighting chance. That was not to be until 1943, over a year to go.

Canada's seventy-odd corvettes had to be doled out carefully. Any reduction in our ocean corvette forces meant disaster even if our men by now had become more proficient against submarines. The merchant seamen and our "corvette cowboys", so named because to sail on one was like riding a bucking bronco, had had no more training than anyone else in this youthful war, but their unwavering morale was probably the greatest miracle of the time. If we lost morale, we lost all. The Navy held firm against any temptation to divert a larger proportion of its strength than absolutely necessary to Gaspé, although five ships originally earmarked for Operation Torch landings later in 1942 in North Africa were diverted to Gaspé instead.

Our merchant fleet was in worse shape. At the outbreak of war, Canada had only thirty-eight ocean-going ships of 5,000 tons or more for a total of less than 250,000 tons. In their best performance months, German U-boats could sink more than that in a fortnight. Even so, Canada would build more than 450 merchant ships of the Liberty class totalling just short of four million tons. These were the famous "Park" ships, named after Canada's National Parks. Our ships would go everywhere and our men would sleep the sleep of the weary, in slung hammocks or crowded mess deck, while others in wet clothes would dream of a meal ashore and a rest between clean sheets. Any ship which could be rounded up until these "Park" ships were ready were called up for wartime use.

In addition, Canadians served their apprenticeship well. By 1942, training depots and schools were able to turn out 10,000 general service ratings a year in addition to 2,000 signalmen, electrical and engineering specialists and sizeable quotas of ASDIC, torpedo, gunnery and Radar personnel, although of the latter, there were still shortages. Nineteen Naval Bases (eleven on the East Coast including Gaspé; four on the West and four in Newfoundland) handled the job of storing, operating, repairing and keeping the ships afloat.

In Gaspé, young high school girls, like Eileen Sams, were recruited to operate the Aldis lamp, signalling incoming ships while the coding room inside would be handled by civilian personnel. Recruitment was a simple knock on the door by a Naval P.O. and the agreement of the mother to let her daughter serve, providing the oath of secrecy was acceptable. Eileen was just 15. The handling of a Naval Code based on numbers could be done by a keen student familiar with mathematics, with only a duty officer responsible for rotation of the codes. The rotation of the codes was a prerequisite to maintaining their secrecy.

When the availability of local girls was exhausted, the Navy brought additional girls from Ottawa. The chief proviso was a Grade 13 education and good marks in mathematics, for which 17 year-old Helen Spratt and a half-dozen others qualified. The robust Ottawa recruiting officer, aware of the huge numbers of men now crowding into Gaspé added one more proviso: "When you get to Gaspé, don't get yourself pregnant."

Following intense training at Halifax, Naval

Some of the Signal Office personnel at HMCS "Fort Ramsay", Gaspé, Quebec. L to r: Miss Eileen Sams O/Cdr.; G. McKinnon, Sig. T.O.; K.A. Grant, S.D.O.; Miss D. O'Leary O/Cdr.; D.R. Mantle, Tel.
— Ian Tate

Sub/Lieut. Murray Westgate, Duty Signals Officer, at HMCS "Fort Ramsay", Gaspé in August 1942.
— Ian Tate

Signal Tower atop the Administration building at HMCS "Fort Ramsay".
— G.J.A. Goulet/PAC/PA-134329

recruits, like Jimmy Stuart of Toronto, would become Signal Officers under Lieutenant Bill Andrews. Another to arrive was Murray Westgate. Westgate would be better known later as 'your friendly Esso Service Station operator' on the Saturday Night Hockey broadcasts with Foster Hewitt.

The gravity of the day was exemplified by the arrival of the Toronto Irish Regiment and by reserves being stationed as far distant as Sussex, N.B. Men like Ron Eakin of Mississauga learned about the old Canadian-built "Carden-Lloyd" tanks, the same ones that smoked out the RCR's when they rolled into Stratford a decade earlier to quell a riot. And they still smoked, even though now they were being used to fight a war and not quell a riot . . . and the war was right here in Canada.

The St. Lawrence Naval Force, from the opening of the campaign in the spring of 1942, to its close in November would consist essentially of two corvettes, five Bangor minesweepers and a handful of Fairmile motor launches. They would be the corvettes HMCS "Weyburn" and "Arrowhead", augmented by "Charlottetown", "Hepatica" and "Lethbridge" later as more corvettes could be spared; while the minesweepers HMCS "Burlington", "Medicine Hat", "Chedabucto", "Clayoquot" and "Drumondville" would be augmented by HMCS "Gananoque", and "Grandmere", "Vegreville", "Red Deer" and "Truro" in turn-about as the year progressed. Initial commissionings of Fairmiles with seemingly inconsequential numbers such as Q057 through to Q085 would help fill the gap also but never more than six would be available at any one time.

Lt. Bill Grand, another RCN(VR), Captain of the Q083 on patrol.   —Ian Tate

The Fairmile Q083 leaves a white bow wave and bubbling stern as it sets out on a submarine patrol.
   —Ian Tate

Torpedoings by U-132, Canada's next protagonist, came with stunning silence and as a complete surprise. Lieutenant Norm Simpson in Q063 and Lieutenant Norm Williams in Q064 were accompanying Lt. Bill Grand in Q083 when the U-132 entered the Gulf and began torpedoing vessels indiscriminately. Simpson's Q063 spotted a torpedo "with his name on it" and turned stern-on just in time. The deadly 'fish' passed harmlessly by. A larger ship would not have been so lucky. Peace, which had returned to the St. Lawrence for the balance of May and June abruptly ended, when, as Grand described it..."All hell broke loose".

On the sixth of July, three merchantmen were sunk in quick succession: the SS "Dinaric'; the SS "Hainnaut"; and the SS "Anastasios Pateras." A fourth ship, the SS "Frederika Lensen" also went down during the month but the exact date was lost in the melee which followed. It was later believed to have been sunk at Grand Valley, a short drive by road downriver from Cap Chat on Gaspé's north shore. Like earlier ships sunk, all would remain secret. George Kruse would find out anyway and the effect would cause him to leave his business and join the Navy as a combatant.

The sinkings by the U-132 raised an understandable furor. Everyone began to talk, especially the civilian employees at "Fort Ramsay". Every bar in town, including Patterson's Cafe, became a hotbed of gossip, and Major Sams became upset at the apparent disregard of secrecy by the civilian employees. Discussing military 'secrets' was too much. Ottawa wanted the 'news' kept silent.

For Canadian Press reporter Brayley, it was a dilemma. Should he send out another 'laundry list' to the News Desk at Montreal? Or just forget the whole thing, knowing any story out of Gaspé would be slugged "Subject to Censor" anyway. He decided against withholding information and rapidly typed ...at least he would have the satisfaction of knowing that Forbes Rhude, at the News Desk in Montreal would know what was happening in Gaspe, even if other Canadians would not.

Unfortunately Forbes was not at his desk when the information arrived in Montreal: his despatch fell into the hands of the senior News Editor. "What the hell is this?" he hollered, "Has Brayley flipped?" "Perhaps the isolation has finally gotten to him", he ruminated as he read, "Three shirts, three shorts and three pairs of sox". In truth, Brayley didn't know just how many subs there were, nor the numbers of torpedoes let go that day, but he did know that three ships were sunk in quick succession, and anyone privy to his code would know.

It wasn't long after that when Commissioner C. Harvison stood before Brayley, reflecting Ottawa's determination to 'nail down everything'. Harvison's tense voice left no doubt; "You've got to stop sending in ship reports." Brayley, unaccustomed to letting a good story go by, gave up at this point. The Fourth Estate in Gaspé was now effectively silenced.

Meanwhile, HMCS "Raccoon" had arrived in Gaspé by late August, stopping there before proceeding upriver to escort more convoys. Lieutenant Simpson, who had enjoyed a brief leave in Halifax before returning to duty, arrived a day late at Gaspé because the train was slow. As a result, he missed "Raccoon's" departure. It would prove to be the luckiest day of his life. His late arrival saved him from death when "Raccoon" was torpedoed by U-132. He returned to the tossing deck of the Fairmile Q063 on which he had earlier served. Simpson would remain as skipper of Q063 in the dark days ahead.

One particular instance in mid-August found Q083 on a rescue mission and Bill Grand remembers when he took off all the men and began hollering to the Captain of the stricken ship. . . . "Jump!"

"I'm not coming", was the astonishing reply," . . . this is the third ship I've had shot from under me . . . and I'm not leaving this time". Grand moved his little boat clear of the freighter so the suction wouldn't pull him under as well. With reduced freeboard resulting from the weight of men threatening to 'pull his Fairmile under', he reluctantly departed. It was the last he would see of the man although the ship was still afloat when Q083 left.

Secure on his own bridge, Lieutenant Grand sorted himself out, lining up again with the convoy when his signalman came hurriedly from below: "A signal's just arrived, sir: Canada has been blooded in Europe; we've gone ashore in Dieppe." All Grand could do was review the horrible events he had just experienced right here in Canada. He merely replied "Thanks" and ordered full speed ahead. It was August 19, 1942.

hartwig in quest of a cross

War, they say, makes paupers of us all; it also makes kings but conflict also, sometimes, becomes the levelling influence that brings king and commoner together. This is what happened ashore and in the waters off Gaspé now.

It seemed to me, after I had settled down in the Kruse Hotel, that the attitude of the people in Gaspé had become...Less delineated: no more could the war be compartmentalized from the niceties of life; all were in it...sink or swim.

Religion, the integral mortar of any family became more important. Although there were many who did not practise their faith, there were many Navy types who attended Morning Divisions regularly but neglected the ritual of services in a Church of God. But the heavy offshore losses in July had made all of us more amenable to prayer and by August even Reverend Wayman's Church of England, at the far end of town, began attracting supplicants.

Secularly, the once strained relations between Mrs. Kruse and Mrs. Patterson (whose husband ran the pulpwood operation and who regularly shipped the valuable product to the McCormick newspaper Empire in the U.S. when that country was neutral and McCormick continued to assert that America wasn't fighting Britain's wars) would also disappear when Mrs. Kruse would have to go 'hat-in-hand' before many weeks were out and beg for a room for Esther, whose arrival by train coincided with the enemy's next attack. The Kruse Hotel would be packed with survivors leaving no room for newcomers.

Ironically, this situation would come about through a man from a foreign land. It was Hartwig and the U-517.

Everyone had turned to prayer following the plundering of our ships in July, yet servicemen were still conspicuous by their absence at the local churches. Nothing concrete came from our newspapers to help enlighten us and Reverend Wayman could count the increase of Naval attendees on one hand.

On one particular Sunday, the Rev. E. Royle described the sermon as "really a learned thesis." Royle was soon to become Padre to all three services in what he liked to call "the Defended Port of Gaspé".

In his sermon, Wayman described 'the beautiful hands of Man'. All of us knew however, that these same 'creative hands' were even now preparing to blow us out of the water. Oddly enough, prior to this particular service, I happened to pass a young acolyte walking in the opposite direction across the iron bridge (Donald's Bridge). We didn't speak as we passed but I noticed he was clothed in appropriate dress of the Seminary, even as I wore the deep navy blue of the sailor. Around his waist he wore a huge green sash which accentuated his swagger with his superior gait suggesting no sympathy for the Navy. His look of apparent scorn reflected what most of us knew by now, that the seminarians felt more of our corvettes should have been here to defend Canada rather than on the North Atlantic helping to supply Britain. I recall returning to the Kruse Hotel despairing of hope for any of us. My meeting on the bridge and even the sermon while in church, had made me wonder at the reasoning of the clergy in general.

The many pilgrimages I had made regularly to the 'Y' Hostel for cheerful conversation among our own men and the occasional dance to help assuage the gloom, was now lost and despair descended like a heavy fog. To make matters worse, we had heard that young fishermen had 'taken to the woods' to avoid service, while our Government, mistakenly I felt, allowed agricultural workers to be given exemptions. Why not fishermen whose products of the sea were equally as important as the farmland? I had proudly assessed the Navy Blue as equally important as the Seminary Green, yet the novitiate never as much as offered a nod as he passed me and he was exempt from service, while the fishermen were not. All this was beginning to negate my earlier image of the clergy even if most, I believed, agreed we needed the services of the Church. At least three naval ratings believed this too. Upon leaving the Naval Service, they would accept gladly the larger service of the Church: Mel Perkes, a Lay Reader; Edward Burton ("Newfie") who, along with Coder Kendrick, would become full-time ministers, and all within the Anglican Communion: Kendrick, in fact, would return to Gaspé as Rev. Kendrick and subsequently serve next door to Rev. Wayman's St. Paul's Gaspé in the neighbouring Parish of Wakeham after the war.

Rev. Wayman remained philosophical about it all, eventually filling his church after accepting Walter Kruse's suggestion to allow sailors to be first in line at the movie across the way providing they attend Evensong. He filled his church in other ways too. A good example was Lieut. Jimmy Stuart's wedding which was celebrated in fine style, helped by crowds of local people: for weeks following the wedding, people stopped Stuart to talk, their only common ground being "I was at your wedding." "Individually, I didn't know any of them from Adam," Stuart recalled later. "It was an 'event' in Gaspé and the local people responded to help bring back a normalcy to their everyday living".

Even the enemy soon would contribute to filling the church in a way which neither Rev. Wayman nor the citizens ever expected; funerals of our men.

Calm returned to Gaspé even if it was a peculiar calm which set everyone on edge. People accustomed to the sea learned early in life of the adage 'the calm before the storm'. Our losses at Dieppe now became a harbinger of terrible things to come for Canada. The only compensation was that the barbarity of war was all 'over there'. Had we realized just how close to us that war really was, our solace might not have been so profound.

George Kruse was to learn sooner than most of us in a most dramatic way.

Sammy Booth, a cox'n with the RCN who boarded with the Kruse's, casually invited George on a fact-finding tour of the North Shore, where he had heard there was a ship aground near Grand Valley. Booth had worked for the Toronto Transportation Commission prior to the war and knew ships, albeit mainly from service on the Island ferries running regularly between downtown Toronto and Centre Island just offshore. He wanted to look at the ship and would George come? He would, but what he found astounded him, for George had zealously maintained his Protestantism in a milieu mainly French and Roman Catholic and to him there were no French Protestants. The idea was preposterous. He received notice of ship sinkings with the same skepticism.

Carefully circumventing the twisting shoreline east and north by car, they soon left behind Cape Gaspé; and Cape Des Rosiers marked by the huge lighthouse of Joseph Ferguson, until they passed Cloridorme and approached Grand Valley. There, like some felled monster, lay the crippled ship, a huge derelict unable to move while the sharp shoreline upon which it rested slowly ground the ship to an inexorable fate. Questions now crowded their minds. Could this have been the freighter which the dis-

traught captain had earlier told his wouldbe rescuers on Fairmile Q083 to "Go to hell, I'm staying"? Had he indeed gotten his ship downriver from Cape Chat where it had been torpedoed earlier, only to lose it here? Here was not only stark proof ships were sinking but a lesson in religious mores which George Kruse had not known. Both men proceeded aboard but found no one, not even the captain. A thorough search revealed only a few personal belongings but even these provided more questions than answers. One item remained fixed in George Kruse's mind; it was a Huguenot Bible of the French Protestants of the 16th and 17th centuries, which he had found in a mess-deck. He had mentioned his find to Booth and Booth had questioned him as to the tremendous importance that this item seemed to have for him. "I didn't know there were French Protestants", Kruse answered. Not long after, Kruse volunteered his services and Skipper/Lieut. Cassivi's prediction had rung true . . . "You'll always be here to help out."

When Kruse volunteered, Mr. Levine breathed easier: one person less at the Hotel would mean improved chances of his remaining; something Mrs. Kruse already had assured him. He would not be turned out like a pauper because of the influx of the Navy. Levine had been a longtime boarder and even Walter Bradley's presence hadn't changed that. Besides, Bradley was more often preoccupied with the giant gun at Fort Prevel and therefore only a casual boarder. Even fitting out a room for my fiancée's pending arrival wouldn't dethrone this 'king'. A converted sewing room would serve Esther.

When Don Clark repaired the radio over which Mr. Levine studiously followed events unfolding in Europe, he helped the situation as well by simply making Levine more comfortable. Levine reciprocated generously by appearing regularly in his accustomed Magician's role at the church hall to entertain church groups and servicemen with his sleight-of-hand. Mrs. Kruse, astute woman that she was, talked Don Clark out of the usual fee for his radio repair services; "I'll just chalk it up against the extra electricity you use running your record player". Clark a 'king' himself, in his own thinking, had expected some remuneration. Instead he felt relegated to the pauper's role.

While 'life' in Gaspé plodded on, the Battle of the Atlantic progressed from bad to worse, and Churchill feared that the battle might well be lost. HMCS "Vegreville" would depart Gaspé in September for the North Atlantic. "Vegreville" no sooner had taken up ocean position when the U-boats in the Atlantic attacked. Out of 36 ships returning to Halifax, eleven were sunk and "Vegreville" helped pick up survivors. There appeared to be no sanctuary, not even in Canada's 'sheltered waters'.

Never a man to miss an opportunity, Doenitz, from his headquarters in France, saw this as the time to deal a death blow to the Allies. With the North Atlantic now being ravaged, Doenitz selected two of his best submarines, the U-517 and the U-165, to stop the flow of war material through what had become Britain's backdoor route, the Straits of Belle Isle. The "King Maker" chose Lt. Cmdr. Paul Hartwig, scion of a German military family, to head up the assault. Hartwig was proud of his tactical ability and popular with his men. He was also a hard drinker, a king among commoners, in a submarine boasting three officers and forty-seven ratings. Before he had finished sinking his first ship, he'd be humbled like the rest. But for now he was like a king in quest of a crown. Hartwig was to try for the coveted Iron Cross, which, for a U-boat Commander, meant that he had to sink 80,000 tons of Allied shipping before returning to Germany.

Hartwig sailed from the huge German Naval Base at Kiel on August 8th, 1942, enjoying the usual "good-luck" sendoff. Actually, it was Hartwig's first command and the U-517's first patrol. The 250 foot gray sub was one of the newest and carried 22 torpedoes and sufficient fuel and supplies including liquor for three months at sea. "We were young and happy and our spirits high" was how he described this latter aspect: "Why not drink?" He had joined the German Navy in 1935 while we'd been preoccupied with disarmament and breadlines. As a young lieutenant in the U-125, he took one patrol with commencement of hostilities in September 1939, followed by a Commander's course and was later promoted to Kapitanlieutenant of the U-517, then being built in Hamburg. Commissioned March 21st, 1942, he was ordered by Doenitz to a site designated on German war maps as "Square A-H", an area near Belle Isle just off the southeastern tip of Labrador. The U-517, accordingly, sailed north of the British

Isles and crossed the Atlantic arriving unscathed. The U-165 left about the same time but by a different route.

Hartwig made landfall on the morning of the 26th of August 1942, and from then on, he worked his way between Cape Bauld and Belle Island. Early next morning he sighted a Sydney-Greenland convoy, (Doenitz had been right) escorted by American Coastguard cutters. The U.S. Bases in Greenland were supplied by convoys under American escort out of Sydney through the Straits of Belle Isle, while materials for the Canadian base in Goose Bay, Labrador, came downriver past Gaspé from Montreal. These were escorted by Canadian warships but both carried valuable cargo for American air bases being built there. One of the ships in the American convoy was the "Chatham," actually a passenger ship carrying American soldiers to Greenland but which Hartwig thought was a freighter. He let go two torpedoes in order to prevent a miss as he "wanted to impress his men." One did miss but the other hit resoundingly and the "Chatham" sank in three minutes. Amazingly, only 23 men died but the "king had served his subjects." Enamoured with his first "kill," Hartwig radioed his success in a short coded signal to U-boat headquarters in Brest, France. It was the first sinking he'd seen but it had a profound impression on Hartwig exactly the opposite of what he expected. Surprisingly, he now addressed the crew over the intercom system not as a king but as a commoner: . . . "You should always remember that it could easily be the other way around, that we ourselves could have been killed." They had to live in a kind of humility, that they would not necessarily be the victors all the time; that while they had a duty to their country so had the other side

One of the Gate Vessels off Sandy Beach at entrance to Gaspé's inner Harbour with a portion of the Submarine net seen in the foreground.
— G. Boutilier

to their country; while they had to be successful they did not have to hate the enemy: in effect, the king had been dethroned. Worse, superiority gave way to desperation. And a desperate man's a dangerous man. Between Hartwig and his coveted Cross stood 80,000 tons of allied shipping that he must sink.

For Doenitz, this first sinking was just a promise of more. They'd found the 'Happy Hunting Ground' and the second 'Happy Time' commenced. Hartwig asked Admiral Karl Doenitz, as head of the entire U-boat force, for permission to enter the Gulf of St. Lawrence; permission Hartwig was eager to receive in order to maintain "crucial figure": the average tonnage sunk per sub per day which, if maintained, assured his Iron Cross. Doenitz simply said "Go ahead."

For Canada, it marked the resumption of St. Lawrence Convoys in earnest, even if now against perilous odds. Now, every ship movement would be a gamble and the only constant remaining would be continued censorship. It would leave all of us unaware of the net that Hartwig was preparing, even if his brief radio exchange had unwittingly altered faithful monitors like Leslie Claxton in tiny Harbour Grace. Claxton's 'Huff-Duff' alerted the military and the race was on. It also signaled a chain of events which would initiate Canada's greatest losses in the St. Lawrence but also begin Hartwig's eventual personal demise falling far short of his necessary 80,000 tons of shipping sunk.

During the afternoon of the 27th, Hartwig sighted a second sub, the U-165, but before they could rendezvous, an approaching search plane forced him to dive. Later, circling leisurely around Belle Isle, he eventually caught up with the U-165 and together encountered the same convoy that he had attacked before. Each U-boat got a ship in the second attack; Hartwig torpedoed the "Arlyn." Hartwig now turned southward down the Strait and by the 29th, U-517 was well into the Gulf reaching the East Cape of Anticosti Island by the afternoon. Patroling next in a zigzag fashion, his monotonous but intense sweep continued until the early evening of September 2nd, when he sighted a northbound Canadian convoy and began shadowing it. The suspense crackled inside the steel hull.

Meanwhile, Canadian warships, from the WLEF (Western Local Escort Force) out of Newfoundland, approached the Gulf towards the Straits. They fell upon the remnants of Hartwig's first strike and proceeded to take on survivors. Survivors from the "Chatham" were everywhere. Unfortunately while dropping heavy liferafts, some of them fell on hapless victims trying to save themselves. One of the escorts, HMCS "Trail," was carrying a young ASDIC officer aboard named James Lamb. He would shortly get his own command but for now, his main job was to try to make some sense out of the primitive equipment he'd been given. Lamb would one day write "The Corvette Navy", a legacy about Canadians surmounting intolerable odds in Canada's Navy. Lamb found, as so many were to subsequently discover, that the "layering effect of the salt and fresh water meeting in the Gulf induced by the thermal effects of the warmer St. Lawrence River meeting colder water of the ocean, made the ASDIC beam bend, rendering it all but useless."

At this particular time, Lamb had 'turned to' and was helping the rescued men. One of the main problems with those being brought aboard was that they were saturated in sticky oil. "We even had to remove oil from their mouths, it was choking them," Lamb said, and he told how they began to rub off the oil from one inert body without seemingly being too successful. It was quickly discovered that the oil had been removed and that the unconscious man would never attain the same shade of skin as Lieutenant Lamb. The man was black.

Curiously, "Chatham's" sinking had a profound effect on Hartwig, not now the pompous drinker but sobered and perhaps even repentant. "We have to remember it could just as easily have been us," he told his men again, reverting back to the cool killer only after remembering his goal.

For myself, a new dimension to the drama unfolded, with the arrival of two Corvettes, HMCS "Arrowhead and HMCS "Charlottetown." On board were two of the original students of our early "R.D.F." group, "Dutch" Davey and Allan Heagy. What might have been a happy reunion however was replaced by urgent work. The opportunity to prove the effectiveness of two distinct Radar Antennae; the "bed-spring" type on "Arrowhead" and the rotating "Yagi" of the "Charlottetown" awaited, unaware that the "nemesis of the Gulf," Hartwig himself, would provide the target. It would result in a success of sorts for "Arrowhead" but tragedy for "Charlottetown."

Meanwhile, HMCS "Weyburn" was coming downriver with a small convoy which included the SS "Donald Stewart" accompanied by HMCS "Shawinigan." "Weyburn" and "Shawinigan" were corvettes and operating from the WLEF. Bert Grant, a crewman on "Donald Stewart," was proud to have joined the laker in Montreal despite the fact that she lacked adequate armament. Unknowingly, he was entering the 'eye of the needle' and the hurricane of events to come would convince him that the Navy, despite its strictures still offered the best opportunity to fight and not DEMS as he thought. "Donald Stewart," loaded with high-octane aviation fuel in 45 gallon drums and holds filled with concrete, was a veritable sitting duck. The cargo was needed for the U.S. Air Base being feverishly built at Goose Bay, in order to provide much-needed air cover for vulnerable convoys. Hartwig already had his eye on her even as Bill Keith returning on SS "Shurwater" in another convoy seemed somehow glad he wasn't on the "Donald Stewart" as they passed going in opposite directions.

The following morning about one-thirty, just as

HMCS "Trail" helped rescue survivors from USS "Chatham" Aug. 1942.

—Maritime Command Museum (MARCOM), Halifax

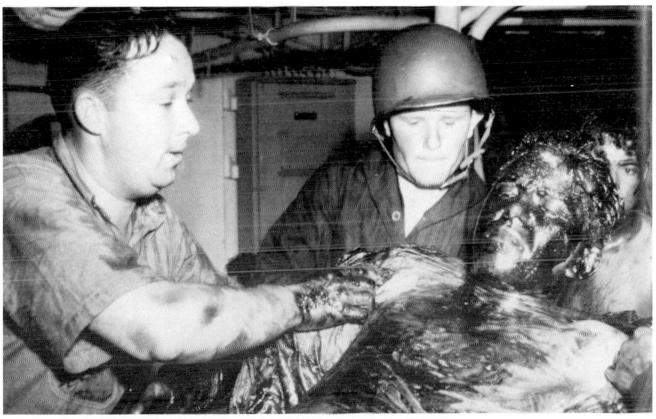

Survivor has oil coating removed by a shipmate.

—Canadian War Museum

The crew of HMCS "Arrowhead" photographed on the foc'sle while in Halifax.

— *"Newfie" Burton*

HMCS "Arrowhead" prepares to join Convoy in the St. Lawrence River, Sept. 1942.

— *"Newfie" Burton*

Crew gather on Foc'sle visiting namesake, "Charlottetown", P.E.I.   —B. McFadyen

The ill-fated "Charlottetown" pictured at Halifax, March 1942.   —Bill McFadyen

HMCS "Weyburn".

—PA 116956

the outward bound convoy passed the inbound one, Hartwig made his move. However, "Weyburn" caught sight of the partially submerged sub from the glistening wash of her conning tower. Aboard "Donald Stewart" the seaman in the crow's nest, unaware of "Weyburn's" sighting, was startled by a gentle tap on the shoulder. He turned and, relieved, looked at the dim outline of Bert Grant barely visible in the faint light.

It was 1:30 am, September 3rd, 1942. "I figured you'd be cold up here" Grant hollered, "I've brought you a hot mug of coffee." The lookout never had a chance to say "Thanks." Suddenly, the night sky was illuminated with a brilliant flash. Grant hailed from Douglastown, a village on the same shore as Gaspé and named after a Scotsman who first founded the community when that burly Scot arrived with the United Empire Loyalists. The Scot had envisaged a community based on good government and kind acts. While his dream never came to pass, natives still carried out his heritage in practical ways and it therefore was natural for Grant to bring a fellow-sailor this warming sustenance. The simple act also afforded a bird's-eye view of the attack, before they, themselves, had to take to the water.

HMCS "Weyburn" had let go illuminating rockets, after Captain Tom Golby had detected the thin initial wisp of foam curling from U-517's periscope. Next, "Weyburn" fired two rounds from her four-inch gun, then bore down to ram. Coolly, the U-517 paused, fired a torpedo towards "Donald Stewart," diving when the corvette was only a thousand yards away. "Weyburn" crossed the swirl of the U-boat's dive and ordered a full pattern of depth charges. But, at the moment of firing, the throwers jammed and only two charges entered the water. They were only sufficient to disturb the already tenuous ASDIC contact and the U-517 slipped away.

Meantime, the torpedo continued its lethal course hitting the "Donald Stewart" near her stern, exploding the high-octane fuel and producing a huge funeral pyre of the doughty laker. Miraculously, only three men died, all in the engine room, while the remainder, including Grant, successfully got boats away or remained in the water until rescued by HMCS "Shawinigan" which withheld further depth charges.

The delaying of depth charges to save our men would be seriously questioned later by a Naval Inquiry. In the meantime, men, who would have been killed by the depth charge concussion, lived and were rescued. (On November 25th, 1944, HMCS "Shawinigan" was sunk in the Cabot Strait between Newfoundland and Nova Scotia; a single torpedo taking the ship and everyone on board.)

HMCS "Weyburn" initiates an attack in the Gulf of St. Lawrence after the "Donald Stewart" was torpedoed. Depth charge projectile has been fired from the starboard waist launch tube.

—Ian Tate

Hartwig suffered only a short blackout of the sub's lighting caused by Weyburn's original two depth charges, while the "Donald Stewart" sank in 7 minutes. The loss of this one ship delayed construction at Goose Bay by 6 months. Captain Tom Golby's hunt for Hartwig over the next half-hour kept the sub at bay. He subsequently rejoined the convoy, which now continued unscathed. Tom Golby was lost less than a year later when "Weyburn" was torpedoed in the Mediterranean. Hartwig swept away on an opposite course and together with the U-165 took up patrol in the Gaspé passage. Here, a surprise awaited but again luck was with him. When one of our aircraft spotted the sub barely awash, the plane dropped from a misty sky placing a bomb squarely on the sub's deck, landing hard against a ready-use locker. The bomb failed to detonate. Assisted by his engineer officer and two ratings, Hartwig succeeded in heaving it overboard.

Meanwhile, the train from Halifax, carrying my fiancée, was already blowing its whistle, as it rounded the last curve before reaching Gaspé Station: on this occasion, nearly on time. The railway actually ran not far from where the submarines were gathering offshore for the next onslaught. My main concern now was that every hotel and rooming house in Gaspé would be overcrowded. I'd watch our grandiose plans for a pleasant time together reduced to those of a pauper. There'd be absolutely no accommodation for Esther as promised earlier by the Kruse Hotel. She would learn upon her arrival that all space had been commandeered by the Government to make room for anticipated survivors. Every Hotel and rooming house by now was packed: crowded by military and civilian workers. The Kruse Hotel was no exception and Mrs. Kruse would announce the news with tears in her eyes, apologetically offering to make amends. She would go to Mrs. Patterson and try for a room there for Esther. Before the day was out, there would be more than mere inconvenience. Sadly, just outside Gaspé Harbour, many would be killed.

The resulting explosion was not sufficient to damage attacking Submarine.   —*Ian Tate*

An unusual "shallow charge" is detonated from a Fairmile—risky to both crew and ship.

for whom the bells toll

Ironically, Labour Day of 1942 fell on a date representing the number long associated with luck, the seventh. But before this day was over, it would be a stunning success only for the enemy, while I'd kick myself for ever inviting Esther to visit Gaspé. The town was now a community, as war-driven as the worst in England and it was too late to cancel out. Even as I waited, what should have been a happy occasion was swallowed up in the events that followed.

The initial murmurings that something was wrong had come earlier in the afternoon about 5 p.m. I was first attracted to the sound of the ringing bells of the great iron bridge just beyond the railway station. It was about four o'clock, Gaspé time. The fact that I had left work an hour earlier was due to the time differential between the Naval Base and the town. Moments later, three ships passed beneath the upraised span, fully steamed and making for the open sea. I could clearly see a conglomerate of war material on board; jeeps, tanks, antiaircraft guns . . . in fact, all the artifacts of war. One was low in the water, obviously another of Canada's "lakers", bearing the name "Oakton." It had a gun on the stern, with several DEMS ratings "closed up" and a huge St. Bernard dog which barked incessantly as if warning the enemy. Two more ships, each somewhat higher in the water, presented the more classic lines of the Greek ocean freighter. They also bulged with war material: monstrous tanks and guns strapped everywhere. What a prize for the enemy, I thought as they cleared the bridge and disappeared down the long Gaspé Gut, past the Boom Defence and into the open sea. I didn't know the enemy had already harassed the convoy. Not since the days of Capt. Donald had merchant ships lay opposite the Robin's Warehouse, now vacant since the Navy's move to Fort Ramsay. Their presence alerted the townspeople that something was stirring even if the newspapers maintained their now accustomed silence. The ships were like old friends returned. However, unlike earlier, these ships had sought out Gaspé for a breather from attack before returning to the fray and continuing their long journey to England. The war was now right at our door.

Don McAllister of the RCAF saw them too. He had recently arrived with #117 Squadron, one of the vanguard of airmen whose buildings were rapidly nearing completion next door to "Fort Ramsay." He had actually seen the ships in early afternoon when they stood anchored opposite Robins Warehouse inward from the bridge. It was McAllister's first leave in a month and he had carefully counted the days since his birthday, a month earlier. He was determined to observe his birthday and thus, Labour Day marked a double occasion to celebrate; he was going to the 'Y' hostel to "tie one on." That's when he saw the ships but didn't know they were moving out. Nor did he know that when he'd return later that same night, his bunk bed, and indeed the whole barracks, would be filled with survivors, mainly Greeks, from these same ships.

The battle actually began on the sixth after U-517 had left a trail of death and destruction in the Straits of Belle Isle. Twenty-three had been killed by the exploding torpedo hitting "Chatham"; nine more on the "Arlyn" and three on the "Donald Stewart". However what went unsaid about "Chatham" was the additional 250 who died from exposure in the icy waters of the Straits.

A much-delayed reunion between "Dutch" Davey and myself revealed the true extent of our losses over the next few weeks. Davey said . . . "We took one convoy of ten ships out of Gaspé and only arrived with one; the ammo ship. If they had got her, none of us would be here to talk about it now". Heagy's account would later be more personal; the enemy would actually sink his own ship right from under him. About the time the "Arlyn" was sunk by the U-517, the U-165, Hartwig's running mate, had torpedoed the U.S. ship "Laramie". However, it cheated the sub by safely limping to port with all hands intact. Piqued at this loss, the U-165 now joined the U-517 and together sought new targets with vengeance. The two submarines reached the area around Cap Chat within 250 miles of Quebec City and waited. They weren't to be disappointed.

Shortly before 10 o'clock, the downriver Quebec-

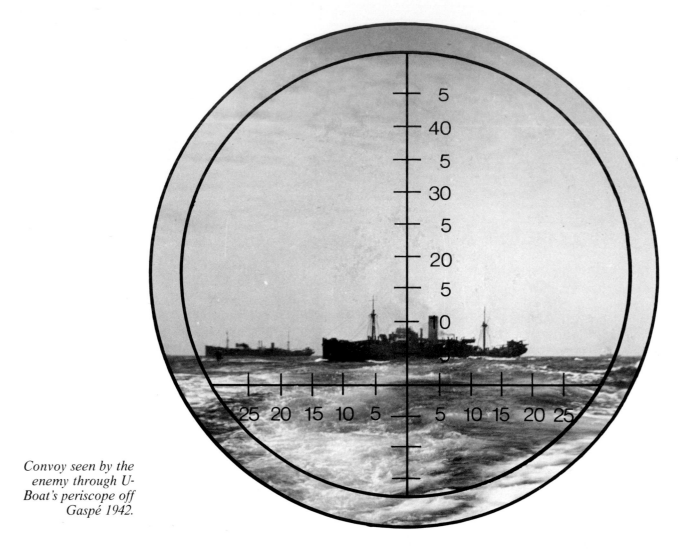

Convoy seen by the enemy through U-Boat's periscope off Gaspé 1942.

Inferno off Gaspé in 1942.

The torpedo strikes.

—Imperial War Museum

—PAC/114397

Fairmile Q064 takes up position as added escort for Convoy going downriver to Gaspé.
—Ian Tate

Gaspé-Sydney Convoy hove into sight. They had sailed after forming up at Bic Island, about 150 miles below Quebec. The Convoy was accompanied by several Fairmiles, two corvettes and the armed yacht HMCS "Raccoon". The Fairmile Q064 already had taken a small convoy up the St. Lawrence, refueling at Rimouski after pausing at Father Point where convoys took on pilots. Part of a seven ship flotilla, the Fairmiles included the Q083 and the recently arrived Q064. HMCS "Charlottetown" with HMCS "Clayoquot" were in reserve at Gaspé, "Charlottetown" equipped with "R.D.F." (Radar). Even at this late date in hostilities, the "Charlottetown" was undermanned. Heagy, in last-minute draft, was to pick up "Charlottetown" when it called in at Rimouski and would thus bring the Radar complement up to three. The two warships departed Gaspé having sufficient fuel for the return trip, while the Fairmiles replenished their smaller fuel capacity at Rimouski. The downriver convoy was considered to be adequately protected. The protagonists in this deadly battle were now about to meet, a battle which would extend well into the following week and would bring both "Clayoquot" and "Charlottetown" into it, and later "Arrowhead."

Lt. Cdr. Willard Bonner, skipper of the "Charlottetown" was considered to be one of the Navy's finest officers. In peacetime he had served as a Marine Officer in the Royal Canadian Mounted Police. Lt. Skinner, skipper of HMCS Arrowhead, on the other hand, had lived on the other side of the law. He was a rumrummer; a profession considered by most in

Nova Scotia as a friendly business. Bonner had regularly chased Skinner and though he had never caught his avowed quarry, Bonner instinctively knew he wasn't "all bad." Both had been Naval Reservists, and both were iconoclasts who abhorred the RCN's penchant for too often belittling the Reservists. It was the Permanent Force Officer who invariably got the sleek sophisticated destroyers while the Reservists drew the workhorses of the Navy, the Corvette or Minsweeper. Curiously, men that in peacetime had been opponents became comrades in war, united now in their actions toward a common enemy, Hartwig.

But fate which had brought these two Canadians together, would now tear them apart for all time. They'd really had opportunity for only a brief reunion when both their ships docked earlier in Gaspé; a meeting which those in the know viewed with much expectation and foreboding. How would an ex-RCMP officer view his quarry now? They need have had no fear. They parted friends, shaking hands some say with tear-filled eyes, each promising to see the other when they returned. Skinner would see neither Bonner nor their mutual friend, Lt. G.N. Smith of HMCS "Raccoon", whom both knew well. Both would disappear from the scene as silently as they came.

Personnel in Canada's Navy numbered close to 40,000 by July 1942, swelling at the rate of some 2,000 per month. Recruiting began now for a Women's Royal Canadian Service to free male service trades for sea duty in Canada's 188 warship Navy.

Fairmiles proceed in "line ahead" formation off Gaspé. — *Gavin Clark*

The official Naval account, by Joseph Schull, described our position . . . "the dry statistics didn't tell the underlying achievement . . . underpinned by heartbreaking failures: our ships and our half-trained men, still scantily equipped and limited manpower, exposed to all kinds of discomforts and terror by night still made it possible with every drab, unmarked day's work to move sixty thousand tons of war supplies each day toward the United Kingdom."

Part of that sixty thousand tons was in the holds of ships now down-bound from Quebec and "Dutch" Davey kept watch-keepers closed up while "Arrowhead" plodded along. Skinner was Senior Officer of the convoy and he wanted a good Radar watch to keep an eye on his charges. For Davey's part, he was more than pleased the ship's "bed-spring antenna" worked so well so far upriver. His Radar was the "hand-me-down" type 286 from the Royal Navy, which long ago had been abandoned for the much superior type 271, now winning laurels in the "Battle of the Atlantic." While the offshore hills in this part of the St. Lawrence effectively shielded reception from distant echoes, the close-in ones were reliable up to a distance of about five miles between "Arrowhead" and shore. Burton came on watch now and Davey addressed him with the affectionate "Hello Newfie". Burton was now an "R.D.F. 2" rating, who had only recently passed 'into the mysterious hallowed halls of science'. More important to the native from Harbour Buffet was that he now considered himself 'a Canadian'. Davey addressed Burton: "The Skipper's stationed "Raccoon" (operators called it

"the Coon") astern . . . watch for it." Pointing to two other blips, Davey added, there are two Fairmiles on the flanks". Davey was pleased he could maintain 'forward watch' as well as directly astern where the 'blip' for "Raccoon" could clearly be seen, due to the ubiquitous faulty "back echoes" which now were actually an advantage. Ahead lay the bulk of the convoy, giving off good echoes.

The bobbing of "Raccoon's" echo aft became one of comfort as Lieut. G.N.Smith 'maintained station' steadily astern of "Arrowhead". Unfortunately, none would be detected from the waiting submarines. The Convoy approached Cap Chat, elated they had now passed the halfway mark between Rimouski and Gaspé's location, now 100 miles downriver. The St. Lawrence widened here almost as if they were now in an endless ocean.

The U-165 and Hartwig's U-157 waited. Aboard one of the Fairmiles, Cox'n Miller felt elated. His early fears of attack had not materialized much like his earlier fears that he might not pass the test for Cox'n. He had 'made it'! Even the bravado taunts of his shipmate George Munger ceased to bother him. Munger had called him a 'chicken-sexer' at one time, because he'd been employed in a chick hatchery in Fergus, Ontario prior to joining up, and had teased him about being born in 'German sounding' Baden, Ontario which was also the birthplace of Sir Adam Beck, the "Father of Ontario Hydro." Baden was a small village but it was as Canadian as apple pie. When another crew member Estwood Davidson entered the friendly argument and revealed that he hailed from a still smaller community of River Bourgeois in Nova Scotia, all comparisons ceased. Munger was from Toronto and all became fast friends. Included in the crew of Q064 was a recent arrival, George Crowell, who took over as wireless operator and sometime Radar watchkeeper.

Meanwhile, in the Radar cabin of "Arrowhead", Davey and Berton were unaware that their skipper Skinner, the rumrunner and Hartwig, the rum drinker now were about to meet. In fact, before the Convoy was through both would be dedicated to killing the other as this Hamlet-like drama unfolded. The two now stealthily approached each other. The convoy and the escorts bore down. Oddly enough, after winning a decoration for service in the Atlantic, Skinner was annoyed to have been sent to the St. Lawrence, which he considered a soft touch. The crew said he bellowed and fumed at the time but the "demotion", as he viewed it, stuck. According to Davey, he didn't go quietly. He enjoyed Skinner's bombast and rhetoric. Like many merchant-service skippers, the long nights at sea offered time for reflection and Skinner's knowledge of oceans and ports developed a peculiar philosophy rare to the city dweller. Skinner called the shots as he saw them and to hell with the consequences. The fact he still liked Navy Rum only improved the eloquence of the recitals which often included Canada's Navy, in which he had an instinctive pride. Before the convoy was through he would have opportunity to justify his calling.

For Hartwig, this convoy appeared to be a pushover. The plan for attack was initiated; U-165 would proceed slightly ahead and make the first contact. Hartwig understandably was somewhat apprehensive about this, for he needed all the sinkings he could get. But there were just so many torpedoes between them and each one had to count, if Doenitz's wishes were to be carried out. Hartwig accordingly waited downriver below Cap Chat.

Begrudgingly, Hartwig watched while the U-165 got the first target. It was the Greek ship "Aeus", torpedoed about ten o'clock the night of the sixth of September. The torpedo killed the wireless operator and one of the firemen. Coming in from the shadow of the hilly shore, five miles distant, it had been an easy target. People in Cap Chat were awakened by the explosion and rushed to their windows, only to see the initial flames dying down. The crew took to boats which hadn't been splintered by the explosion. All that remained was for the escorts to pick up the survivors. Aboard the Q064, cox'n Miller's idyll had been shattered. Miller wondered if this was going to be another of those nights. He felt a pang in his stomach much like he had felt when he first went to sea on the destroyer "Ottawa". On that trip he had been seasick, spewing all over the deck. Standing orders were that crewmen must 'swab up' their own mess. He managed to keep his stomach this time but wondered how the war affected different people.

The curses of the demented seamen in the water still rang in his ears, and the captain, who refused to be saved earlier, contrasted to the sensitivity that had been attuned as he listened to regular Bible reading at the Sunday School that he attended in Baden. Munger tried to console Miller after both watched men die all around them in the St. Lawrence. These horrible facts of life stupefied both of them: that it could happen "right here in Canada!!"

"Dutch" Davey, Leading RDF of HMCS "Arrowhead."
—Beacon-Herald, Stratford

Aboard "Arrowhead", Davey kept the watch-keepers closed up, actually pleased his "bed-spring" antenna worked so well so far downriver. He had five miles of vacant water free from land echoes and he worked this to the full. Davey was especially pleased the fault with "back-echoes", cursed earlier, now lent itself admirably by allowing the Radar to monitor "Raccoon" behind, at the same time as the forward echoes bounced in. But the U-165 was not "seen" on the Radar, obliterated by the clutter of wave echoes which made detection of a mere periscope difficult. But Davey was suspicious now. He called by the ASDIC cabin and in an instant summarized the events. There sat Smith, staring into space . . . muttering something about . . . "I knew it was a sub." Davey asked Smith . . . "Are you all right?" All he got back was Smith repeating over and over again . . . "I'm sure it was a sub," as Davey listened, despairingly. "I'm sure because I told the bridge . . . good doppler . . . good echo . . . running right clear down the ship it did" Smith reiterated; then he blurted, "No one believed me." The case was all too familiar to Davey who'd heard "Cry Wolf" before. "Perhaps the new 'Subby' on the bridge suspected just another ruse also" thought Davey, "I'll see what I can do". On the bridge, Davey found the Sub-Lieutenant, a new entry who had just joined the ship, with no previous seatime, was obviously confused. Should he risk condemnation by calling the 'old man' even if he'd already left strict orders he wasn't to be disturbed? The 'Subby' knew the Skipper already had had a tough night keeping the group together after losing one ship. The Skipper was determined to get some shuteye before dawn action stations, the accustomed time for an attack with the usual 'first light' and the young officer-of-the-watch decided to do nothing.

Davey returned to find the Radar operator fuming about another problem. He'd lost the back-echo. "Raccoon's not on the trace." "It's just the switching motor," Davey suspected, "I've seen it before." With that, Davey asked to 'borrow' the key-chain that a seaman was wearing on his wrist. "The key chain" Davey had hollered, reaching for it hungrily. The seamen watched in disbelief as Davey, hurriedly yet methodically, pulled each interlocking ball from the other until the seaman's keepsake was reduced to a palm-full of shiny little balls. "This'll do it" as Davey then offered a curt "thanks" and began filling the ball-race of the recalcitrant electric motor with the, now, all-important parts of the chain. Except for small individual holes, they were perfectly round, and the idea worked. However there still was no back-echo. Davey suspected that the motor was merely acting up again and gave the set a kick. Almost at the same instant he heard the explosion. It came from astern of them; so powerful that it penetrated the sealed cabin itself. And the customary "pip" in the stern quadrant was gone. "Raccoon" by the early morning of September 7th, literally had disappeared and the Radar set was working properly.

The explosion woke the 'old man' and he rushed to the bridge. "Arrowhead's first reaction was that "Raccoon" had sighted a sub and was dropping depth charges. However, a horrible silence followed; unusual for a ship which normally would follow a first pattern and drop more. Actually, U-165 had torpedoed "Raccoon" and the tiny armed yacht with its 38 men had vanished. Their requiem, "Lights in the Night", had been sung in one brilliant flash. Skinner's Newfoundland anger swept over him and the accompanying invectives left little doubt about how he felt. He had left the Atlantic figuring that his posting would be too dull only to find he was in the thick of it now, but unprepared. "Drop a full pattern of depth charges" he ordered "and keep moving".

Hartwig had been lured to the activity of U-165 and now wanted part of the action. The U-165 now had this ship to its credit while he had none. The only salutary thing about it all to the Canadians was that Smith had been right; he had detected the U-165

ASDIC operators on board a Canadian warship plot a German submarine "somewhere off an East Coast Port".
— W.S. Leggett PAC/134330

but by now, any calls from the ASDIC were suspect. Skinner was having none of this 'ASDIC business' and just 'shot from the hip'. Hartwig came in at the wrong time.

The U-517 couldn't dive as deep as Hartwig would have liked even though he had some 900 feet of water below him at this part of the St. Lawrence. He made a run for it. Then, Skinner's depth charges let go. Not just a few of the lights in the sub went out this time, but all the electrical wiring providing necessary illumination was jarred loose. This signalled an imminent rupture. It was the time to bring out Hitler's favourite and cherished idea . . . the "Pillenwerfer", a metal gadget about the size of a large tomato can. U-boats in trouble could blow one of these cans out of a torpedo tube, and, on contact with the water, they let out a stream of bubbles. These reflected our ASDIC beams to nearly approximate those of the actual sub itself and the pursuer invariably followed the stream of bubbles, while the sub slipped quietly away, frustrating the most talented and experienced ASDIC operator. Smith had only recently joined "Arrowhead", without experience, and "Arrowhead" was unable to score "a kill."

Hartwig escaped with only a severe shaking up. He had a new respect for those Canadians whom Hitler had reportedly said at one time . . . "leave them alone and they'll sink themselves." Hartwig resolved to be twice as wary next time. He didn't realize the opportunity would come so soon. The convoy made it safely to Gaspé dropping off three freighters for a breather before continuing on.

Mr. Levine never saw the three freighters leave. He was too busy minding the hardware store even for a quick look. By five o'clock, he hurried 'home' to the Kruse Hotel on the chance that the news—the radio worked perfectly now—might report at least something of the intense activity now enveloping Gaspé. Everyone in town became as involved in the war as the servicemen. Each day the newspapers were scoured for even a hint of what was going on. Ears strained for every word of the static-laden overseas radio broadcasts reporting the latest stages of the war in Europe, but nothing was ever said about Canada. Levine could tell there was 'something up' by the grim look on our faces as we poured into the dining room for our meals. Mr. Levine, now old and tired, wanted to help but he knew he was being left out. "Can I help" he feebly asked while Don Messer's regular "Down East" music continued to thunder out from the loudspeaker, preempting any news which might have been important. Only the Marine Weather forecasts continued. "A for Apple is to be carried out": decoded it meant all secondary lights were to be extinguished; the enemy was in the vicinity.

It was Hartwig's plan to wait for dusk. Accordingly, on the following day, he warily made his way to within 15 miles of Cape Gaspé and waited. By evening of the seventh, he moved in just as the three ships made a break for the open water to join up with the remnants of the convoy from Quebec City. Just past 5 p.m., after an hour's steaming down the long Gut, Hartwig with his usual daring moved past the inadequate escort as they formed up again.

Dead ahead of Hartwig was the Greek ship "Mount Pindus." Following was her sister 'tramp' which had been one of the three in Gaspé, the "Mount Tayegetos." Swinging his periscope around he saw the Canadian "Oakton" dead astern. Virtually unchecked and in bravado fashion, he exercised what would be his greatest feat: he fired both fore and aft torpedoes simultaneously; three lethal 'fish' emerging, two from the bow and one from the stern, all within a matter of seconds. All three hit their marks. In the "Mount Tayegetos" carrying 28 men, five were killed in the engine room. "Mount Pindus" lost her engineer and fireman. The rest of her crew of 35, shivering, cursing sailors, hollering in a dozen different languages, were picked up along with 23 survivors from the "Mount Tayegetos." The brave laker "Oakton" lost men in the same location as so many other ships; the 'hell holes' as they were called, losing one oiler and two firemen also a St. Bernard dog despite his brave stand on the gun platform. They hadn't even time to close up the gun crew. Seventeen men survived "Oakton." Hartwig made good his escape safely submerged in the Gaspé passage between Anticosti Island and the mainland. But he was perplexed. Despite his stunning success, he feared he had stirred up a hornet's nest. Already Hudson bombers from Mont Joli were patrolling and near misses had come close to sinking him earlier. An estimated 27 bombs already had caused damage, and "Arrowhead's" pounding almost spelled doom for the U-517.

On his hydrophone, he could hear the peripheral searching ASDIC waves bouncing from shoals or rock-bed only to be absorbed by the mud below. The Canadians proved they were fighters and Hartwig wondered how they kept coming on despite their obviously inadequate equipment. One day they'd get him and a cornered man is a dangerous man. The alarm was out and he was no better than a hunted criminal with the hounds already nipping at his heels. The U-517 shuddered as it put on an extra burst of speed. Hartwig was also determined to increase his bag.

What of the survivors? The answer came not in an instant but days later as the remnants floated ashore in bits and pieces; life jackets forgotten in the melee; oars and wooden crates, Carley floats and rope. Whether at Cape Gaspé or at Cape Des Rosiers, where Ferguson helplessly watched the drama unfold in the sea before his lighthouse, or along the opposite shore at Fort Prevel or Percé, those survivors who managed to make shore were hurriedly loaded into horsecart or truck and despatched along the bumpy road back to Gaspé.

For Mr. Levine, who watched the not-entirely-

SS "Oakton", hauling pulpwood in better times.   —PA 33129

unexpected arrival of the first oil-soaked survivors, the seed of an idea was born. He first gave up his bed; the rest would come later. For Mrs. Kruse, the routine was now familiar: she selected clothing from the huge cardboard box she had earlier filled, matching odd pants or a suit to each man's needs, forgetting size which wasn't important while covering them the best she could. For those men dropped off at McAllister's barracks, a quick stop at the Naval stores first produced a warm Navy blanket to throw around each shivering person and then to a hastily requisitioned bunk, including McAllister's who had unsuspectingly climbed into bed upon his return, only to find a Greek already occupying it.

For the rest of us at the Kruse Hotel, all rooms were politely taken over. When they were full, the overflow slept on the floor. For myself, the train's arrival was the height of frustration. However it was made bearable by the prompt response of Mrs. Kruse and the rediscovered friendship of Mrs. Patterson, who found a place for Esther to sleep in her home. What a time to arrive for a weekend visit!! Not only was the weekend lost but the next four days as well. Apart from a brief tour of the town and one dance at the "Y," what might have been a fun-filled week became a recital of emergencies. Attending to the needs at the Base or the more important requirements of helping ships prepare for sea with the enemy now just offshore meant little time at the

Hotel for me. For Esther, an indoctrination on how to run a Hotel in the face of instant guests became part of her routine, a difficult adjustment for a young lady trained as a typist but now immersed in a war. Friday of the week was taken up mostly preparing for Esther's return to Halifax. Irvin Brethen kept quoting the Scriptures on the seriousness of marriage and pointing the way to Wayman's Church, where already several Naval officers had been married. But it was too late. That very day, Hartwig prepared his response and before another week began, Rev. Wayman would be burying our dead, not performing marriages.

No one in Canada would know of the unexpected guests who arrived in the night. Someone would snap a picture of Mrs. Kruse by the early light of the following morning as she bade farewell to the men she had helped before they were whisked away by special train. This picture was proudly displayed by her son Earl on the wall of his home: it showed "the Fighting Lady" surrounded by the men she had befriended, their ill-fitting clothes a testimony to her determination and charity, but it was never reproduced in any newspaper, anywhere.

Canada should not have worried about the Gaspé people not being able to face up to the enemy, but rather a Government which itself was afraid to own up to Canada's peril and share the danger with all its citizens.

"The fighting Lady", Mrs. Alfred Kruse, stands proudly before a group of survivors plucked from the waters after their ship had been torpedoed off Gaspé on Sept. 11, 1942. Survivors wear ill-fitting clothes hastily provided by Mrs. Kruse and the ladies of the town. They were shipped out the next morning by special train. Picture was taken in front of the Kruse Hotel just before they embarked from the CN Station.

— Earl Kruse

unlucky thirteen

September, 1942, marked the apex of the war in the St. Lawrence. John Robinson was just two years old and his brother Ken already had begun school. Their mother, the wife of Sgt. A.L. Robinson, of the RCAF at Mont Joli, Quebec, had decided that English-speaking kids shouldn't be deprived of an education because their father wished to have them with him instead of sitting out the war back in Orillia, Ontario. Consequently, Mrs. Robinson organized an English-language school at the Air Force Base. For Mrs. Robinson, education was really secondary in her thoughts now. Her first concern, when the night sky lit up, was the increased sorties by newly arrived Hudson Bombers along the St. Lawrence. She now had second thoughts about having come. She hoped the Navy's recent battle with submarines wouldn't go unanswered, meanwhile she searched the daily newspapers for an explanation and found none. They revealed not a hint, leaving her to rely like most people, on gossip which now circulated along the shore as far distant as Octave Gendron's Lighthouse at Metis Point. While Mrs. Robinson taught the "three R's", Nazi submarines offshore taught Canada the "three S's" . . . suspicion, subterfuge and surprise.

Don McAllister at Gaspé knew what was going on; so did all those young men and women who monitored signals from ships around the clock. The Navy Signals room at "Fort Ramsay" now had become part of Air Operations and together they received a running commentary of the battle of the 6th and 7th of September via the myriad of Naval Signals and codes which crossed their desks. They could only take their hats off in salute to the brave men (really only kids) who now went regularly in ships to meet the enemy offshore.

Meanwhile I was preparing to watch the train chuff out of Gaspé in the early morning. Like most in Gaspé, I was concerned just where the enemy might attack next and I became apprehensive that the subs might try to shell the train. Raoul Babin, a conductor on the Ocean Limited, had told me he was ordered to draw all the blinds while that train ran along track paralleling the St. Lawrence to prevent the possibility of drawing enemy fire. Esther's train ran along this unprotected coastline before reaching Matapedia. But I realized my own personal dilemma in the greater affairs of men was really inconsequential. Despite all the perils of war, Esther returned safely to Halifax and our plans would just have to be put aside.

September 11th dawned bright if generally foggy but we had no idea the dilemma HMCS "Clayoquot" together with "Charlottetown" now faced. Apparently the two had just delivered their convoy successfully upriver to Bic Island, being spared "Arrowhead's" and "Raccoon's" baptism of fire four days earlier. This was their first joint operation and they felt confident and, therefore they would not need additional help from Fairmiles, resulting in the two returning alone to Gaspé. Fairmiles Q064, Q065, Q080, and Q083 hadn't the requisite fuel reserves as had the two larger warships, so they dropped off at Rimouski to 'top up' while "Clayoquot" and "Charlottetown" continued towards Cap Chat some 90 miles downriver from Rimouski. It was a fatal move.

Cox'n Lyle Miller wasn't sorry for the delay; the early morning fog "was atrocious" and they'd get no help from their SW1C Radar which Miller described as "primitive". When Skipper Norm Williams ordered the delay, Cox'n Miller felt as elated as when Williams had granted him permission to grow a beard: in the Navy this was a sign of coming of age and Miller had been the envy of his shipmates ever since. He was somewhat apprehensive, however, by the fact that weeks had gone by since his request and all he could show for a beard was a little fuzz on his chin. By comparison, Allan Heagy on board 'the big ship Charlottetown' sported a King George V type beard as epitomized on the packages of Player's Cigarettes that the boys smoked.

It seemed perfectly natural to Al Heagy to grow a beard. After all, he had toughed it out on the North-Atlantic run, and the beard seemed a fitting climax for one who now counted the whole world his stage. Heagy grasped the heavy-handed "Chevy"

One of the youngest cox'ns in the Canadian Navy, 17 year old Lyle Miller from Baden, Ontario is shown at the wheel of the Q064. — Ian Tate

Allan Heagy wearing coveted Navy Beard. Insignia indicated "Leading-Hand" on left arm while "Masquerading Wireless Badge" is worn on right arm.

steering wheel on his SW1C Radar with confidence, after departing Rimouski and the cluster of Fairmiles berthed nearby. He went on duty at 8 A.M. Obviously, Heagy didn't know what his classmate "Dutch" Davey had endured in these same waters only a few nights earlier, nor that "Raccoon" was now missing and presumed lost. The newspapers hadn't announced it and like most of us, all he knew was what he read in the papers. He'd come straight from Halifax on draft to Rimouski and had only gotten settled aboard when "Charlottetown" piped 'leaving harbour routine'. Now, they were doing a good 11 knots with "Clayoquot" just off the port side but far enough away to avoid the half-mile blackout range of the SW1C. He could monitor "Clayoquot", at the same time ranging on land six miles distant.

On the bridge, the officer-of-the-watch had succeeded in obtaining a "fix" using a church spire glimpsed with a slight lift in the fog and the Radar range called out earlier. Miraculously, it confirmed the distance. But the Radar failed to pickup a telltale wisp of water curling from a periscope.

At "Fort Ramsay," McAllister banged out positions on the teletype, but he never expected the tumult of events which were to follow.

At Fontonelle, just across the harbour from "Fort Ramsay" Bob Wallace helped relay signals from his own vantage point atop the Gaspé mountains surrounding the harbour. Wallace was one of a dozen men who lived most of the year in isolation so they could send our signals over the metal-encrusted hills allowing them to be received on the river on the other side of nature's shield. It was so high that on a clear day, Wallace could see clear across to Anti-

costi and the dreaded Gaspé passage. Wallace had been mystified by all the heavy aircraft activity as the Hudson bombers from Mont Joli were joined by the PBY's now stationed at Gaspé. Only last week they had officially opened a huge hangar at "Fort Ramsay" to accommodate the PBY's. I had played band music on Don Clark's record player for the march-past as the Base was still lacking a proper military band. That was Sunday, Sept. 6th, just one day before the submarines struck Gaspé.

After the 7th of September attack, Sub. Lieut. Ian Tate had been despatched to St. Yvon, where one of the torpedoes from the attack had run astray. Instead of hitting a merchantman, this one travelled all the way past Ferguson's Lighthouse at Cap Des Rosiers, running up on the shore at St. Yvon with a violent blast, knocking out all the windows in fishermen's homes. Tate and his entourage motored along the North Shore approaching St. Yvon with guns drawn for any eventuality. They recovered part of the torpedo to return to Gaspé. In the opposite direction across the harbour mouth at St. Georges des Malbaie, a single lifeboat was found empty, mute evidence of the struggle that had taken place and the ferocity of Hartwig's attack.

Aboard "Charlottetown," Ldg. Signalman Wesley Vincent was just returning from the Wireless office located near the towering Radar Hut noting Heagy had closed up his watch on the SW1C. He knew it was working because the heavy Yagi antenna slowly jerked on its cumbersome conduit running up to the masthead as Heagy made each labourious turn of the heavy Chevy steering wheel. Vincent gained the mess-deck and just had time to put a cup of apple

Twin-engined PBY aircraft provides fitting background for Sunday morning "Divisions".

—Ian Tate

"Eyes Right!" The combined Navy and Air Force march in the Sunday morning sunshine. With no military band available marching precision was helped by the use of a record player and public address system, both of which were loaned by P.O. Don Clark, while the playing of the record was done by the author. Note the hastily erected aircraft hangar at the left. HMCS "Fort Ramsay".

—Ian Tate

PBY successfully lands on Gaspé Harbour.   —*Ian Tate*

Lifeboat washed ashore, one of several found at the Harbour's outer perimeter off Gaspé resulting from ships sunk by Submarine U-517.   —*Ian Tate*

The road to St. Yvon! It was here that a German submarine, attempting to sink the merchantman "Meadcliffe Hall", fired a torpedo which missed the ship and came up on the beach where it exploded. The "True North Strong and Free" had been violated.　　　　　　　—Ian Tate.

Curious villagers and children gather to view the remains of a torpedo which shattered windows in the community of St. Yvon a half-mile away in Sept. 1942.　　　　　　　—Ian Tate

juice to his lips when it happened: 'there was a deafening explosion when the first torpedo hit and all the lights went out. I was just going up the hatch when a second one hit. I got to the deck and saw the stern, a twisted mass of torn steel. The ship took a sharp list to starboard almost immediately. I grabbed a lifebelt and after some of the fellows got a life raft over the side following 'Abandon ship' order, I went over the side, too."

Topside, stoker Bill McFadyen of Collingwood, miraculously still alive (his mate in the stoke-hole was killed with the first blast) saw Captain Bonner. Stunned for a moment by the surprise, Bonner already had the men organized trying to launch the port lifeboat. But the ship was sloping opposite and the falls fell inward making the task impossible. Undaunted, he then ordered the starboard boat away. Because of the list, the starboard boat was lowered away more easily. The Captain hollered "Jump boys, we're not going to make it." Over the side went Carley floats; boxes; anything that would float. One man clung to a bully beef container while others scrambled for the lifeboat or rafts now bobbing in the water. But the captain remained behind.

What followed next was completely unexpected. When the first torpedo hit, it loosed the depth charge brackets aft, spilling the lethal drums all over the rear of the ship, fouling their safety settings. As they slipped off the quarterdeck they began to sink and the water pressure caused about six to explode, sending up a huge geyser of water. A rescued sailor reported "some of the boys seemed to be right in the middle of the explosion. It was terrible. The charges are effective up to 500 yards and they were only 100 yards away". One of those in the explosion was Captain Bonner, who, in the best tradition of the service, was the last to leave his ship.

Hartwig, watching impassively from below suddenly saw "Clayoquot" swerve towards him for an attack. Topside, the gunnery officer of "Clayoquot" ordered "fire", but Captain Lade at the last moment belayed the order. Later, McFadyen claimed Lade thereby saved many men still struggling in the water by witholding additional depth charges. "He only continued the attack when clear". Captain Lade would subsequently lose his own life when his ship was torpedoed off Halifax on Christmas Eve, 1944. "Charlottetown" settled at the stern, lifting her bow as if in proud defiance, revealing a seaman still clinging gamely to the wreckage. It was Seaman Garland, who earlier had risked his own life by passing out lifejackets for others, depriving himself of one. "Jump" the men hollered; but he refused. "I'm not leaving without the dog," he hollered back; a mascot they'd had since earlier calls at Newfoundland. He didn't know that the dog was already safely aboard a Carley float; but it was too late. Another massive explosion and the ship was gone, carrying Garland with it. Another sailor had rushed back to get his girl friend's picture. He was never seen again

HMCS "Clayoquot" taking on survivors from sole lifeboat which successfully cleared HMCS "Charlottetown" before she went down off Cap Chat near Gaspé.   —*A. Heagy*

With no room in the lifeboat, survivors from HMCS "Charlottetown" are rescued by Carley-float; Allan Heagy (seen in white lifejacket) gave up his place in lifeboat for injured crewman.

Fairmiles on patrol. — *Gilbert A. Milne/PAC-134325*

Examination vessel "HDPC-7" skippered by Lt. G. Allard RCN (R) departs Gaspé Naval Base searching for survivors of the torpedoed "Charlottetown".

— *Ian Tate*

either. Some couldn't swim; others learned to swim almost immediately. Fred Rush of Winnipeg took a chance of losing his life by giving up his lifebelt to a fellow seaman who couldn't swim. Rush was found floundering about in the oil-soaked water and was subsequently picked up by a raft, somehow uninjured by the depth charges. Heagy, who earlier had managed to get into the crowded lifeboat, gave up his place for the injured seaman, electing to hang onto the side of a raft instead. SBA Bateman did what he could to aid the injured until his portable supplies were exhausted. Bonner's body was recovered after an hour and a half search of the icy 44F degree water. His body was lovingly lifted into the already overloaded boat by executive officer G.M. Moors. He then recovered more injured from the uncomfortable Carley floats before making for shore. It was apparent that Bonner's body would have to be taken out of the boat and the men helped lash Capt. Bonner's body to the rudder to accommodate the additional men, many groaning pitifully from injuries sustained. After rowing for about an hour, the rudder was torn adrift by the weight and Bonner was regrettably left behind. They could make better time this way. It was almost as if in death the faithful Capt. Bonner was still serving his men. The shore was just two miles away.

For Hartwig, Doenitz's dictum not to hazard his men unduly had been forgotten because of "Charlottetown" and "Clayoquot." It was either them or him; two warships against one submarine. After he let his torpedoes go, he exercised his "escape weapon" again, the Pillenwerfer, as "Clayoquot" initiated her counterattack. Once again the device burst forth its stream of lifesaving bubbles, fouling Clayoquot's ASDIC which never managed to get a firm fix on the U-517.

On hearing news of the sinking, the Fairmiles, now topped up with fuel, were despatched immediately from Rimouski. Additional rescue ships began to arrive from Gaspé, including George Allard in the "HPD7," the latest examination vessel replacing the earlier "Oracle". When they burst through the fog, the now-muffled explosions of depth charges from "Clayoquot" could be heard still valiantly trying to make up for "Charlottetown's" loss. Allard brushed aside the urge to want to kill Hartwig himself "with my own bare hands". If Hartwig surfaced, Allard would have had to use 'his bare hands', for the "HPD7" had no guns nor depth charges aboard. As the fog lifted, it revealed a mass of jetsam and flotsam where once sailed a proud ship. For Allard, the tragedy of the war had been played out almost as surely as a curtain closes the last act. What he had long feared before the war broke out had come to pass; Canada's own boys were being killed right in our own waters by the enemy. Allard's own heart, now heavy as a stone over the loss, felt like crying out . . . "Canadians are being killed right here in Canada and no one seems to . . ." He stopped

Survivors from HMCS "Charlottetown" pictured outside Naval barracks at HMCS "Fort Ramsay"; Note rescued ship's mascot in front row.   —P.O. J. Wheeler

short at this point for he knew Canada's own cared; were they not right here dying, coming down to the sea in ships, meeting the enemy bravely? But their brave deeds were trapped by our own secrecy. "Damn," Allard cursed, "the young die first." He wept silently, then recovering, Allard ordered "full speed ahead" and returned to Gaspé with the tiny armada. Hartwig, now free of danger, made good another escape. But it wasn't without remorse. Once free, Hartwig said to his own crew, "I feel sorry for the crew of that ship, because they were killed by their own weapons."

Ashore, Dorothy German was busy laying the injured, like cordwood, on her carpeted living room floor, oblivious to the steward who ceremoniously appeared by the doorway, reminding her that the oil-splattered bodies would spoil the carpet. She continued to place them one by one on the floor anyway, only concerned that each one had a place to lie. Those who were in the water when the depth charges let go were the worst off; the concussion bursts the blood vessels and you die a slow death. Retching and coughing blood are the unmistakeable signs. When Dorothy German's husband, Cmdr. Barry German came in, he took one look at them and ordered all of them to be taken immediately to the Hospital in Gaspé. He knew Dr. Guy Fortier was the only one who could help them now. Some didn't make it.

Telegrapher Bill Bean of "Clayoquot" certain that "Charlottetown's" second torpedo was meant for "Clayoquot," watched thankfully after docking safely at "Fort Ramsay" with survivors following the fruitless search for the U-517. They had found the lifeboat with the crew singing lustily, still determined and still paddling for the shore. However, "Clayoquot's" timely intervention kept more from dying. Telegraphist Edmund Robinson was an example of determination. When put ashore he insisted on walking, only to fall flat onto the jetty unaware of the severity of his injuries. He died 5 days later in the Hotel Dieu Hospital. Fifty-seven were rescued, five died with the ship and four later died in hospital.

Censorship moved in as promptly as had the enemy. Those of us who remained at the Base but who should have known, weren't told. I only found out about "Charlottetown's" sinking the next morning when Heagy apeared unceremoniously at my workbench in the "R.D.F." office. Dressed not in the rig-of-the-day but in an old turtleneck sweater and baggy pants, he was symbolic of other survivors I'd seen earlier at the Kruse Hotel. My initial reaction was wonderment, followed by immutable anger to think my friend was now also a victim. He had somehow learned through the barracks, where they'd all spent the night, that I was here; Heagy made the triumvirate of University of Western Ontario graduates at Gaspé complete. He didn't know that Davey on "Arrowhead" was by now well on his way through the Gulf heading for Sydney with their downriver Convoy. It was hardly a reunion but Heagy made a simple statement profound in its implication, " . . . I told you they'd never get me". Dennis Bright, who had been on HMCS "Windflower" was gone; Davey's welfare on "Arrowhead" was now uncertain; but Heagy had made it and he wanted me to know.

The relatively sleepy town of Gaspé, pleased with its recently acquired ability to "keep secrets," remained ignorant of the disaster until the funeral service the following Monday Sept. 14, 1942. Wayman's Church was at long last filled to capacity. Even so, no word of this made it to the rest of Canada. The survivors, to a man were confined to barracks over the weekend before being whisked to the "outside world." And no one talked when questioned except relating their own suffering, for suffering is hard to hide, but no one gave the location where they had been torpedoed; to a man each abided by his vow of secrecy.

The Government issued its own brief account from Ottawa, revealing "Charlottetown" had been "torpedoed in Northern waters where enemy subs have been active". One account even suggested it was in waters off "an East Coast Port" but that's as close as the newspaper reported. That was all; but the wall of secrecy was beginning to crumble. It would be accelerated, in a month's time, when the CNS Ferry "Caribou" would be sunk by enemy action while sailing between Sydney and Port Aux Basques, Newfoundland. One hundred and thirty-six lives including women and children were lost when the ferry was torpedoed on Oct. 14th, 1942.

For the Navy's part, Naval Minister MacDonald already had released this rejoinder: "Naval losses are part of the price which must be paid in order that protection may be given the merchant ships carrying supplies to the battlefronts."

Gaspé had become the Front Line. And the long-delayed reunion between Davey, Heagy and myself, apart from the brief appearance of Heagy, was now postponed indefinitely. In fact, I would not see him again in Gaspé. Canada had now lost nine warships on the high seas: "Charlottetown," was the third warship lost in the St. Lawrence and already seamen were needed elsewhere to replace losses considered to be more important than Gaspé.

Funeral at St. Paul's Church, Gaspé of Donald Bowser, Able Seaman, lost when HMCS "Charlottetown" was sunk off Gaspé on Sept. 11, 1942.
— Ian Tate

Parish of Gaspé
(ANGLICAN)

St. John's Church
SANDY BEACH

St. Paul's Church
GASPÉ

RECTOR:

ARCHDEACON OF GASPÉ AND THE NORTH SHORE

P.O. BOX 466

GASPÉ, QUEBEC

TEL.: 368-2564

Donald Bowser, a native of England, Able Seaman (A5207)
R.C.N.V.R., H.M.C.S. 'Charlottetown', aged twenty one
years, died of wounds received at sea in action on the
eleventh day of September Anno Domini Nineteen hundred
and forty two, and was buried in the graveyard of the
United Church of Canada, Gaspé, Québec, on the fourteenth
day of the same month in the same year.

In the presence of:
A. R. Perkins
Reg deGruchy.

By me,
J. W. Wayman
Archdeacon of Gaspé

Canadian sailors burial plot was located near St. Paul's Church in the neighbouring United Church cemetery. —*Cassidy's Photos*

Funeral cortege for victims of HMCS "Charlottetown" torpedoed off Gaspé Sept. 11, 1942 leaves St. Paul's Anglican Church following service conducted by the Rev. J. Wayman, Gaspé's inner harbour forms a sombre background while the hospital, where sailors from the "Charlottetown" later succumbed to wounds, may be seen left of centre. —*Reg de Gruchy*

fraternity in battle

Dead men tell no tales!! . . . or do they. Unlike the newspapers of the day, bound as they were by an ever tightening censorship, the discovery of Russ McConnell's body on the shores of Anticosti Island spoke volumes.

As an irony of the war, Anticosti, long coveted by Hitler, was now the resting place for a brave Canadian who likely never knew of the political posturing for the island, which went on while he was still in school. The Navy decided to provide a burial at sea befitting a brave sailor. The Fairmile Q064 had the unhappy task of fetching the body, located earlier by aircraft, to Gaspé. Cox'n Lyle Miller was given the sorrowful task of searching the body for identification. Miller studiously noted on the report that "three toes were missing as was most of the flesh from the torso." He confirmed that the deceased, indeed, was McConnell. The body was placed in an appropriate shroud, and was gently lowered over the side to a sailor's grave three miles off Gaspé. None of the other thirty-seven of the crew of "Raccoon" were ever found although bits and pieces of the ship eventually came down river with the inexorable flow of the mighty St. Lawrence.

About this time, three more recruits Wayne Freer, Fred Walker and Gerald Wright entered the military. Freer who was from Petrolia, Ontario, chose the Navy, joining up at HMCS "Star", the Hamilton Naval Reserve. Walker from Hamilton, chose the Army while Wright from St. Marys, chose the Air Force. All would end up in the Gaspé; Wright at Mont Joli's Air Base; Walker at "Fort Prevel"; while Freer would be posted to "Fort Ramsay" in Gaspé. Imagine their surprise when they arrived at what should have been peaceful Canadian bases only to find guns booming, ships sinking and Canadians being killed right in Canada. Walker was sure "All hell prevailed" when he reached Fort Prevel and heard the 'Big Gun' boom for the first time. The only thing good about the gun, Walker recalled, was George Bernard's proud boast . . . "This gun can shoot eight miles out to sea." Although this was impressive, as it turned out all German submarines had to do was to skillfully surface within our convoys, as Hartwig had done, thus preventing the gun from firing for fear of hitting our own ships. Against submarines, it was useless.

Percy Dallner's complaint after finding a war on our own doorstep was, "Why didn't they tell us what to expect before we got here?" Martin J. Lester and Frank Farrell were two more who wanted to know the same thing. Both hailed from neighbouring Kitchener; Lester serving as ground crew in Mont Joli while Farrell would fly hundreds of sorties out of St. Hubert's airfield in Montreal past Mont Joli down the St. Lawrence where he had a bird's-eye view of everything that went on. Freer would serve on the Boom Defence where his job although far less spectacular, was to maintain an old Ford V-8 gasoline engine which operated the winch that controled the anti-submarine net. If it failed to start, he'd give it a kick. If that didn't work, he would strip it down even if it meant for the moment that the submarine gate was immobile. The huge iron-meshed net stretched from his port (or red) Gate vessel on the one side of the Harbour entrance to the starboard (or green) Gate on the opposite side. One evening he almost prevented a convoy from gaining the sanctuary of the inner harbour. Humber Gentile and James Lukeman, stationed in the opposite Gate, realized that Freer's engine wasn't working but he managed to get it repaired and the engine suddenly burst into life and the ponderous chain-mesh gate slowly opened; all breathed a long sigh of relief. This device had originally been put in place during Captain Donald's tenure. Had the gate failed, it would have left the convoy to the mercy of the enemy.

Freer loved to argue and his favourite statement was that Canada really couldn't afford to have a war because "We all end up shooting our own relatives": a point that one 'Canadian' seemed to find embarrassing. He had come from the Stratford-Kitchener area and still had first generation relatives in Germany. At Gaspé, as it was in all Canadian outposts, the displaying of family photos pasted on lockers revealed Ukrainians from the West; English, Irish and Scottish from the U.K.; Poles from Europe

Fairmile Q064 proceeds to Anticosti Island where the body of Lt. Russ McConnell, crewman of HMCS "Racoon" was found.
— Lyle Miller

and a miscellany of countries between. Their owners, though Canadians, were all called by the appropriate nickname, "Limey", "Uke", "Pollack" or "Kraut". The latter name was familiar to Canadians who came from the area of Kitchener which was noted for it's hockey team and it's famous "Kraut" line of Bauer, Schmidt and Dumart. Wayne Freer, merely prided himself on being 'a Canadian' supported by a little French, learned from people in nearby Windsor. Needless to say, the German-Canadian to whom he had made his original statement about 'shooting our relations', wasn't convinced, even if before the war ended, Freer's words would have proved to be prophetic.

While Hartwig continued to harass our Coast, the girl in the CNR station, had telegraphed McConnell's next-of-kin in Montreal about his death. At the Kruse Hotel, the finding of the body set in motion a pattern of activity not seen before. Gaspé attempted now to alleviate the tension for the young servicemen. Mrs. Kruse, her daughter-in-law, Mrs. Walter Kruse and Mrs. Jean DeGruchy, set up a social committee to make the 'boys' feel at home. Everyone contributed, even the Ursuline Sisters, and Rev. Wayman provided the Parish Hall for entertainment. I still recall Mr. Levine's star performace, gowned in a long robe and a magician's hat, making the servicemen forget their cares, if only for the moment.

The Air Force, which up until now had somehow maintained a low profile, came through admirably with the visit of the chef from their Officer's Mess, who came bearing gifts from his kitchen, which enhanced the otherwise sparse table of sandwiches and lemonade. The host of icing-clad buns, huge chocolate cakes and dainty rolls certainly filled more than just the stomachs of the men.

Unfortunately, the men at Fort Prevel missed the Parish Hall concert and the 'goodies' that were served afterwards and they had been 'left out' so to speak. It was decided by a group of about twelve of the local Gaspé girls that if Don Clark and I would provide the music that they would go to Fort Prevel and have a party. Accordingly, we drove the eighteen miles over the rough, gravel roads in jeeps and Army trucks. When we arrived, we made one rule . . . we would have to depart for Gaspé at eleven o'clock.

There were two reasons for the early departure. We had almost an hours' drive back and Don and I had a problem to solve with the SW1C Radar and required an early morning start. Whenever our ships used the SW1C Radar, the electrical interference caused the regular wireless aboard the corvettes to become useless and valuable transmissions and messages were missed. We believed that we could solve this problem by hand winding an electrical filter which would deaden the interference of the Radar without affecting its own operation. However our experiment was to take place the next morning and for now, the party was the more important item.

I had just made the announcement at eleven o'clock that this would be the last dance, when the young officer in charge of Fort Prevel appeared by my side at the record player. In a style reminiscent of the frontier days, and hand on his pistol, he said, "This is the best time my men have had since we got posted to this Godforsaken country, and you'll continue to play until I say stop." The music continued and the girls puffed and wheezed and a hundred men continued to literally dance them off their feet. An hour later, reason prevailed and the young officer removed his hand from his holster. His warning hadn't been ignored and we finally got away from the party sometime after midnight.

Clark and I resolved the problem of the SW1C interference in the morning through heavy-lidded eyes. Our hand wound coils worked and Radar on our corvettes became 'noise free.' And just in time as Hartwig returned for a third appearance. This time, his target was an upbound convoy from Sydney headed for Quebec City. When the convoy was about eight miles off Cape Des Rosiers, he struck.

The escort was stronger than usual this time, thanks to the presence in the escort of a British destroyer. Hartwig recognized a problem but not before the pounding that this submarine would receive would end his tour of attacks in the St. Lawrence.

By September, Fairmiles hadn't yet put in their appearance in sufficient numbers to do any good and freeze up was still two months away. We had to use the few larger warships that were available to us almost continuously before Nature would rescue us. The War Cabinet had attempted, unsuccessfully, to provide the RCN with more long-range aircraft and destroyers, trying at the same time not to rely solely on British Naval assistance. Less self-reliance might have assured a better balanced defence on our coastal waters, in other words more British than Canadian ships, but this was not what either party wished. Canada should develop its own unique defence and the corvette was admirably suited to do just that. The trouble was that the detecting equipment wasn't adequate, even if we had the ships. The Canadian Naval Staff themselves, had been reluctant to accept the new type 271 Radar now proving out so well in the Royal Navy. "Because it was not Canadian" according to James Lamb, "when we were offered 271 by the British when we were overseas, earlier,

Quebec-Sydney Convoy; sails past Gaspé while a Signalman on the "Port" Gate Vessel signals "Gate Open" to the opposite "Starboard" Gate Vessel at the entrance to Gaspé Harbour. Sandy Beach Light is in the background.
                                                    —*Ian Tate, Gilbert Boutilier*

word came down we were to refuse." Apparently the Hierarchy was even reluctant to equip our ships with "Huff-Duff" when it was first offered, mainly because the decision-makers in Ottawa were ignorant of its performance at sea. Yet the RN proved it was the one indispensable weapon, aside from Radar, which could detect a sub's presence. Canada, in its defence, was considered to be "the poor relation" and as such, no pressure was put on to have us accept it. The Magnetron went to the U.S. and not Canada when first introduced and the new aircraft (the PBY's that Capt. Donald so desperately needed earlier) were at first denied Canada because Britain had more need. "The determination to support defence in the Eastern Atlantic off Britain couldn't be argued," said one historian, "yet, the Western Defence, considering supplies to support that defence all came from the New World, should have been given more consideration." As it was, Canada argued and with time, eventually gained control of our own offshore waters and the Gulf. Canada had to prove in the interim that she could defend herself, but at what a price.

As Joseph Schull later remarked in his historical account of Canada's Navy as seen at this time . . . "Angelic harmony was neither attained nor greatly desired, but there was a steadily growing community of respect. The ships themselves were becoming entities and close-knit families; each one priding itself on a personality recognized if not applauded by the others; and the various groups of ships were larger families of families."

The St. Lawrence Force, already thin, was now two warships short; "Raccoon" was gone and the pride of them all, "Charlottetown" lay at the bottom. Joseph Ferguson's young daughter, Yvonne Ferguson, saw the next attack. She was heading for her father's lighthouse at noon on September 15th, when the Nazi struck. "The convoy was just sailing past my father's lighthouse in line formation when, to my horror, I saw first one burst into fire, then another, followed by loud explosions. Our ships were sailing about six miles offshore and as I watched helplessly, first one slipped beneath the water, then another . . . it was terrible." I found out about the attack from 'Dutch' Davey when I talked with him later on the quarterdeck after he had successfully made Port. He was standing duty, (a revolver strapped to his waist was mute witness that they had been prepared for anything) and he described the event. The U-517, again, working from within the convoy, was able to sink the Norwegian "Inger Elizabeth" and the Dutch "Saturnus," both within six minutes. When Hartwig made his escape shortly after, the Canadians and the single RN warship dropped everything they had, but it was too late to save anything, neither our ships nor our National Pride.

Hartwig was severely shaken, more so than the last two attacks he miraculously survived. This convoy, the SQ36, had at least seven of the 22 ships as escorting warships, but again lacking good ASDIC, the U-517 escaped. By now, Hartwig had survived 100 depth charges, with the last one close enough to damage his torpedo firing gear. His distilling equipment was down to 10 gallons per day from the usual 50 and he now had a difficult decision to make. Should he shadow the convoy proceeding upriver for Quebec, or flee while he still had a few torpedoes left? He chose to shadow the convoy, even if by now, aircraft had finally appeared.

Early next morning, the convoy reached a point near Mechins. Here, U-517 moved in. He torpedoed the Greek ship "Joannis" which mercifully sank slowly allowing all her crew to get off and make shore over four miles away. He then torpedoed the British ship "Essex Lance," which broke in half, but didn't sink. The two pieces later were towed to Quebec and rejoined. Only a year before she'd been machine-gunned and bombed by German aircraft in the English Channel and survived. Now, one of her crew was killed. Hartwig's luck was running out. He had four torpedoes left and he decided to turn tail and make for the Straits of Belle Isle from whence he had entered nearly two months before.

One clear night he came upon a Greenland-bound convoy. It was a large convoy with several escorts accompanying it. He had noticed earlier that there had been sub-hunting aircraft above so he had to be extra careful. Again, worming his way into the convoy centre, he let go his four remaining torpedoes in what was to have been his parting gesture. Because of the damaged firing gear, all four missed their targets. With no torpedoes left and far short of his coveted 80,000 tons of Allied shipping, he left the St. Lawrence. He had sunk over 31,000 tons of Allied ships including one Canadian warship and killed an estimated 286 men, all in the St. Lawrence River and its approaches.

He reached Lorient in France on October 15th and received a "heroes welcome," even if his recorded tonnage was far short for an Iron Cross. However, a grateful Fuehrer gave him the award anyway doubtless out of recognition for having carried the war so far inland into North America. No sooner had Hartwig departed the St. Lawrence River than a fourth, fifth and possibly sixth submarine crept into the Gulf.

Meanwhile, "Arrowhead" licked its wounds and prepared to bring another convoy up the St. Lawrence. While docked in Quebec City, a reunion, of sorts, took place with "Arrowhead" inviting officers of HMCS "Trail" to the wardroom. I'd already had my reunion with 'Dutch' Davey when "Arrowhead" called in at Gaspé earlier, and the talk was mostly of regrets at not having Al Heagy share our company, but delighted that Hartwig hadn't got him. Davey's own brush with death was coming next.

better left unsaid: Q-083 on the rocks

Censorship for us now had become a way of life, accepted only begrudgingly perhaps, like all limitations of freedom that come with service life. Some ratings were singled out and specifically told "not to talk to the newspapers." For those of us serving ashore in Gaspé, this wasn't too unusual, considering it had been only a few months since Brayley's admonition from the R.C.M.P. about reporting ships. But censorship could not be maintained when "Caribou" was sunk because it was so poignant and affected so many people that it couldn't be hushed up. Another episode was about to unfold and the people of Gaspé would once more have to depend on word-of-mouth for news.

Convoy N.L.-9 sailed from Labrador for Quebec City in early October, going upriver past Métis Point, about 180 miles above Gaspé on the St. Lawrence. It was an unusually small convoy of four ships and had just two escorts; the Corvettes "Arrowhead" and "Hepatica." Larger convoys were the norm as Canada pressed all available shipping in order to continue supplying war-ravaged Britain's insatiable appetite. But these few ships were going the other way and empty. They shouldn't have been attacked.

Octave Gendron was the lightkeeper at Métis Point and when the night sky lit up just after midnight, he knew an attack was underway. He also concluded that the nearby RCAF Base at Mont Joli should be told. But to do this, he would have to drive the 3½ miles to the nearest telephone located in the next village. The Government had refused to install a phone in the lighthouse.

He thought of his dozen kids asleep in the house nearby. Perhaps his house would be shelled next. Although he was already racing down the road in the black family car, he turned around and went back while the ground under him shook from the powerful explosions. He woke the kids and piled them into the huge touring car. Racing for the village, he dropped the kids off at the roadside where he knew they'd be safe, with instructions to remain until Papa returned. Then he drove the remaining distance over the bumpy road and phoned in his report over a payphone. He had only hung up the receiver when the roar of aircraft could be heard taking off from Mont Joli.

Out on the river, "Arrowhead's" crew sighted the first telltale wake even if Davey and Burton, the latter proud he'd only recently "passed-muster" and was now a "Leading-seaman R.D.F. 2", failed to detect the sub by Radar, providing further evidence of failure. But this torpedo "had their name on it" and when Davey received the lookout's sighting, all he thought of was Al Heagy and "Charlottetown". Topside on the bridge, Skinner recognized the torpedoes track lay directly at them and he nudged a last ounce of speed from his ship. Everyone waited for the inevitable. Miraculously, the phospherescent wake of the torpedo, easily seen in the black, cold waters of the St. Lawrence, raced past the stern missing "Arrowhead" by only inches. (Within 24 months, when the German acoustic torpedo would be introduced into the St. Lawrence, an attack like this would have finished "Arrowhead.") This torpedo was a conventional one with no "sound-seeking" capability such as those to come. Unfortunately, the SS "Carolus" a British freighter with a mostly foreign crew had difficulty following orders and was slightly ahead of the Convoy. She would suffer the consequences now. It was October 9th, 1942.

Unsuspectingly, Bob Dowson, one of four Canadians aboard "Carolus," had just broken off conversation with his mate, Dick Barrett of Montreal and prepared to leave the stoke-hole while Barrett remained. They'd been talking about how Dowson had only been married one month to the day and how a mutual friend in DEMS, Jack Cook of Oakville, had been posted to Montreal with DEMS by "Daddy" Woodward, just in time to be 'Best Man'. Both hoped to rejoin Cook in Montreal after a tiring journey from Labrador where they'd been delivering fuel and supplies. The other Canadians aboard "Carolus" were a wireless operator who Barrett only knew as John and who hailed from Nova Scotia; a cabin boy from Verdun named Milmine and a fourth engineer "a

Dutch chap but now a Canadian". All had attended Dowson's wedding in Montreal on September 9th, 1942.

The explosion came as a complete surprise, according to Dowson: "It was like a heavy sledgehammer followed by the smell of gunpowder as the ship suddenly shuddered; everyone below . . . rushed to get out; I was the last one up the stairwell and found my life jacket was missing from the rack above. I grabbed a remaining white cork one and ran, the shoulder strap catching me around one of my legs. Consequently, the four pieces of the cork were all down around my front. As I reached the deck . . . the normally vertical hatchway became suddenly horizontal and I knew she was going over . . . I was hanging now onto the hatch-frame with the stern standing almost straight up. The bow appeared to do likewise; we were hit in the centre . . . The ship was going down fast and the hatches flew apart and the empty drums came rolling out. I couldn't swim so I didn't want to let go even as the drums cascaded about. One must have struck me for I was unconscious when I popped up out of the water, my arm still through the life jacket. I could see the Corvette running about trying to locate the sub, but the river gives off false echoes so a sub is difficult to locate . . . . I hung on for three hours in the icy water supported only by a plank which floated by, having my jacket ripped off when she went down. I heard a lot of yelling trying to locate survivors. "Arrowhead" finally came along dragging a huge scramble net and you must grab the net on first pass, tough to do when your hands are frozen; but one failure and you're under the ships' propellers and a goner." The sub never harassed them again. Was it sunk? Perhaps it became one of the some eighty percent of U-boats which never did return to their home Bases in Lorient and Brest, although neither ship was credited with a "Kill." Seaman Doug Vincent had a comical experience in the midst of the pathos of the situation. As "Hepatica" began picking up survivors, Vincent, after struggling valiantly with the very fat Captain of "Carolus," finally got him aboard. He told Vincent he was lucky to be safe on "Hepatica" because when "Carolus" went down the suction was so great it had pulled his pants off — leaving only his money belt. It had been loaded with money he'd gotten from liquor that he'd bought while in Quebec City and sold to workmen in Labrador.

For Dowson, this episode provided a telling criticism, not only of Canada's woeful lack of defence but our Censorship policy. When the Convoy remnants arrived safely in Quebec City, they were told not to speak to the newspapers nor to tell any reporter what happened. Despite this, Jack Cook already in Quebec City, received a cryptic phone call from Dowson, simply saying . . . "no matter what you hear, I'm all right" . . . and he hung up. The survivors included Dick Barrett, who escaped from the stoke-hole but not the cabin boy nor the

fourth-class Engineer who called himself a Canadian. They were lost.

Dowson managed to wangle a brief hour to see his wife, before the survivors were all put aboard the Halifax-bound train, denied the customary "survivor's leave" to which all were entitled. The Government didn't want this latest episode getting out of hand and they were more determined than ever 'to keep the lid on.' Twenty-four hours later, the survivors arrived in Halifax. Dowson had had a sleepless night and couldn't bear to have the light off in his cramped upper berth. He didn't even remove his clothes. At Halifax an ambulance waited, and they were then driven by a circuitous route around town, ending finally outside Admiralty House, next door to the Stadacona barracks. The rear door was flung open unceremoniously revealing a young sub-lieutenant, who indifferently peered inside and said, "Where did you guys come from and who are you?" "I want to go to a hospital," cried Dowson. "I've had no sleep and I've just been . . ." The Drafting office at Montreal had warned them not to speak to anyone about what had happened on the river, so he shut up. The young officer apparently miffed at being refused an answer started to question the survivors again, "I asked you a question," he said. "What happened to you and where did you come from?" Dowson replied, "I want to see 'Daddy' Woodward." The magic words worked. All he remembers was being put between clean sheets in the nearby Naval Hospital.

Woodward would later have Dowson drafted back to Montreal where he would continue to help outfit guns on our ships and continue sailing in the St. Lawrence. Bill Keith also continued to serve having attained the age of 17 by now, and having nearly a dozen trips to his credit. His service record was interrupted only when he fell down an open hatch and broke his back. He recovered and despite his parent's protestations, he immediately volunteered for the Royal Canadian Navy. As he said . . . "to be where the action is." He served aboard a Fairmile for the remainder of the war. He was one of the 'indispensables' who went back time after time to face an equally determined enemy.

Censorship of a frightened Government made strangers of father and son, husband and wife, brother and sister, even English Canadian and French-Canadian. The shore from Gaspé, along the Bay of Chaleur to neighbouring New Brunswick, had to depend on word-of-mouth for news, and although the Gaspasians and the servicemen in the area were brought closer together, it effectively isolated us from the rest of Canada. Only the catastrophic sinking of "Caribou" on Oct. 14th couldn't be hidden. Certainly, the sinking of an insignificant Laker which succumbed to the enemy three days earlier, on Oct. 11th even though it carried the symbols of a free press with the tons of newsprint aboard, would never see the front page of Canada's newspapers.

For Bob Dowson, Convoy NL-9, five days earlier

Quarterdeck crew of HMCS "Hepatica" stand astride loaded depth charge racks. Similar racks on HMCS "Charlottetown" resulted in several crewman being killed, including its Captain, Lt. Willard Bonner, when an enemy torpedo struck the stern.
—*Ian Tate*

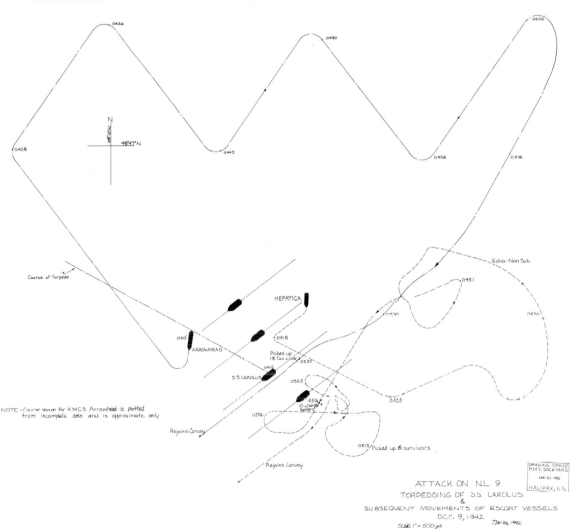

ATTACK ON N.L. 9
TORPEDOING OF S.S. CAROLUS
&
SUBSEQUENT MOVEMENTS OF ESCORT VESSELS
OCT. 9, 1942
Scale 1" = 500 yd.

Plan of attack on Convoy NL-9; note near miss of torpedo on HMCS "Arrowhead". HMCS "Hepatica" joined in the search for the submarine, later assisting "Arrowhead" to rescue survivors from the SS "Carolus". The attack took place near the fashionable summer resort of Metis, within miles of Quebec City.
—*PAC*

was just as damaging in morale. Comprising the tiny Laker "Waterton" accompanied by a sole escort, an armed yacht named HMCS "Vison," miraculously rescued all "Waterton's" crew but nothing was said about it in the newspapers. The Sub used the same methodical form of attack. "Vison" was only a few hundred yards away when the first torpedo hit "Waterton". A second tore through the hold sending newsprint flying in all directions, mixed with fragments of steel deck and live steam. "Waterton" erupted with terrific force. The entire crew somehow was spared. They managed to get off the ship and were rescued by "Vison" while roles of newsprint like giant strands of toilet tissue, unrolled upon the waters. But again the sub got away, likely because the Germans by now recognized that Canadians weren't a warlike people and that they would rather spare their own people than depth charge their own men on the chance they'd hit the enemy below. The safest place appeared to be right under our own ships. This "lying in wait" was practiced with tragic consequences in the case of "Caribou."

Meanwhile, at Gaspe', the concern of Cmdr. German and COAC Admiral Murray, visiting from distant Halifax, was understandable. A program of expansion of Convoy protection was announced, even while CNS "Caribou" prepared to make its next schedule run to Port-Aux-Basque. "Caribou" was hit in the early hours of October 14th, 1942. The two hundred and thirty-eight people aboard included her crew of fifteen, twenty-four women and nine children. In a sense the ship was a scheduled troopship, 117 of her passengers were Canadian and American soldiers, sailors and airmen. For months, the Navy had lived with the fear that if the Germans knew this, they would be laying for her. Chief cook Harold Janes later said he'd slept in his clothes because "somehow there was that feeling that we were likely to be torpedoed." On Oct. 13th she departed from Sydney, exactly on time. Early Wednesday morning, she was attacked when only 25 miles short of harbour at Port Aux Basques and in one of the deepest spots in the Cabot Strait. Earlier, Coder Kendrick on the escort vessel overheard the skipper of HMCS "Grand Mére", Lt. J. Rose, RCNVR, express the fear that sticking too close to schedule would make her an easy target. Kendrick believed that the German Sub waited at the bottom, free of detection, then merely struck when "Caribou" passed overhead.

This was the only attack in which Canada admitted that there was something wrong in the St. Lawrence. No ASDIC or Radar could have detected this submarine and Navy Minister MacDonald made much of this premeditated attack in which 136 were lost. The torpedo had charged right through "Caribou," passing from the starboard side clear through and going out the port side. The high loss of life caused MacDonald to state in the Press that, "those for whom our hearts bleed most are the score and more of women and children who were either killed by the blast of the Nazi torpedo or who were drowned in the waters of Cabot Strait; . . . if there were any Canadians who did not realize that we were up against a ruthless and remorseless enemy, there can be no such Canadian now." MacDonald rightly called it the "hideousness of Nazi warfare."

The fact that "Arrowhead" had survived Convoy NL-9 became a welcome antidote needed to help offset the growing despair from increased sinkings. "Dutch" Davey like Al Heagy had not only survived but, unlike "Charlottetown," his ship had been spared as well. But neither this fact nor the unhappy news that neither "Carolus" nor "Waterton" had survived and were now at the bottom of the St. Lawrence was mentioned by the Government even if both were sunk within the same week as "Caribou." We were back to strict censorship again. "Caribou" contained propoganda value, not seen since Kapitanleutnant Fritz-Ludwig Lemp in the U-30, torpedoed the passenger liner "Athenia" on Sept. 4, 1939, plunging 120 men, women and children into the Atlantic. In 1939, the ground-swell of public indignation helped assuage the crisis of going to war. Doubtless, "Caribou's" demise would help sustain our resolve to continue the war and so it made the headlines in the Canadian Press.

Cmdr. Barry German never needed proof that the Canadian sailor "had what it takes," however, incontrovertible proof of Canada's scientific failure appeared now. Not surprisingly, it appeared when the Navy was battling insurmountable odds to save life. By late October, preparations had begun for winter. The out-going NOIC CMDR Barry German was preparing for Lt. Commander George Bernard's arrival due in early January 1943, when a signal came in announcing that a U.S. plane was down somewhere in the Gulf.

Cmdr. German summoned two Fairmiles, Bill Grand's Q083 and Norm Simpson's Q063, to conduct a search, with Q083 moving out first, despite a threatening fog. Reaching Cape Gaspé at the harbour entrance, Q083 prepared for the open water of the Gulf with the SW1C closed up and apparently operating satisfactorily. They almost cleared the point but, in doing so, the operator mistook nefarious "back echoes," caused by the inherent fault of the Radar for "land ahead" noting it to be several miles away. Actually, the "echoes" showing on the Radar were the hills behind them, Cape Gaspé being "hidden" within the half-mile "blackout" characteristic of the SW1C. They were now heading right for it. Unsuspectingly, Q083 proceeded only to come crashing with full force at the base of Cape Gaspé, still invisible in the fog. The order came next: "Abandon ship." The sole casualty, turned out to be a seaman who, to his complete surprise, landed on solid ground instead of the icy water that he had expected. Instead of being in the icy Gulf, he had sprained his ankle on dry land. With first light, the Q083 was found to be spiked high and dry on a rocky ledge, quite immobile.

Cmdr. Barry German RCN, N.O.I.C. "Fort Ramsay"; Admiral L.W. Murray RCN, C.O.A.C. (Commanding Officer Atlantic Command) accompanied by Aides on an inspection tour of Gaspé. Lengthening shadows reflect sombre mood.

At first light, the bow of Q083 was found pointing skyward, clutched by the precipitous rock of Cape Gaspé.

— Gilbert Boutilier

Remote from his Gaspé home, George Kruse watched the demise of our ships, on the huge impersonal map at NSHQ, Ottawa, where he had been drafted from Halifax. Each loss, including the Q083, was displayed in cold indifference. So great were the losses by Christmas of 1942, Kruse was convinced we had lost the war. It was tough medicine for an otherwise peaceful Canadian. In Gaspé, sailors like Lorne Hutchinson of Q056, who hailed from Brantford, could still get home on "Agricultural Leave" in order to help with the harvest. There was no leave for Kruse. He was stationed in Ottawa and the only harvest he could recall was the harvest of war. Kruse had barely survived the "new-entry" training at Halifax and he could still hear Pullen's hated argument that the "cat 'o nine tails had been abolished too soon." Kruse had seen green recruits wilt as they fed 45 pound shells into the breech at the Gunnery School. Men like Pullen, Kruse felt, were enamoured too much with the blood-and-guts of a Royal Navy of a century earlier. Kruse saw Pullen as a caricature of life and not the real thing, much as I viewed the Canadian-built SW1C. Our own pregenitors of the SW1C in Canadian industry were of the same stripe as Pullen, where the fanfare of introduc-tion far exceeded SW1C's capabilities. Despite millions of dollars spent on its creation, it proved far inferior to the British type 271 built on a shoestring. The dozens of failures already, and more to come, fortunately would make the authorities recant. The grounding of Q083 was the latest failure but fortunately it had a happy ending.

"We're not going to lose that ship," hollered Lt. Paul Belanger as he swung the tug "Pat McQueen" from the jetty at "Fort Ramsay" and proceeded to Cape Gaspé. Astern was the "Venning," with the irascible "Knobby" Clark down below handling the engine. In Belanger's view, handling engines was the only good thing Clark would ever do during his long stay on the "Venning." It must be remembered that Belanger had skippered the "Venning" only six months before. Together, they hoped to pull Q083 free providing Clark did as he was told. This time Belanger didn't return empty-handed. Using superb seamanship and patient planning, Belanger not only got the Q083 off the rocks, but with his consummate skill and the engine-handling of Clark on the "Venning", at high tide, they got her off intact.

It was a symbolic act and a harbinger of better days to come for Gaspé.

With high tide by late afternoon and a good pull, Q083 swings free from the clutches of Cape Gaspé.

G. —Boutilier

praise the lord and...a spy in our midst.

The return of winter 1942 proved more welcome than usual. Nature's intervention meant we could recoup our losses and lick our wounds before the inevitable return of the submarines in the spring. Somehow, this ceased to engender fear; for spring meant soft summer breezes and ice breakup, as once more the Gaspé hills would break forth in a mantle of green: more than a welcome antidote to what the enemy might offer next.

Meanwhile, Q083 was taken in tow and successfully reached Weymouth, Nova Scotia on the Atlantic ice-free shore before winter closed Gaspé. There, the Fairmile was given a new keel and returned to service.

Meanwhile, back in Gaspé men confined to barracks found their own way of passing the winter as the weather closed in and the Subs disappeared for a season. An ice-rink was built and hockey leagues initiated. Teams from Gaspé were dominated by the "Clerics St. Viateur"; the brothers proved to be masters of hockey as well as prayer. Navy boys called them the "RC Highlanders", their long habits waving like kilts as they skated.

Some of us even thought the dam of Censorship might break to at least reveal to the folks back home just what Gaspé had endured at the hands of the enemy. But a happening occurred just before freeze-up that put us back into the dark ages of Censorship. Even Jack Brayley, despite being privy to what happened next, couldn't talk and while we waited patiently in the cold outside the railway station opposite the Kruse Hotel the lid of censorship was hammered on tighter than ever. Canada had a spy on our shores . . . a genuine German spy and we were hoping to get a look at him. We never did see the spy and the events were only revealed much later when Commissioner Harvison would write about it in a book, long after we had all gone home.

He wrote; "After discussing this development with headquarters and requesting that arrangements be made for the close censorship of any news stories coming out of the Gaspé Peninsula, the Officer Commanding (Cmdr. Barry German) directed that I leave at once by car for New Carlisle." The magnitude of the event was too big for most of us to comprehend. The story itself was as good as any spy thriller from Hollywood that we could see at Kruse's neighbourhood movie house, with the bed-sheet screen. We, however, had to be satisfied with picked up pieces of information and rumours. Real life was different than Hollywood. But censorship itself still smacked redundant; why shouldn't Canadians know about their brave sons fighting an enemy offshore, and, in particular, enemy spies that now were discovered on our soil? Even Harvison's motor trip from Ottawa to Gaspé was a thriller in itself and should have been told but, where spies are concerned, the Government decreed and we remained committed to silence.

We now know that Harvison's odyssey was well-planned and executed.

"I was accompanied by Sergeant "Pete" Bordeleau (later to become Deputy Commissioner) and a special constable who spoke German and who was to act as interpreter", Harvison would write. Considering the fact the ill-used roads were mostly sheer ice, making the trip from Ottawa in two days says something about their determination. But even before Harvison arrived, Cmdr. Barry German had already assisted Signals Officer Jimmy Stuart in "Fort Ramsay" to initiate the capture. In fact, together they successfully frustrated Germany's first real attempt to launch a spy into Canada.

It was November 8th, 1942, when Canada was still licking her wounds from the previous summer's onslaught, that Stuart first intercepted a coded message. At first Stuart thought it was one of our ships making a routine call. Because it contained the correct cyphers, it lead him to think it was merely one of our ships offshore. However, investigation revealed we had no ships in that coordinate and Stuart became suspicious.

The struggle for intelligence supremacy had been ongoing since war's start, actually, going back as far as 1939 when the Germans had the advantage with their Naval cryptanalysis service known as "B. Dienst." They had penetrated the British Naval cyphers (which of course were Canada's, too) and this was a dilemma that the staff at Gaspé had to deal with. Stewart's suspicions were understandable and, after discussion with Barry German, they became alarming.

"Darn it all, Jimmy," Barry said, "if you think the code's not quite right, copy it down and I'll alert Ottawa." Further examination revealed that the signals not only were clandestine but proved to have come from a German sub located right off our shore just south of Gaspé. The Gemans had had a clear idea of Allied shipping movement as early as 1940. With the emergence of the German "Enigma" machine, their cyphers remained secure and they felt, therefore, that they could duplicate our ship movements undetected. When the German Submarine U-110, commanded by Fritz Lemp, was captured intact, British sailors recovered the German "Enigma machine" which was needed to help break the German's code; and, one of the valuable coding insights fell into Allied hands. Gaspé alerted the RCMP and things moved fast.

By the time Harvison arrived at New Carlisle, the Sub had quietly slipped away but had abandoned their spy ashore.

Werner Janowski first hid in an abandoned barn. Mrs. Babin, the mother of CN conductor Raoul Babin, had had the building hauled onto her property to replace her barn which had burned down. Because of this seemingly innocent connection, all of Raoul Babin's mail from his mother, would subsequently be censored and would bear the censor's stamp. When Janowski moved to the local New Carlisle Hotel managed by Earl Annett Jr., Annett became suspicious. The spy asked if he could be provided with a room and a bath. Annett says that he reeked of diesel fumes typical of a person harboured in the close quarters of a submarine.

By November 10th, Annett knew it was time to act on his suspicions; Janowski had proffered a large Canadian one dollar bill, of the type Canada had used prior to the Depression and had since reduced in size. The Gestapo in Germany had apparently failed to take this into account. Annett attempted to delay the spy, alerting first the Quebec Provincial Police, who in turn alerted the RCMP. Janowski refused to be delayed and boarded the train at New Carlisle heading south. However, at Bonaventure, the next station stop, QPP Sergeant Normandeau who also boarded the same train at New Carlisle, gently touched Janowski on the shoulder and said "You're under arrest." Inspection revealed that the heavy valise he carried contained a powerful radio transmitter along with personal things.

During heavy interrogation in the Jail at New Carlisle where he was detained, Harvison included the threat of hanging if Janowski didn't reveal everything. The threat of hanging appeared to be most motivating, according to Harvison. Janowski had been on his way to Montreal to join up with the known Fascist, Adrienne Arcand, who apparently had hundrds of followers in Montreal. Significantly, in his book, Harvison revealed it was the sight of Canadian Veterans parading to the Cenotaph in the Common just below the barred windows of the New Carlisle Jail, which further moved Janowski and persuaded him that "we weren't such bad people after all." Janowski confessed and he later became a double-agent, doing valuable work for the Allied cause. One example was revealed later when the Nazi's made their next attempt the following summer in the same Bay of Chaleur nearer the New Brunswick coast. There, the Germans attempted to rescue nineteen prisoners-of-war who had earlier escaped from the Grand-Linge Camp south of Montreal. The prisoners, seven of whom were expert submarine engineers, were desperately needed to replenish Hitler's harassed undersea fleet now being 'hammered' everywhere in the "Battle of the Atlantic." The submarine coming to rescue them was detected by intercepting their signal and by breaking their code beforehand. The escape was stopped by Gaspé's efforts. Part of this was attributed to Earl Annett Jr.'s earlier work and Bernard made sure that he was duly recognized by a grateful Government. Bernard also saw to it that Joseph Ferguson was credited with detecting our first Sub from his Lighthouse at Cape des Rosiers earlier in the war and accordingly, he was recognized with a suitable plaque.

Bernard settled in as the new N.O.I.C., reading profusely in order to catch up on events he knew little about. The familiar plaint of his generation . . . "all I know is what I read in the newspapers" was redundant where Gaspé was concerned. Bernard came from HMCS "York" in downtown Toronto where newspapers daily splashed headlines about the war in Europe but not a word about what was happening in Canada. The only thing he knew about "Caribou's" loss, was that it had been the last ship to have been lost in 1942. That was the only chink in the heavy armour of Government censorship and the fact that the heavy loss of life provided an obvious propoganda foil, didn't endear this report to Bernard, nor anyone who knew what really was going on. It was, after all, a propoganda weapon on a par with Lemp's untimely sinking of "Athenia." With the loss of "Athenia," Canada entered the war within the week; with the loss of "Caribou," Canadians were doing nothing; only the relatively isolated group at Gaspé was carrying the war to the enemy, a war which continued peculiarly silent to the rest of Canada.

The winter's pause gave time to Bernard to restock Gaspé with the artifacts of war which, if 1942 was a harbinger of things to come, he would truly need. It also provided personnel to restock the Navy's Spiritual needs. Thus, the Rev. Cecil Royle arrived and took over the church operations, in Bernard's view,

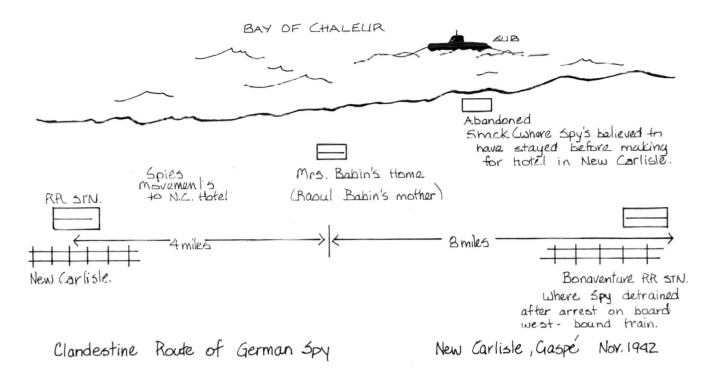

BAY OF CHALEUR

SUB

Abandoned Shack (where Spy's believed to have stayed before making for Hotel in New Carlisle.

Spies movements to N.C. Hotel

Mrs. Babin's Home (Raoul Babin's mother)

RR. STN.

New Carlisle.

←———— 4 miles ————→|←———— 8 miles ————→

Bonaventure RR STN. where Spy detrained after arrest on board west-bound train.

Clandestine Route of German Spy

New Carlisle, Gaspé Nov. 1942

Sketch showing escape route of Nazi Spy from shore to New Carlisle Hotel below Gaspé.
—*Author*

too long neglected. For Royle, his obvious pride in this posting was understandable. Earlier, he'd been Padre to only a handful of men at isolated shore "Radar" installations such as those at Cloridorme and Fox River. Here, he was named Head Protestant Padre for not only the Navy but the Army and Air Force as well. This somewhat heady responsibility prompted Royle to change his address from passive "Fort Ramsay" to the more active-sounding "Defended Port of Gaspé." This was really more descriptive realizing that additional warships were already slated for Gaspé and would arrive with ice-breakup. The additional air sorties now being flown, coupled with the extra warships should make the Nazis think twice before entering the St. Lawrence as they had done on an unprecedented scale in 1942. The trust would prove to be well placed. There would actually be no recorded submarine attacks in 1943 and only two in 1944, when HMCS "Magog" and the freighter "Fort Thompson" would fall prey to Germany's newest secret weapon, the Acoustic Torpedo.

"Anglican" Bernard also requested that a Roman Catholic Chaplain be supplied for his troops. Father Quellet was surprised to be met at the railway station by a Protestant Padre when he arrived. However, they got on famously and Royle described this man

later, as "a very simple, lovable and devout man". Quellet also later confided he never planned to become a "Service Man's Padre."

"When I was first interviewed for the job by the Senior RC Padre in Ottawa," he said, "the Senior Padre noted 'So you are the Priest who wishes to become a military Chaplain.'" Quellet replied, "No, Colonel, I am the Priest who was *TOLD* that he would be a Chaplain."

As RC Padre to the Forces, he now insisted that every serviceman attend Church Parade. Within two weeks, Church attendance had increased!

Royle's duties included visiting barracks, planes and ships, as well as the Hotel Dieu Hospital in Gaspé, but he never quite got used to having his car's headlights painted for black out purposes, nor being challenged by armed men when visits took him to other outlying areas to bring the Word of God to Canada's men. He, like almost all Canadians, was unaware that the Nazi menace had reached the shores of Canada and penetrated within its boundaries. The "Defended Port of Gaspé" was now the official address of the base and letters to loved ones, urged to be written by the 'Padres', gave evidence to the recipients that the war was not all "over there" but right here in Canada.

Ball team representing Army, Navy and Air Force gather for picture prior to game at HMCS "Fort Ramsay".
— Ian Tate

Ice remains in the Harbour at Gaspé long after spring arrives. This photo was taken in May 1942.
— G. Boutilier

Admiral Percy Nelles and recently posted N.O.I.C. Cmdr. George Bernard in black cap stands to the right of Nelles during a brief visit to HMCS "Fort Ramsay".

a surprise ending: the tide of victory slowly turns

Closing down a Base is often more difficult than opening one. True, Capt. Colin Donald RCN had had about as insurmountable a problem as anyone, but once begun, Gaspé became a fighting Base propelled along by an insatiable desire 'to get even'. Bernard, the fifth and last C.O. was supposed to have only a temporary appointment but he would spend his remaining service as a VR Officer in Gaspé doing what most of us had come to suspect; a rear guard action designed to hole up the enemy in the St. Lawrence, and no more. Bernard however had the singular privilege of being the only Voluntary Reserve Officer to hold such a post. Complete command of a major Base, as Gaspé had become, was a role usually reserved for Permanent Force Officers. Bernard knew what war was all about. He had survived the "Hungry Thirties," rising to head up the Canadian Manufacturing Association. Before that he had served with distinction in the Royal Navy and he knew exactly what had to be done. It was obvious to Bernard, now a full Commander RCNVR, that it was necessary to keep the pressure on everyone because he knew that the subs could come again. And this time our role would be different.

Bernard took satisfaction in the fact that Paul Hartwig now recognized to be one of Germany's top aces, had been held at bay in the St. Lawrence by Gaspé's efforts. You don't do this without a price and we had paid in full. The Base took particular delight when Hartwig's Log Book was circulated, soon after Bernard's arrival in early 1943, courtesy of the Royal Navy. Bernard was especially pleased when he learned that Hartwig had been captured, along with his crew, before the U-517 went down for the final plunge in the Bay of Biscay on November 21, 1942, at the hands of superior British forces. Hartwig was now a prisoner of war in Canada.

1943 also brought a well-deserved hiatus for Gaspé; a breather when long neglected matters could be addressed. One was the need for continued recreation and since hockey flourished in winter, baseball would be tried in the summer. Another was to prepare for the rotation of men by bringing in 'fresh blood' to replace those men already war-weary from nerve-wracking nights on lonely escort sweeps in the Gulf and River.

At the same time, sailors who had spent two years or more at sea, some without letup, would find here, a well deserved rest.

Some sailors, like Bob Dick, were still at sea. He had arrived in Halifax about the same time as I did, and was assigned to a corvette in the Atlantic. She had her stern blown off and he was, therefore, a survivor as well as a veteran. Assigned now to HMCS "Noranda," he was doggedly coding signals as his ship escorted the "Kyle," the successor to "Caribou" as she plied the straits between Sydney and Port Aux Basque.

Despite the hard lesson of "Caribou," the Port Aux Basque ferries continued to make the passage on fairly strict schedules, and the sister ferry to "Kyle," the "Burgeo," although never subject to torpedo attack itself, was instrumental in the loss of her escort, HMCS "Shawinigan," to the submarines.

She was returning from Port Aux Basque after safely delivering "Burgeo" when in the dim light, somewhere in the icy waters of the Cabot Strait, she went down, lost with all hands and "believed torpedoed." She sank so fast that there was "no time to even get out a radio message." 94 crewmen perished. A day or two later only fragments of wreckage were found. It was November 25, 1944.

The following month, the Nazi U-boats attacked with even more reckless abandon. On December 21, 1944, a Liberty ship was torpedoed while forming up in a convoy just off Halifax and on Christmas Eve, the faithful "Clayoquot", which did yeoman service off Gaspé in the early days of the war, was hit herself. Under Captain Lade, she had rescued many of the survivors of "Charlottetown" but this time she was the victim and included in the list of eight casualties was Captain Lade. She had been lost, while ashore the Christmas lights twinkled in recognition of the arrival of the 'most holy of Holy Days.'

In the meantime, the movement of our men

HMCS "Clayoquot" fires depth charge in the Gulf of St. Lawrence.
—Ian Tate

Captain of HMCS "Clayoquot", Lt. H.E. Lade RCN (R) is seen controlling action from the bridge.
—Ian Tate

HMCS "Clayoquot" tied alongside jetty at Naval Base HMCS "Fort Ramsay".

Crewman from HMCS "Clayoquot" struggle in the water on Christmas Eve, after being torpedoed by the enemy right in the Halifax approaches. —PAC/PA-134342

continued towards the East. Replacement crews went to Sydney, Halifax and Shelburne: the war was apparently bypassing Gaspé. The main interest was to help reinforce Canada's Atlantic Coast as the war reached its critical phase and anything could happen.

In Gaspé, Bernard even had time to fulfill his long-cherished wish to meet Bishop Ross; something that should have been done at the very start of the build-up of the military in Gaspé "But you're an Anglican" interjected his wife Monica, fearing the Bishop might think her husband presumptuous. "Cmdr. Barry German was RC; he should have gone" she added emphatically. "Barry had his hands full . . . and so did Colin Donald before him," returned Bernard, undeterred, taking the Staff car to Town. Besides, he had a personal request of the Bishop. It was some time after the huge black staff car had rolled up before the "Bishop's Palace," as Bernard later described it, and after he had sat unbearably uncomfortable for some time in a stiff-backed chair, the Bishop appeared. To Bernard's pleasant surprise, the greeting was amicable and they immediately fell into animated conversation.

"Ah, there's the matter of uniform time" Bernard interrupted at one point, after his audience had extended into a half-hour, "Can you help here?" Bishop Ross would, and did. The town of Gaspé subsequently adopted "Fort Ramsay" time. This resulted in our men "going ashore" for the first time, not having to stand around for an hour before things opened up. The lovable, but now aging, Rev. Wayman's "Evensong" at neighbouring St. Paul's was apparently the only casualty. The need to attend Evensong, first, in order to gain a preferred place in the lineups outside the Kruse Theatre for Sunday night's shows was eliminated. Bishop Ross, of course, had a request of his own in return. It came a few mornings later when Bernard awoke at the Base to find farm equipment rolling towards "Fort Ramsay, as far as the eye could see." The equipment had been in poor repair with the military getting priority on metal and parts and Ross requested Navy help to put all the implements back in good repair. Bishop Ross reciprocated by having the Brothers from the Seminary install a beautiful vegetable garden right behind Bernard's home on the Base. Later, when the

Anglican Archbishop Carrington arrived from the Church of England headquarters for the Province at Quebec, Carrington glanced from the window and noticed the garden, now in full bloom.

"Why, who put in such a beautiful garden? he asked Bernard.

"Oh," Bernard returned, glowing, "Let's just say, some of our Roman Catholic Brethren". Cooperation between Church and State was at its peak in Gaspé.

Our numbers of warships continued to increase and Canada also learned how to fight better. Stealing a lesson from the German "Milch Cows" used earlier by the enemy to replenish their Subs, Canada now supplied our frail Fairmiles with the aid of HMCS "Provider," a veritable floating Base right in the St. Lawrence. Headed up by Comdr. Joe Heenan RCN(R), an ex-Royal Navy veteran who first went before the mast at the turn of the century, HMCS "Provider" turned the Gulf into a fortress by operating on the St. Lawrence out of Sept Isles across from Gaspé.

The "little ships" as Heenan was to describe them later, dropped depth charges on anything and everything following Skinner's earlier dictum to 'shoot from the hip'. Canadian authorities finally realized a new look at our scientific war was needed if we were to successfully combat the sub. Better ASDIC was put into use and the 'S.W.1.C.' gradually gave place to the British 271 Radar on all ships, with correspondingly improved performance. "Arrowhead" went to a well-deserved rest and refit, with leave for the crew. Subsequently, corvettes and 'sweepers were gradually fitted out with type 271 and "Kills" increased, with one Canadian Convoy returning from the U.K., for example, under an all-Canadian escort with the loss of not one ship. Decisions of far-reaching importance made earlier in January 1943 now had their salutary effect. The Atlantic was at last recognized, by Roosevelt and Churchill in their third Casablanca Conference dealing with the Atlantic tonnage war, as having absolute priority. The St. Lawrence War wound down and the enemy Subs now moved to the outer perimeter of the Gulf.

As John Swettenham in his book "Canada's Atlantic War" was to point out: "Doenitz, with some 130 U-boats in the North Atlantic in May 1943, the highest number so far, refused to recognize defeat until the Allies forced the lesson home. Morale in the U-Boat crews was declining. Commanders who had become experienced when Allied defences were weak, had nevertheless gone to the bottom one by one; they were replaced by raw commanders who, faced with experienced anti-sub tactics and advanced technology . . . succumbed more quickly: Doenitz was to lose 41 U-boats in May (including one commanded by his son) and this was a price he could no longer afford to pay. On the 24th of May 1943 an incredulous British Intelligence team decrypted Doenitz's message to his U-Boats ordering them to withdraw from the North Atlantic. It was unexpected, almost too much to hope for, but Doenitz in his memoirs admitted that in May, he knew that the Atlantic Battle could not be won.

Gaspé by now had received sufficient Fairmiles minesweepers and Frigates to even have some left over to help the U.S. They were still suffering losses off their own East Coast and in the neighbouring Caribbean, where German subs apparently sought a "Third Happy Time." It didn't occur. Canada sent

Cmdr. Joe Heenan RCN (R) returns the salute crossing the quarterdeck of a recently arrived Fairmile.
— Gavin Clark

two flotillas south, the 72nd and73rd, leaving the 76th to patrol the Halifax approaches. This new defence proved successful with one exception. According to Robert Hewitson, this came while everyone's attention was focussed on the all-pervading fear of the submarine (which didn't transpire in 1943) ignoring the usual hazards when ships operate in close quarters. When the cable ship "Lord Kelvin" collided with HMCS "Chedabucto" sending that unfortunate ship to the bottom, he learned just what this meant. HMCS "Swift Current," which he'd just joined, was detailed to pickup survivors before clearing the Gulf for the North Atlantic with no chance for shore-leave. Equally disappointing was the experience of 17 year-old Bob Bruce from Toronto. Bruce would sail into Gaspé on HMCS "Thetford Mines" a year later. Like Hewitson he

Fairmiles enjoying summer weather at HMCS "Fort Ramsay",   — *G.A. Milne/PAC/PA-134324*

Winter: Fairmiles of the 82nd Flotilla stop off at Gaspé for a well-deserved rest after buffeting winter storms on the way down the St. Lawrence to Halifax.   — *G.P.B. Murison/PAC/PA-13438*

The Fairmile Q065 on a sub chase dropping depth charges off Gaspé.   *—Author*

would find his ship was required in the larger theatre reaching a critical phase in the Atlantic and left before he could get ashore in what was now the friendliest port in Canada.

Canadian ships that had gone overseas earlier in the war were now coming home to help meet the anticipated threat along our East Coast as Canada's defence circle expanded. The Navy was concentrating on the Cabot Strait, where the Gulf joins the Atlantic and along the East Coast of Nova Scotia. One sub did succeed in penetrating this shield, launching the first acoustic torpedo, in the St. Lawrence on Oct. 14th, 1944. Lt. James Plomer who had served during the most crucial Atlantic Battles commanding an R.N. ship already had returned and others like Jeffry Brock, John Robarts and John Toye would follow. Plomer's introduction to the St. Lawrence was to stay up all night, writing a definitive report on the torpedoing of HMCS "Magog." His effort was met by a now, thoroughly war-weary Admiral Murray, who merely said, following the briefing next morning . . . "very interesting" . . . and walked out. This, in spite of the fact "Magog" had been torpedoed by the enemy within 200 miles of Quebec City. Worse, a few days later, the freighter "Fort Thompson" was also hit closer to Quebec City by 30 miles, as she steamed upriver. Both occurred near Point Des Monts, just opposite Cap Chat where the "Charlottetown" had gone down just two years earlier.

Lt. John Toye's return proved interesting to me for he had served for several years on British men-o'-war maintaining "R.D.F." He was one of the original University of Toronto "R.D.F." trainees who graduated about the same time as we did from the University of Western Ontario. Both Robarts and Toye would be chosen for posting to Canada's entry to the "big ship Navy" concept when our first full-fledged cruiser, HMS "Uganda," was received as a gift from the Royal Navy. The Canadian "Uganda" would have an all-Canadian crew and the Radar staff would include myself, chosen, as the Navy put it . . . "because you're the only lower-deck rating with previous cruiser experience." I wondered at their perspicacity as I only had experience on a converted auxiliary cruiser, HMCS "Prince Robert," and had only operated obsolete SW1C Radar, at that. But I would leave Gaspé, pausing only long enough in Halifax to marry Esther, before moving off to the Pacific following a brief upgrading in Radar at HMC "St. Hyacinth", Quebec, by now the largest Signal School in the British Empire.

Rumours and counter-rumours were now going the rounds that a German surrender was imminent. "D-Day" came on June 6th, 1944, and it drew both men and ships from Gaspé. Even Fort Prevel's big gun fell silent after the Fort all but emptied sending Army men to Europe to help stem the anticipated bloodletting in France. Our navy's contribution fell

The first German acoustic torpedo is launched and finds its mark on the stern of HMCS "Magog" sailing in the St. Lawrence off Point Des Monts opposite Cape Chat Oct. 14,1944.
—PAC

Like a sitting duck, HMCS "Magog", helpless, awaits a tow
—PAC

mostly to our minesweepers; ships which had successfully swept the St. Lawrence and the approaches to Halifax and St. John's where the enemy had tried to stop our convoys with deadly mines. John Davies, better known as "the Lionhearted" an apt description earned when he had sailed under the very noses of the recalcitrant Germans to relieve the starving garrison at Tobruk, taught our sailors how "to sweep" and he taught them well. His appellation was also descriptive of our sailors—both Navy and DEMS; many of them having learned this new art first in the St. Lawrence and they were now sweeping the English Channel off Cherbourg, making possible the Army's continued landings in France. The great wheel was turning, bringing sailors home from the sea while the Army still went overseas, and the Battle of the Seas wound down. Many sailors now arrived at Gaspé to be under Bernard's care, exchanging places with ratings like Ed Palk of Brantford, Ontario. Palk came here inexperienced in 1941 but was now a thoroughly trained officer overseas taking part in the Allied landing at Cherbourg.

Bernard knew the end of the road had come for "The Defended Port." Helped by dedicated and self-effacing men, Bernard maintained the Base in fighting trim while receiving back "the broken and the tired." The lack of further German attacks testified it hadn't all been in vain. His only respite was to occasionally lounge in Del Aitcheson's barber chair, a sanctuary Admiral Murray had suggested during one of his brief visits. Aitcheson had no substantive rating. He had left Dundalk, Ontario for Halifax in 1943 but he fell ill. Since Canada needed all the men she could get, Aitcheson was kept on despite this because of his barbering skill. He was sent to Gaspé and Murray suggested "crossed scissors and a comb" as a suitable badge and the Navy thus instituted a new category. It was while barbering that Aitcheson got his first taste of war. One of our Fairmiles blew up right at the Jetty below his shop, sending shock waves throughout the community, and fear into everyone at first, that the enemy had arrived. Instead, it was merely the culmination of what every Fairmile skipper dreaded; the fear of a spark igniting the volatile high-octane fuel that the "little ships" carried. This Fairmile blew up when the cook lit up the galley stove. Two men were killed instantly. One crewman jumped into the icy waters and saved his shipmate and was later awarded an Oak Leaf for bravery. Aitcheson and all the Base knew about this but the newspapers told no one.

High-octane fuel used by Fairmiles was a constant threat to safety. Picture shows what happened when fumes ignited when the cook, in the galley, prepared breakfast for crew. Two crewman were killed. Another received an oakleaf, a bravery citation, for jumping in the water and rescuing his mate.
—PAC

Nor did they reveal the inevitable closing down of the Base. F/O Art Killam, of Liverpool, N.S., first got an inkling of the Base closure, when he was sent from No. 5 E D Moncton, N.B. on April 1st, 1945, to help close down the PBY operation. By this time patrols in the St. Lawrence had become redundant, favouring the move towards the coast in anticipation of German U-boat attacks there. Captain Colin Donald had earlier requested the use of the giant PBYs which he couldn't have while in Gaspé but now, several would arrive to help out in his new command at Shelburne, N.S.

Both Bernard in Gaspé and Donald in Shelburne waited, not without some trepidation, for the final

his part wasn't reticent either about the fact that Gaspé by now 'had the most powerful radio voice in the East'; the best reason he could think of to be chosen for the job of calling for surrender.

The behaviour of the submarines, in most cases, was correct but it is interesting to note that the Captain of the U-532 signalled Doenitz to find out if last-minute sinkings could be credited for possible promotion later! The Allies had to be careful. Our own Bangor class minesweeper, HMCS "Esquimalt," had been sunk in the Halifax approaches on April 16th, 1945, less than a month before "V-E Day." "Esquimalt" was the last Canadian casualty of the war; thirty-nine Canadians had died out of a crew of

Naval ratings form up to observe V-E Day in Gaspé.

— G.C. Bernard

word of the German surrender in Europe. Both knew that their respective barracks were already overcrowded and that when the end finally came that their men would need looking after as pent-up emotions surfaced and men realized that they would soon be homeward bound. Thus Donald, like Bernard, had planned a giant "V-E Day" banquet to help calm the situation. This was perhaps of little importance to newspapers who likely wouldn't have published it anyway given their record of performance for things military, but when Admiral Murray in Halifax would mistakenly announce "Open Gangway" and the sailors would pour into Halifax streets disenchanted with what had been the uncorrected festering sore of a too-long-neglected "Stadacona," the papers would scream headlines. Nothing had been planned by the Navy in Halifax, as it had been by Donald and Bernard, and the restless sailors went berserk. The result was the infamous V.E. Day Halifax Riot.

Donald now waited to receive the first surrendered sub, reportedly just off Shelburne. Bernard for

sixty-five. In the final twenty-four hour period before the official surrender, German subs sank two Allied ships.

At one minute after ten, on the night of May 8th, the German High Command under Allied dictation, made available to all of our wireless stations, an order to its U-boats still at sea. They had actually been ordered to stand down as early as May 4th, when German Admiralty orders officially ended the submarine war; it wasn't the wish of the sub commanders themselves who eschewed the termination of their vaunted fleet. German sources reported that 39,000 men served, and of these, some 27,491 were lost and an estimated 5,000 were prisoners of war.

Appropriately perhaps, Captain Colin Donald RCN received the first surrendered sub. The Canadian frigates HMCS "Dunvegan" and "Rockcliffe" arrived upon the U-889 after an American Liberator aircraft had sighted the sub two hundred and fifty miles southeast of Cape Race, flying a black flag as instructed and proceeding on the surface. The two ships gave it a course for Shelburne, before continu-

HMCS "Buckingham" and "Inch Arran" formally take surrender of U-889 at 3:24 pm A.D.T. about two miles off Shelburne, N.S. Capt. E.R. Miles RCN, Chief of Staff to the Commander of the Canadian North-West Atlantic accepted the formal surrender while Capt. Colin Donald RCN received the submarine at Shelburne, N.S. on May 13th 1945; shown is HMCS "Buckingham".

—J. Ritcey.

Black and sinister U-Boat lies on surface in surrender. This dramatic photo of the captured U-889 was taken through the cross hairs of his gun sight on board "HMCS Buckingham" 200 miles off Newfoundland by John Ritcey, May 11th, 1945.

ing with their convoy. Relieved by the frigates HMCS "Buckingham" and "Inch Arran," and with the sub safely between them, they provided escort to Shelburne where the undersea boat was officially surrendered to Capt. G.R. Miles OBE, RCN, Chief-of-Staff to the Commander-in-Chief Canadian North-west Atlantic. The U-889 was the first to surrender before the floodtide poured other submarines from the North Atlantic into Bay Bulls, Newfoundland. The U-190 was near there when the surrender call came and was picked up by HMCS "Victoriaville" and "Thorlock." The sub had apparently first reported her position on the evening of the 11th, and the Canadian ships had arrived shortly before midnight. By 2 a.m. a boarding party had crossed over to the U-boat where the Captain signed a three-line declaration on ordinary DND letterhead paper: "I hereby unconditionally surrender German Submarine U-190 to the Royal Canadian Navy through the Flag Officer Newfoundland."

In Shelburne, Freer's company watched from jetty-side, where Capt. Colin Donald had lined them up, preparatory to accepting the surrender. There was nothing unusual about this, for about the next few days, all the major ports along the East Coast would witness the same surrender, including Gaspé. But something was to happen here, which Freer at his joking-best wouldn't have believed; it had to do with what he'd said in jest earlier about "Canadians shooting relatives." Overhead, a PBY made a fly-past, the drone of the engines adding a sombre note to what everyone anticipated would be a happy event. Offshore aboard HMCS "Buckingham" the tension was mounting and John Ritcey, manning the Port gun, photographed the compelling moment through the gun sight, symbolically capturing what the moment meant for himself and Canada.

Upon arrival, the German crew, usually "pusser" to the extreme by always taking care to present themselves in the best military light, this time lolled listlessly about the Conning Tower. This was in marked contrast with their commissioning day only a few months earlier in Germany. This submarine, one of the most modern available, carried the Schnorkel, an apparatus which enabled the sub to "breathe" while submerged, a weapon which had proven devastating to our Convoys. When commissioned, the same crew lustily saluted "Heil Hitler" with great fervor; the submarine's 26 year old Captain Freidrich Bronecker, of Hamburg, Germany, was to endure the ignominy most of them feared; capture by the enemy. But the revelation from one Canadian who stood at attention next to Freer was even more revealing. When he began to fidget, Freer admonished him, "Don't you know Donald's a stickler for protocol?" But Donald was too engrossed to notice, while the submarine came to rest with a gentle "thump" against the Jetty. Suddenly, the rating broke rank and, turning to Freer asked him to look in the direction that his arm was pointed. All that Freer

Commanding Officer Frierich Breuecher of Hamburg, Germany gives a sardonic smile when pictured aboard the U-889 after being taken into custody. He appeared far more friendly in captivity.

—Fred Davis—PAC 134321

John Ritcey ("Lofty" to his shipmates), is photographed on HMCS "Buckingham" off Newfoundland.

PBY aircraft of the RCAF 161 Squadron roars overhead as the captured German Sub U-889 hauls down its flag and the Navy's White Ensign is hoisted on the Conning Tower, May, 1945.

—PAC 116720

Surrendered German submarine is pictured under escort by the Q085 as it sails into Gaspé following V-E Day.

—H.J. Dow

Photograph of U-889 taken in Germany only months prior to its capture in Canada. Note the "Heil Hitler" salutes and enthusiasm of the crew. This was in marked contrast to their photo when captured. This photo was given to a Canadian seaman by a German submariner upon the latter's internment in Canada. It transpired that they were actually cousins.

could see was an unusually blonde youngster; one of the "pure-bred" Aryans coveted by Hitler and who now was the object of his friend's excited attention. The young Nazi on the Conning Tower certainly wasn't anything to get excited about, so far as Freer was concerned. Then, Freer's mate looked him full in the face and cried: "It's just like you said in Gaspé," acknowledging Freer's earlier assertion. "See that kid up there" he said motioning with his arm . . . "that's my . . . cousin." Then, looking quietly to the ground as if in abject apology, he added, but much quieter now; "See, . . . I've been trying to kill my own cousin. All this time, we've been trying to kill one another."

It happened in Canada, and Canada didn't know for Canada had never been told. This was Canada's Unknown War . . . This was Victory in the St. Lawrence.

What are his thoughts? A Nazi submarine officer is shown with one of his crewmen after surrendering in waters off Newfoundland.

— George Bernard.

"Charlottetown" (II)

— Bill Mundell

epilogue

There were two exceptions to the news "blackout" during WW 2 at Gaspé. I subsequently learned of the one from Bill Grand and the other from George Kruse. Both men had served in Gaspé during the months of the "Deep Silence". When Bill Grand returned home on leave in 1943 and inquired why there was so much fuss being made over him, "I learned over the car radio that you were a hero", his brother responded. "While I was driving home from Muskoka, the radio said you'd just rescued 78 survivors with your boat off an 'East Coast Port' ". It was July 1943 when he heard this and Bill Grand recognized that his brother was talking about a rescue that had happened months earlier, not off an East Coast Port but right in the St. Lawrence.

George Kruse's experience with censorship was equally gratuitous. In Newfoundland in the spring of 1945, he was surprised to meet an old Sea Captain who once knew his father, Alfred Kruse. But what was more surprising was to find out that only now the old man was learning about the "Battle of the St. Lawrence". "That's gettin' pretty close to home" he said to Kruse, mentioning that ship which had run aground at Grand Vallée after being torpedoed in the river.

"But that was only one ship he knew about; he never knew about all the others and it had been run aground in 1942. The 'news' he was quoting was three years old". Kruse concluded "Canada clearly wasn't giving anything away".

Another example of our "silent press" came only recently when I happened to notice a store window decorated for November 11th. It was an inauspicious yet sincere display honouring Remembrance Day, 1983. Included was a picture of a Canadian warship and a Coder's uniform of the RCNVR. I confess I wasn't entirely taken aback because I'd already met the proprietor, by chance, a decade earlier during the Kitchener-Waterloo Naval Vet's Reunion. However contrary to the customary vet's reunion, "where everything usually hangs out", Bill Mundell never mentioned his ship to me at the time nor the part they played in the closing years of the war, when his ship helped the torpedoed HMCS "Magog". This time he talked: perhaps prompted by the fact that I was delivering my manuscript about this very war to the publisher, which, as it happened was located just down the street in Erin, Ontario. Mundell's ship turned out to have been the successor to the earlier ill-fated "Charlottetown," a frigate and a much-improved version of that earlier ship bearing the same name.

"I stood on the deck of my ship and watched the sinister bubbling wake of the torpedo as it passed nearby heading for its quarry to hit with a loud explosion into the stern of 'Magog'", Mundell explained. "We dropped everything we had and pounded that sub unmercifully, so much so that he left the wounded "Magog" alone." Later, "Magog" was successfully towed to Quebec City but the sub was never found, nor did it attack again. Nobody knew his story, for Canadians had never been told.

We held a Memorial Service in Gaspé in 1979, throwing wreaths on the waters to honour our dead. A total of eight ships, "Bras D'Or", "Otter", "Raccoon", "Charlottetown", "Chedabucto", "Shawinigan", "Clayoquot" and "Esquimalt", were sunk defending Canada's coastal waters. While a monument stands today in Point Pleasant Park in Halifax honouring the dead of the Battle of the Atlantic, nothing marks the loss of so many sailors fighting Canada's war in the St. Lawrence.

I couldn't help thinking while researching this book that a grateful Government could, at least, erect a monument to honour our sailors who went out and did battle with a determined enemy; many never to return. It could, and should, at least acknowledge their sacrifice and it should lift the veil of secrecy on these unsung patriots.

Many have questioned the lack of knowledge of our Navy's St. Lawrence battles and the continued 'blackout' of Canada's Unknown War. Hopefully, now, the 'blackout' has been lifted and some acknowledgement of these brave men has been made.....

acknowledgements

I wish to express my gratitude to the many Army, Air Force and Navy Veterans who appear in this book as well as many others who sent photos, made telephone calls and granted interviews in order to make this book possible. I would also like to thank James and Jean Filby who, by their untiring efforts proof-reading maintained the whole in orderly progression reinforced by John Denison who captained the project and laid out the book. Special mention should be made to Mr. James Plomer whose own enthusiasm for the Navy sustained the rest of us as we despaired for the flagging interest in our post-war Navy. I'd also like to single out Mr. Warren Mackenzie who took us over often inaccessible roads providing transportation; to my son Mr. David Essex for persevering with camera and taping equipment; and to Mr. Philip Dunn, local historian who filled in unexpected blanks. And to James Lamb, whose own writing about sailors in "The Corvette Navy" has left us all richer and who, for some reason or another said to me when I first broached the subject of this book, "You're the one to write it". Finally to Mr. Peter Donald, son of the first Commanding Officer of Gaspé, Captain Colin Donald whose early reminiscences helped set the stage for what followed; and to Mr. Julian Bernard, son of the final Commanding Officer of HMCS "Fort Ramsay" in Gaspé in 1945, who cheerfully stepped in when his father George Bernard passed away June 1982 and helped.

Regarding research assistance, I wish to publicly thank the Kitchener Public Library, the Waterloo County Libraries, the Stratford-Perth County Archives and the Public Archives of Canada for their untiring efforts tracking down endless facts, dates and places long forgotten in the intervening four or five decades. And of course, George Allard of Gaspé.

The inferences drawn and interpretation of events are my own and any shortcomings or errors in the work are my own although all reasonable care in recording dates and happenings has been scrupulously observed and every effort has been made to relate them accurately.

James W. Essex

Troops arrive home on the "Pasteur".

bibliography

The Great Lakes—St. Lawrence Waterway,
The Grolier Society, 1931
The Dark, Broad Seas, Jeffry Brock, McClelland &
Stewart, Toronto
Murray, the Martyred Admiral, James M. Cameron,
Lancelot Press 1981, Hantsport, N.S.
Duplessis, Conrad Black, McClelland & Stewart,
1977
U-Boats offshore; when Hitler Struck America,
Edwin P. Hoyt, Stein and Day, New York 1978
Night of the U-Boats, Paul Lund and Harry Ludlam,
Foulsham, London 1973
The Ultra Secret, F.W. Winterbotham, 1974
Harper & Row
Canadians at War 1939-45, Reader's Digest
Parts 1 & 2
Canada's Atlantic War, John Swettenham,
Samuel-Stevens, Toronto, 1979
Pictorial History of the German Navy in WW2,
E.P. Von der Porten
The Far Distant Ships, Joseph Schull, 1950, Dept.
of Nat'l. Defence Ottawa
The Secret War, Brian D.G. Johnson, 1978,
The BBC, London, England
The Horsemen, C.W. Harvison, Commissioner
RCMP, McClelland & Stewart, 1967
The Armed Yachts of Canada, Fraser McKee,
Boston Mills Press, 1983

articles and newspapers:

Globe & Mail, Toronto, Ont., May 13th, 1942 edition
Beacon-Herald, Stratford, Ont., Sept. 18th,
1942 edition
The Star, Toronto, Ont. Sept. 18th, 1942 edition
Telegram, Toronto, Ont. Sept. 18th, 1942 edition
"Battle of the St. Lawrence", Jack McNaught,
Maclean's, Nov., 1946
"Battle of the Gulf", James B. Lamb, *Mayfair
Magazine,* November, 1946
"Picturesque But No Longer Poor", Anderson
Charters, *Financial Post,* Nov. 3/79 Toronto, Ont.
"The Second World War Battle We Lost At Home"
The Canadian Magazine, Feb. 26/72, by Peter Moon
"Wartime Role of Sydney, N.S.," and associated
description of RCN operations in the Gulf of
St. Lawrence, *Chronicle-Herald,* Halifax, files for
May 13/67 and Nov. 11/72